THE FRONTLINE

THE FRONTLINE

An account of the life of a football devotee,
chronicling thirty-seven years following
Middlesbrough Football Club

John Theone

MILO BOOKS

First published in October 2003 by Milo Books

ISBN 1 903854 18 0

Typeset in Plantin Light by Avon DataSet Ltd,
Bidford on Avon, Warwickshire, B50 4JH

Printed and bound in Great Britain by
Cox & Wyman Ltd, Reading, Berkshire

MILO BOOKS
10 Park Street
Lytham
Lancs FY8 5LU
info@milobooks.com

Dedications

Fred (Custer)
Ernie Ragbo
Bunty
Ferret
Salty
Frenchy
Rest in peace you wonderful reds

Acknowledgements

Best mate Bri

Stevo (contributions)

Samantha & Steve Simpson
(rescued the document when I lost it on the PC, doh!)

Craggsy (photographic contributions)

All the lads I've been associated with over the years,
you know who you are, without whose camaraderie
this book would not have been possible.

My wife, mother and family for putting up with all the
worry and stress I've caused them over the years.

Finally but not least Middlesbrough Football Club,
who I will follow till the day I die.

Contents

Introduction

THIS STORY CHARTS my life following Middlesbrough Football Club from 1966 to 2003. The events described are all true to the best of my recollection. However, some names have been changed to protect the identities of those concerned.

As you read on, the choice of title should become apparent. 'The Frontline' is where most up and coming 'boys' aim to establish themselves. Every town or city has its own 'firm' or 'crew' and every firm has its leader(s). Some firms have one, some have several. The leader will also have his main boys. These are the ones who never run: the Frontliners.

In the mid-Sixties, firms didn't really exist, although football violence did rear its head now and again. Most kick-offs happened spontaneously, as the result of a goal scored or an insult hurled towards opposing fans. This usually ended in an away supporter being subjected to a good kicking. This in turn made people think, *well if I'm going there again, I'm gonna take a bit of back-up next time*. This was the start of firms being established.

Initially it was just the odd coach being organised, usually by a respected club official or working men's club committee. Then during the Seventies, younger, more streetwise lads started to use trains and to hire vans, and arranged to meet at well-known locations to march in mob-handed. Sometimes as many as 2,000 would meet up for a sortie into enemy territory. As we progressed through to the Eighties, firms became more organised and battles were being arranged between consenting parties. The Nineties ushered in the age of mobile phones and the internet. However firms were now reduced to smaller yet often more effective numbers, with pre-arranged meetings usually away from the football ground.

The following is a chronological account of how I progressed from a young, impressionable eight-year-old to a full-blooded Frontliner, ending with my 'retirement' to 'normal' football fan culture.

CHAPTER ONE

The Ayresome Angels

JUNE 1966, THE World Cup was in England and Ayresome Park had been chosen as a venue for the early group stages. I was eight years old and had never been to a football match. I had only recently arrived back in England from South Africa with my mam and brother following the split-up of my parents. My dad chose to stay in Africa, where we had been for the previous three years. My mam hated the place, it was too hot and there were too many strange insects and other animals that chose to invade our house. Our family had emigrated there in 1963 when I was five. I had started my schooling there and it wasn't nice; this white English kid with the strange accent didn't go down too well with the Afrikaans kids. From my first day at school I was bullied by the 'yarpies', as they were known, subsequently having two fights in my first week. Although my brother was older than me, I was the bigger and ended up having to fight most of his battles as well.

I was happier than most when my mam decided she'd had enough and came back to Blighty, only now I had this horrible Afrikaans accent that I picked up and was as brown as a berry. This didn't go down too well at Ravensworth Junior school in Teesville, the estate where we lived, situated to the east of Middlesbrough in the Borough of Eston. Once again I was subjected to more bullyboy tactics. My African experiences meant I was more able to hold my own and had soon made most of the local kids aware that I don't back down to anyone very easily. Mind, I received my fair share of second prizes.

I was keen to get involved with the World Cup party atmosphere, which by today's standards was very sedate; in fact the only time anyone got remotely excited was when England played. This would bring out a few union flags flying from the odd house here and there (the union flag was recognised as the England flag those days, as opposed to the St George Cross which would later become more prevalent). At the start of the competition even England weren't expected to do too much and the press were calling for the head of Sir Alf Ramsey following a goal-less draw in the first game. A couple of older lads I went to school with were going to the Italy v North Korea match so I went along with them. Most people in the crowd wanted Italy to win but I shouted for the Koreans. I always had a soft spot for the underdog, even at that tender age.

There I was shouting, 'Come on the little fellas,' in my strange Afrikaans accent, then the little buggers go and score. I felt a punch on the right side of my face, I immediately fell to the floor clutching my rapidly swelling eye, crying for all I was worth. I looked to the lads I was with for some back-up, as this other kid who had hit me must have been a good three years older and a foot taller. One of the lads I was with told me to just take it and say nowt. 'His dad is Italian, and the whole family are as hard as fuck,' he informed me. By now my eye was coming up like a ripened plum. I stood whimpering for a while, glancing across at the lad who hit me. He just stared at me as if to say, 'Do you want some more?' Not likely – the first punch had nearly killed. The Koreans held on to win the game 1–0 and I afforded myself a wry smile of satisfaction. *Fuck you*, I thought to myself. When I got home my mam went apeshit, threatening to find the 'Italian bastard' and black both of his eyes, and his mother's, for bringing such an arsehole into this world. After she calmed down, she laughed when I told her the full story and saw the funny side of it.

So my first-ever game saw me sample the sweet taste of victory along with the pain of disappointment, but I had caught the bug. This was ten times better than rugby in South Africa.

My mam banned me from going to any more World Cup games so I had to content myself with watching on TV. The final was amazing, going into extra time with more drama and twists and turns than one could imagine. Eventually, as everyone is fully aware, we won: England 4 Germany 2. My mother came in from the club absolutely rat-arsed. 'Your father would've loved this,' she slobbered. 'He loved his football, your dad.' My mam knew how to celebrate, and how to 'torture' me and our kid; we both ended up covered in lipstick. My dad would have loved it too, but South Africa didn't have TV until the 1970s. Unlucky pops.

When the euphoria of the World Cup had died down, it was back to basics in the league, and believe me we are talking basics here. Middlesbrough (the Boro) were in dire straits, having been relegated to the Third Division the previous season. This didn't bother me, as I hadn't seen any Boro matches before in any case. Boro had always been regarded as a top-flight club, noted for never having won anything but always having the potential. This once great club had been accustomed to internationals such as Wilf Mannion, George Hardwick, Brian Clough and George Camsell (who held the league scoring record of fifty-nine goals in a season) playing for them. Now they had hit the bottom of the barrel, going into the Third Division for the first ever time. A guy named Stan Anderson (an ex-Boro, Sunderland and Newcastle player who captained all three) was charged with the job of getting Boro back up at the first attempt, but it was not an easy league to get out of.

The first game I went to was between Boro and Bristol Rovers. I can't remember the score but the one thing that lives in the memory is standing in the boys' end watching and listening to the 'Ayresome Angels'. They were the equivalent of today's kop-end singers. The Angels stood in the Holgate end of the ground and were fiercely loyal to Boro, travelling all over the country to sing and chant for the lads in red and white. I was captivated by their togetherness and camaraderie and the way they dressed: works hardhats painted red and white, long white butchers' coats adorned with players' names, heavy hobnail boots, scarves tied around the wrist or head and the customary rattle. The manner in which they would spontaneously burst into a song or chant often related to what was happening on the pitch or came in answer to a chant by the opposing fans. It was this togetherness that drew me back to Ayresome Park over and over again for the next thirty-seven years, not the quality of football played, although some of that was quite good at times as well!

During the rest of the season, which turned out quite exciting, I was content with standing in the boys' end (a reserved section of the ground reserved for youngsters under sixteen which cost 1/- 6d to enter, about 7.5 pence) watching the football and soaking up the atmosphere, especially the final game of the season when we played Oxford United. We had to win to be promoted back to the Second Division. A crowd of 40,000 packed into the ground, with thousands more outside still trying to get in. At the back of the boys' end where I stood came a loud crashing noise, so being young and curious I climbed the wall to get a better look. I couldn't believe the scenes as hundreds of fans came charging through the space where the gates used to be. Eventually the police managed to take control but not until what must have been a couple of thousand fans had got in to the ground. This surge of fans entering all at once caused a domino reaction on the terraces, resulting in the wall at the front collapsing and several hundred fans spilled onto the track at the side of the pitch. When order was restored the police allowed people to sit on the track so that the game could proceed, and although I didn't need to, I made my way to the pitch side and joined them – anything to get near that hallowed carpet of a pitch. By half-time I was in the Holgate End with the Ayresome Angels, who were in full voice. A big, rough-looking lad of about fifteen grabbed me and lifted me onto the barrier, encouraging me to join in with the songs. One I'll always remember from that night is still well known today:

> Hello, hello, we are the Boro boys
> Hello, hello, we are the Boro boys
> We are the Ayresome Angels and we never miss a match
> We will follow the Boro.

The song, or rather chant, was normally directed towards the away fans, but on this night there were none to be seen. During a run-of-the-mill game the chanting and singing would involve around 300 to 400 fans, but this was no ordinary game and the whole ground was joining in. The atmosphere that night will live long in my memory. As soon as the ref blew the final whistle, there was a pitch invasion from all sides of the ground and the party began. Boro had won 4–1 with one of my early heroes John 'give us a goal' O'Rourke bagging a hat-trick.

After my first taste of life in the Holgate, I had to have more. However, there was a problem that was to stay with me for a few more seasons – I couldn't afford to pay in the Holgate every match. Where there's a will there's a way, and the way was found via the 'squeeze'. The squeeze was a way of getting into the ground without paying. The way it worked was simple. First you found a 'gadgie' (a term used on Teesside to describe a bloke, usually large), then you ask him for a squeeze. If he said yes, you would pretend to be his son for the next minute or so until you were in the ground. In those days men who took their kids to the match would take them through the turnstile for free by squeezing in two at a time. Asking for a squeeze could be dangerous, especially if the gadgie had been on the piss, resulting in a painfully squashed arm or, worse still, a very sore nipple. Failing to get a squeeze, the next option was to try sneaking under the turnstile when the operator wasn't looking, but if you were caught this could result in more pain via a good kick up your arse. Another option to get in the Holgate was to pay at the boys' end and nick your way round under the fences that separated each paddock. I received my first good hiding using this method when we played Millwall in 1970.

I WENT TO the Millwall game in late November 1970 with a few of my mates. Everyone managed to get a squeeze except me, so I had to pay in the boys' end and try nicking round to the Holgate. The previous season there'd been some 'chew' (chew is Teesside-speak for trouble/getting on one's nerves/baiting) at the Den between Boro and Millwall fans, so there was a distinct air about the place and talk was of a big showdown. As I was getting from the Bob End to the East End seats, I stood on the foot of another lad who I suppose was doing the same thing. He called me a wanker and pushed me into the fence. As I turned to retaliate, one of the sweetest right hooks I've ever had the misfortune to take hit me right on the button. If that wasn't enough, another punch hit me on my left eye. As I went down, all I could feel was the thud of boots coming at me from all over; either this lad was very fast or there were a few of them, I don't know. The next thing I remember, a steward was picking me up from the floor and asking if I was all right. I told him I was okay, then he said he had chased them all away and informed me that I had one hell of a clock to look forward to the next day.

Suddenly there was a bit of a commotion further up the stand. A crew of Millwall fans had come into the ground chanting, 'We are Millwall.' There were only about fifty but all of them were geezers. Most of the fans in this part of the ground were kids or old codgers not really up to fighting, and a lot got on their toes, causing a big space to appear. The Millwall crew stood with their arms out, beckoning and shouting, 'You'll never take the Millwall.' Most of these Londoners were dressed in donkey jackets with jeans and heavy boots. Their hair was a lot longer than ours and they were all between twenty and thirty-five years old. A few gadgies had stood their ground and started chanting, 'You'll never take the Bob End.' Then there was a free-for-all, followed by a dozen coppers moving in to calm things down, with several fans being ejected from the ground. Witnessing this at close quarters gave me one hell of a buzz; it was hand-to-hand fighting and I have to say that the Millwall crew more than held their own.

When everything had calmed down, I resumed my quest to reach the Holgate End, passing a few tasty-looking gadgies moving in the opposite direction, their motives being patently obvious. On reaching the Holgate, my mates asked what happened to me, as by now I had a big fat lip and my eye was up the size of an apple. 'Fucking hell, what happened to you John, were you fighting with the Millwall?' Before I could say anything, who should appear but the lad who'd given me the good hiding, with a few of his mates. One of the lads I was with said, 'Ow ya fucking tosser, think yer hard picking on someone on his own? Get out the back at half-time and fight him one to one.'

Fucking hell, thanks a lot, I thought. Most of the lads had come to regard me as a fiery fucker who would fight anyone. I couldn't refuse, if only to save face. When half-time arrived we all went out the back but he was nowhere to be seen and personally I was quite happy about that, as I didn't fancy my chances due to the fact I had one eye shut and a lip bigger than Mick Jagger's. During half-time there was a big kick-off between Boro and Millwall in the Bob End, so we all rushed back onto the terraces to get a better look. It was all over in thirty seconds as the law moved in and more ejections were made. This time I'd say Boro got the upper hand; mind you, they outnumbered the Londoners three or four to one.

So I'd had my first taste of soccer violence, and to be honest I loved it. For the next few years I got to know who the main lads were in the Holgate. Most were aged between fourteen and eighteen, with names like Sharky, Dapper, Nailer and Winker – everyone had a nickname. These were the frontline troops and no battling took place without them being involved in some shape or form. The only problem was that they weren't very well organised. Most lads stuck in their own little clique, normally with lads from their own area. This caused problems during any battles, often leading to a punch from one of your own fans through mistaken identity.

I came from Teesville, a council estate purposely built to house the workers needed for Dorman Long (later British Steel) and the ICI Wilton petro-chemical sites, roughly six miles from Middlesbrough. The estate was bordered by the longer-established areas of Grangetown and South Bank, very dodgy places in their own right. South Bank was a particularly hazardous area to venture into, even though I lived just up the road. Some hard fuckers came out of that place. My mam, who had by now got divorced from my dad, had hitched up with a bloke called Bill who had lived in South Bank for a couple of years. He told me how dangerous it was to cross a South Banker: 'They're funny people who you need to keep close but not too close. Never cross them or you're in trouble.' Sound advice which I took on board, making friends with a lad known as 'Bounce' in my class at school. Through him I slowly got to know a lot of the main faces, which has stood me in good stead to this day. Sharky was a huge mountain of a guy, six feet-plus with a bit of weight to back it up. Dapper, as his name suggests, was one for the ladies, always smartly dressed in the latest fashions and good looking as well. Nailer was very unkempt with straggly blond hair and a gap where he had lost two front teeth during a skirmish with Millwall. Winker was nearer my age but a lot bigger and slightly overweight, not the sort you'd want your sister to go out with.

Where you came from meant quite a lot in Boro. For example, during the early Seventies the main gadgies in the Holgate were from Middlesbrough and Grangetown. They normally occupied the centre section of the terracing. Being from the 'G-town' area myself, I was okay to stand in the centre section, as I knew most of the big lads. This was the beginning of my apprenticeship as a Holgate Ender. Grangetown was a similar area to South Bank, having close-knit terraced streets with back alleys. There always seemed to be stray dogs roaming around (even they were fucking hard). Middlesbrough itself consisted of the town centre with its terraced housing and outlying council estates: there were the B Farm boys (Brambles Farm estate) led by Ernie; the Border boot boys (St Hilda's estate, an area known as 'over the border'); the Park End crew (Park End estate), usually led by Mad Frankie; the Whinny Banks boys (Whinny Banks estate); the Newport gang; and the Doggy boys (North Ormesby – I don't know to this day how the place got the name Doggy). Then there was the Stockton firm, the Haverton Hill mob, the Port boys (Port Clarence), the Redcar Reds (later to become the Casuals). Every little area had its firm (if I've missed anyone, sorry), all led by their own main gadgie. These leaders would change as the years passed and people moved on.

CHAPTER TWO

The Boro Boot Boys

DURING THE 1971–72 season the skinhead/suedehead culture had started to blossom, with fans a lot more fashion-conscious than ever before. Where once there were 'X brand' jeans (cheap denims usually from Woolworths) and even school trousers worn at the match, maybe with a scarf thrown around the shoulders and a bobble hat in the team colours, now it was Wrangler or Levi jeans, Dr Marten boots, Fred Perry shirts and the scarf was round the wrist. Yes, the age of the boot boy was here, and this fad was to stay for some time, filling umpteen thousand inches of tabloid column space.

My first taste of derby match violence was to come in this season, at home to the 'Mackems', or Sunderland to those of you who are unfamiliar with the term. Earlier in the season we had played the Mackems up at 'Joker' Park. It had been a night match and the Boro had taken a mob into the Fulwell. Sharky had arranged for a crew to go in incognito to do as much damage as possible then get out sharpish like. Sharky was a sound bloke who didn't suffer fools gladly. He didn't like bullies or anyone who ran, however he didn't stand giving orders out like some jumped-up general. Sharky instilled you with confidence and with him at the front others had much stronger self-belief.

While waiting in the queue outside, one of the lads got cold feet and started to chant:

Boro boys we are here, woah-oh, woah-oh.
Boro boys we are here, woah-oh woah-oh.

At that the police moved in and escorted most of the mob round to the Roker end, abandoning about fifty lads who had already got in. These fifty included Sharky, Lou, Nailer and a few others. The Mackems were all fired up, looking around knowing that some must have got in. Ten minutes into the game, Sharky led the small but game crew into the middle of the Fulwell. The Mackems knew they must be Boro and a big gap opened up. Right in the middle stood Sharky, 6ft 2ins, fifteen stone, offering everyone out (people swear to this day that he had a shotgun under his donkey jacket). A bit of a rumble took place and the small Boro crew were escorted round the pitch to a standing ovation from those stood in the Roker end. As for the football, we were hammered 4–1.

So now we had the Mackems at home. All the stories were going round: pubs full of them in the town, three trainloads arriving at 12.30, big battle on the Newport Bridge, some fucker thrown off the Transporter Bridge – all half-truths possibly with some fragment of fact. The Newport Bridge straddles the Tees and was the main gateway to Middlesbrough from the North; the Transporter is the one famously dismantled in *Auf Wiedersehen Pet* and no Mackems would ever cross the Tees using this one. One rumour that was really strong was that the Mackems were coming in the Holgate. If so this was one day I had to go in, even if it meant paying full price. I didn't have a pair of DMs so I put a pair of steel-tipped work boots on with three pairs of footie socks, as they were two sizes too big. I had also stolen a toilet chain from school which I had in my pocket (don't ask me why, it seemed the 'hard' thing to do at the time).

On approaching the turnstiles I noticed that everyone was being searched, so I nipped down an alley and dumped my chain. Being slightly scared about whether the police would notice my steely boots, I was oblivious to the fact that I was queuing with Mackems to get in the ground. As I entered and started making my way towards the middle section everyone around me started shouting, 'Sun-der-land,' followed by a volley of rapid claps. The reply came from the other side of the terrace: 'You're gonna get your fucking heads kicked in.' All I could see was a sea of arms clapping and pointing in unison towards where I was stood. I was right in the middle of Sunderland's finest. *Time to get to our lads*, I thought, *and the sooner the better*. I was lucky I was only thirteen years old, which made me relatively unnoticeable. I made my way down to the front and slowly edged towards Boro's section, passing what can only be described as no man's land, where the two sets of fans began and ended. Every now and then the lines would be breached and a melee would ensue, resulting in police helmets flying and a constant stream of bodies being removed from the ground. The Mackems, fair play to them, had about a third of the Holgate, and as they were all boys who were up for it, with police everywhere we just had to live with it.

Boro won the game 2–0, with big John Hickton grabbing both goals to thrill a crowd of 34,000. At the end of the game we met the Mackems in Boot Boy Alley for one hell of a battle – no police, just 2–3,000 going for it good style. Boot Boy Alley runs down one side of the ground from the Holgate to the Main Stand. If you've ever heard the song 'My old man said be a Boro fan and don't dilly dally on the way', then listen to the Mackem version. One verse goes: 'We dillied and dallied, then knacked 'em in the alley.' This apparently refers to this day when obviously they claim to have turned Boro over (so I was told by a Mackem anyway). Half the time no one knew who was who during in the battle, but after what seemed like twenty minutes – but was probably more like five – the Mackems started backing off and eventually running away, with the Boro on their heels. All the way to the station there were sporadic outbreaks, with Boro generally doing the business. However, in the papers the next day it was Sunderland fans who got the most coverage.

Shortly after the Sunderland match, we were drawn away to Millwall in the FA Cup fifth round. This brought everyone's passion to the fore, and I was on my way to my first away game. Sharky had organised a coach for all the G-town lads to travel down to London. I was lucky to get a seat, as the big lads weren't too keen on taking any young kids with them, however Sharky said I was okay as I had stood my ground against Sunderland. We boarded the coach early on the Saturday morning and set off for the big city. Most of the talk was of the game a couple of seasons back when there was a big rumble with Millwall up at our gaff. I must admit I was shitting myself at the thought of what could happen over the next few hours, especially after Nailer leaned over to me.

'Ow son, wait till ya see these fuckers in action. See this?' He removed his teeth to show me a gap where his front gnashers used to be. 'Fucking Millwall did that last time we played the cockney twats.'

His breath smelled of stale beer and I was soaked with spit on each word as he slavered his hatred of their firm. All the seasoned veterans were crowing at the thought of a full-scale battle with the most notorious crew in the land on their own turf, buoyed by the fact there were another couple of thousand Boro travelling down to the Den, some of whom we met at service stations *en route*. At these stop-offs I was amazed to notice that no one bought a thing; it was sheer theft on a grand scale, a sort of mass shoplifting expedition which I feverishly joined in.

On arriving in London, Sharky ordered the driver to drop us at Kings Cross station, telling him to pick us up there at 6 p.m. As it was only 11 a.m., we had a lot of time to kill before heading through to Millwall, so we found a cafe and had some breakfast. This was all good crack and every now and then a few more Boro turned up to add to our numbers. Eventually we numbered about seventy-five as we left the cafe to meet the lads coming in off the train. What a sight it was to see that train trundle in to Kings Cross, especially when 2–300 Boro marched off the platform in full voice singing, 'Hello, hello, we are the Boro boys,' which echoed through the station. Everyone marched straight down to the tube and we began to make our way to the Den; my nerves by now had evaporated and I was full of confidence. Who wouldn't be with such a big mob?

On arriving at the Den, we went straight to the nearest pub, which had a few Millwall gadgies in it. As we numbered so many they decided to concede the ground and left peacefully, promising, 'We'll be back mate wiv our firm.' One or two Boro lads took exception to this threat and gave them a slap as they left. Sharky pulled the Boro lads up.

'Ow, fucking leave 'em alone, ya daft twats. Boro don't do easy prey like that. Fucking hell, man. You could've had the fucking law down on us. I want a fucking good drink, not coppers beefing us. Hey and don't worry son, them fucking cockneys'll be back with their firm. I hope yer as fucking game then.'

During the next hour or so, we didn't have the slightest hint of trouble, just Boro songs being chanted at full voice. Then suddenly half the windows in the pub seemed to go through simultaneously and both doorways had some of the biggest gadgies I'd ever seen pouring in, knocking out lads left, right and centre. This was it, the lads we saw earlier had fulfilled their promise. I hid behind a table with bottles and glasses flying everywhere. After a while the Millwall were forced outside and the battle continued in the street. I watched from the relative safety of the pub.

In the middle of the road was this enormous gadgie who was taking everyone on. He was dressed in a long trenchcoat with hair flowing across his shoulders. He must have put about five Boro lads on their arses before Goldie caught him with a DM right in the knackers, which poleaxed him where he stood. Goldie got his nickname through wearing Dr Martens painted gold. He was very clever and astute, always with the latest fashion on. As a few lads started to put the boot in, the law turned up, scattering everyone. This had the desired effect for the Millwall crew, as we were now split all over the place.

Back in the pub only six or seven of us remained, no big lads just youngsters, me being the junior of the lot. The question now was what to do. The landlord had locked the doors while the fighting was outside and told us to wait till everyone had gone before he would let us out. This meant we were on our own so we made our way up the ground. When we entered the ground we could see a pocket of Boro fans chanting but before we could get to them Millwall were at them like a pack of wild dogs, resulting in a mass dispersion on the terraces. We decided to keep quiet for the time being so as to suss out where everyone had got to. The game had started and most of the crowd settled to watch the match. Then there was this mournful, almost ghost-like chant from the home crowd: 'Miiiilllwaaallll.' I practically shit my pants on the spot. I mean, these were not lads in their mid-teens, they were all big fuck-off dockers and they were literally laughing at the state of our crew, calling us babies and kids.

Then just before half-time, John Hickton goes and scores to put us one up. There was an immediate surge from behind and I was sent crashing to the floor by the crowd. When I got up again, only Kingie was left out of our lads. He suggested we stay put and keep our gobs zipped. Good advice, I thought. Well into the second half and we both thought we were all right. Nothing serious had happened so we got a bit confident, until Kingie noticed his legs getting warm and wet. I turned round to see four big gadgies, one of whom was having a piss down the back of Kingie's legs. He looked at me and just said,

'Awight mate,' with a big smile on his face. Who was I to argue?'

'Yeah, sound mate. Look, we're just kids an' we don't want any trouble,' I said nervously.

'Who's facking causing trouble, hey?'

I looked him in the eye and said, 'Not me mate, we just want to watch the game.'

'Ah well, that's cushty then son, innit.'

I agreed with him and Kingie and I slipped away into the crowd. My heart was pounding.

The game finished 2–2. As we left the ground, I noticed mobs of Millwall on every street corner, picking out Boro fans and chasing them all over. This had me quaking for the third time that day and I was almost on the verge of asking a copper for protection (a big no-no). Suddenly Kingie noticed Sharky and a load of Boro lads under police escort, heading towards the station with hundreds of Millwall following on both sides of the road. Every now and then there was a charge by the Millwall and scuffles would break out, resulting in the law moving in to break it up. Eventually we managed to catch up and join them on the platform. The police decided to leave all the Boro unguarded and loads of Millwall crammed onto the platform with us, forcing us to one end. Where the two sets of supporters met it was mayhem. Something had to give and it happened when a bloke fell onto the electric line, causing total confusion. I heard the guy died as a result of this. Rumour has it he was one of Millwall's top lads and to this day they have never forgiven us. We all made it back safely and Boro won the replay 2–1 to set us up with a quarter-final tie away to Manchester United.

I COULDN'T AFFORD to go through to Manchester for the cup game, however Boro managed a draw 0–0 and brought the famous Man Utd back to Ayresome for a replay. These were the days of power cuts and three-day week, so the game had to be held on an afternoon instead of in the evening. We queued throughout the Saturday night in freezing conditions for the coveted tickets, playing football to try to keep warm. On the day of the game, half the schoolkids in Teesside played truant to go (we all got detention the following day).

Now Man Utd had the biggest following in the country and about 10,000 of them were coming to Boro. Seven thousand had tickets and the rest were hopeful of buying on the black market or, as happened, just bursting their way into the ground. My mates and I could only afford to go in the boys' end, so we decided to nick round to the Holgate from there. When we had reached as far as the East End seats, a steward chased us out the back, and as we got to the exit stairway my heart almost stopped. I saw what must have been hundreds of United fans coming up the stairs, chanting, 'U-NI-TED!' It was all we could do to get onto the grass bank out of their way. One or two of them noticed us and at first they were going to give us it, but one of them said, 'Leave them alone, they're only kids,' and they steamed into the stand, sending men women and kids running for their lives. When they realised they were in the seats they all came running back out, hotly pursued by the local plod. I was fascinated by all of this and the adrenalin rush ran through me like a steam train. I even hoped they would invade the pitch, if only to see the reaction from the Holgate.

When order was finally restored, we managed to find some seats and settled to watch the match, which as it turned out was comfortably won by United 3–0, Best, Charlton and co. being on top form. The rest of that season petered out to an uneventful finale with Boro finishing in ninth position.

The following season didn't offer much in the way of excitement. We beat the Mackems, they beat us, gates were down to an all-time low averaging just 10,000, we had no cup runs and not a great deal happened on the terraces, except for a bit of a do away to Oxford United – yes, even Oxford, every team seemed to have a firm in those days. I even went to see a game at Hartlepool versus Darlington. Now these two do have a bit of history. The gate was only 5–6,000 but Darlo had a healthy crew of about 1,500 boys and the 'Moosemen' (Pool's mob) were well up for it. All the regular chants were thrown at each other (along with bricks, bottles and cups of Oxo). The one chant that seemed to get it all going was by the Darlo fans – 'Monkey, monkey hangers' – this being a reference to an old tale about the people of Hartlepool hanging a monkey as a French spy during the Napoleonic Wars, the inference being that Poolies were thick as fuck due to the fact that they thought a Frog looked like a monkey. Mind I could see where they were coming from; the French are ugly fuckers at the best of times.

Darlo is a rural town with a very strong tradition of market days, where the pubs have special licences on certain days throughout the year. Their main lads, known as the Bank Top 200, have a strong England following and are a close-knit firm who have been known to hold their own on many occasions against supposedly bigger outfits (Boro have firsthand experience of this, but more of that later). Their greatest rivals are Hartlepool, who they hate with a passion. Hartlepool is more of an industrial town, famous as the home of comic-strip character Andy Capp and Peter Mandelson the MP. Being near the coast they have a strong seafaring tradition and the construction of oil and gas rigs is their main industry nowadays. They are a bit more friendly to Boro folk, although it's not the place I would recommend for a night out (every time I've had one there I've had a bit of chew). It is, however, an excellent place for getting fixed up with the ladies. We used to go through now and again for Sunday afternoon strip shows in the late Seventies and early Eighties. A workmate of mine once got fixed up with a stripper when he was invited on stage. As she stripped him he had a hard on (he was a big lad);

the stripper took one look at his tackle and arranged to meet him later on. Nuff said.

After such a poor season it was quite obvious that Stan Anderson had taken Boro as far as he could, and a fresh face was needed to inject that extra bit of sparkle to get the fans going again. That man was found in big Jack Charlton, a no-nonsense character who'd had a distinguished career with Leeds and England. The whole town was buzzing at the new appointment, although some of the older generation reserved judgement.

The start to the season was a bit cagey but after the first seven or so games Boro got into their stride and hit top spot, never to lose it for the rest of a record-breaking season. I was in my last year at school and found myself with a bit more money in my pocket than before. Thus began my regular visits to away grounds. This was 1973, I was fifteen years old and, although slim, a sizeable five feet eleven inches. I was able to get in most pubs and was well accepted into the Holgate end culture, regularly standing on the barrier, scarf on wrist, leading some of the communal singing. I had noticed some big black lads had become major players in the Holgate, having their own barrier in the centre section. They were a well-known family from Middlesbrough town area and had been travelling all over with the lads. This was quite unusual, as only West Ham had ever had black boys following them up to now. They were handy lads as well and even joined in with some of the racial-style chants that were on the go at these times.

I had served my time at home and now it was time to get involved with some of the away sorties that were talked about with such relish in the Holgate. I had been to Millwall and made the odd trip to Sunderland; now I wanted to taste some real action. The first away game that season for me was at Blackpool. We must have taken about 5,000 fans, most of which were boot boys. Blackpool, to their credit, had a good mob out but Boro just took over the place. I travelled on an organised trip through a lad I knew from Eston, arriving at around lunchtime, and went straight into a pub with a few Blackpool fans in, although they didn't want any trouble. It wasn't long before the pub was packed to bursting and people were being refused entry. The landlord had some heavies on the door to stop any more coming in, but when a crowd of Boro fans were knocked back, a battle broke out with the bouncers at the door. We in turn attacked them from inside. The poor buggers didn't stand a chance and got a right pasting until the law emptied the pub and closed it.

As it was getting close to kick-off, we headed to the ground. Bloomfield Road was quite a decent stadium then and the Kop was a huge open end, which rapidly filled with Boro. We had lads in their end, in the paddock, even on the pitch at one stage and they couldn't live with us. One cheeky sod ran across the pitch and punted the ball away as their keeper was about to take a goal kick. He was quickly pursued by a couple of coppers, who gave up when he dived back into the Kop and the protection of his mates. *Fuck me*, I thought, *if everywhere is like this, how do I hear stories of our lads getting turned over now and again?* I was about to find out a few matches later at Sheffield Wednesday.

BORO HAD BEEN taking several thousand fans away from home on a regular basis, and due to the team setting the division alight, everywhere we went was like a cup final to other teams in the league. This in turn brought out all the local kick-off merchants. The main names playing for the Boro in those days were Graeme Souness, David Mills, Bobby Murdoch, John Hickton, David 'Spike' Armstrong and Jim Platt.

When we visited Sheffield Wednesday we had got a bit cocksure and decided to go in their kop. Big mistake. The gate was only 12,000, with about 4,000 or so from Boro.

Wednesday were in deep relegation trouble and we thought it would be a walkover. We took over a couple of pubs near the ground and had no chew all day, so a few of the top boys decided we were going in their end for a laugh and to embarrass them. About 300 of us queued up to get in the kop, which was a big open end at the time. The Wednesday fans could see over the back and knew we were coming in. Obviously they had a fierce pride in their end and we got the shock of our lives when we got in. Before we got halfway up the back stairs they were at us, hurling bricks and all sorts. Eventually we made our way onto the terracing right behind the goal, only to be met by several hundred Wednesday fans coming at us from both sides and from behind. We were left with one place to go: on the pitch.

As we spilled onto the grass the Wednesday followed. It was now hand-to-hand fighting, with police baton-charging and us running toward where the Boro were congregated on the far side, our lesson learned. About thirty-odd of our lot got lifted and when they went to court there was another welcome committee from Sheffield waiting for them. One lad ended up in hospital with a fractured jaw as well as a £50 fine for soccer hooliganism. This was the first time I had heard that phrase but it wasn't to be the last.

The rest of the season went along similar lines: the usual chew with Sunderland at home, while Nottingham Forest away was dodgy to say the least. Hull turned out to be on the same lines as Blackpool: thousands of Boro took over the place and a new fad had arrived, the taking of trophies from opposition fans. This involved sparking a rival and taking his scarf as a trophy, resulting in deep humiliation for the victim, as no fan worth his salt would give up his colours without a fight. I managed to come away with a Hull scarf and beanie-style cap, but Jacko had about eight scarves and countless hats when he got back to the coach. Some who had not been so successful bought them off him, pretending to their mates that they had won them during battle. After away games it was customary to wear your trophy to the next match alongside your Boro colours, to show that you had been to the game and had done the lads proud.

Sunderland away was probably the biggest test for our new-found reputation, as we had never really fared too well up there. We must have had up to 15,000 fans there, mostly packed into the Roker end, with a few thousand in the side paddocks. And fuck me, what a day that was. Our kid had gone on the local working men's club coach with the old fella (Bill had married my mam and was now my stepdad) but I was not allowed on because I wasn't old enough – club rules and all that. So I decided to hitchhike, which wouldn't be a problem considering the following we were taking.

Sure enough I got a lift straight away in a works van. Ten right rough-looking gadgies sat in the back. I recognised one of them from the Holgate and later found out the rest of them were from a new firm known as the Bob End Crew. I made conversation about the match and how we were going to stuff the Mackems on the park. All they talked about was how many Mackems they were gonna kick fuck out of. One of them, known only as Billy, showed me his flag. It was too big to unfurl in the van but all it said was, 'Boro kick to kill'. *Fuck me*, I thought, *these gadgies don't mess about*. They were all aged about twenty to twenty-five, ancient by boot boy standards but I knew I was in good company if there was any chew. I tried to make conversation about the game.

'Hope we beat these Mackem fuckers.'

'As long as I put one of the fuckers in hospital I don't care,' snarled Billy. 'Fucking hate these Mackem bastards me, fucking hate 'em.'

I could feel the anger in his voice. He hated all things Mackem. I didn't dare tell him I was of Mackem parents and half my cousins would be shouting for them today.

'Have you ever had chew here before then?' I enquired.

'Fucking chew? Sunland, yer always get the fucker here, they're all fucking animals, fucking jumped by hundreds of 'em last season, kicked the shit out of us. Mind, I bit one fucker's ear off, fucking blood everywhere, fucking screaming he was. D'ya remember that Dobbo? Fucking screamin', wasn't he, eh?'

Dobbo looked at me, smiled, rolled his eyes and tutted, as if to say, 'He tells everyone that story.'

'Yeah Billy, you copped a fucking good kicking though din't ya?' Dobbo joked.

'Fucken revenge time today, old son, though. WE HATE SUNLAND.' Billy broke into a loud chant, which everyone including me joined in with, banging on the side of the van. *We may well just see a bit of chew today, we may well.*

And so it proved: chew, chew and more fucking chew. We had been in Sunderland five minutes when one of the lads I was with decided to kick the holy shit out of this Mackem who'd had the audacity to call Boro shite. No he wasn't alone, he was stood in a pub doorway with dozens of his mates inside. The rest of the lads I was with held the whole pub at bay by bricking the doorway. Those inside were too wary to come out, like no one wanted to be the first to get smacked. As this was happening, fifty other Boro stormed the pub, smashing the windows to boot. As we moved away the Mackems all came out, hurling bottles and glasses. Now it was getting really hot. We were holding our ground on a roundabout but their numbers were growing as more and more came at us from all directions.

As if by magic the law turned up, probably saving our arses. The Mackems ran back inside the pub and we made haste towards the ground. I never noticed the name of the pub at the time but I now know it to be the Wheatsheaf. Another pub nearby called the Terminus was probably where the rest of them came from. On our trek to the ground it seemed every pub wanted to have a portion of chew with us. Even at the stadium there was a battle going on outside the Derby between another mob of Boro and Sunderland. Obviously we joined in, and I had the utmost pleasure in putting this Mackem on his arse, whereupon two Boro lads proceeded to finish him off with the help of red-tuxtoned DMs.

Sunderland had always had an immense rivalry with Newcastle, bordering on pure hatred, right down to the fact that fathers wouldn't let their sons or daughters marry into the 'enemy's' clan. It all stemmed back to the early part of the century when unions on each river, the Tyne and the Wear, refused to allow workers from the other river to work on their contracts. Geordies always regarded themselves as higher-born than Mackems, which even showed during general elections, Sunderland being staunch Labour and Newcastle tending to vote Conservative. The rivalry between the Mackems/Geordies and Teessiders was not as intense. They hated us, for sure, but not with the same venom. This always rankled a bit with Teessiders. We hated them and I suppose we were a little jealous of their rivalry, especially when they sometimes disregarded us as a proper derby match. So you could say the rivalry was a bit one-sided; the Mackems would look forward to playing the Geordies and treat us like any other game. Us Boro fans always found it harder going at Sunderland, probably due to the fact that we never really invaded their ground like they did ours. Also their 'away' end, if you can call it that (the Roker end), was a massive open terrace behind one goal which was always full of their lads. At our place they were always given a full end of their own.

When I made it into the ground I was collared by the old fella and our kid, so I had to behave myself and put up with watching the aggro without joining in. The atmosphere during the game was unbelievable, with over 41,000 in the ground, a constant stream of lads getting taken out by the police, two players sent off and a 2–0 victory for the mighty reds. It wasn't over either. When we left the ground, hordes of

Mackems were waiting outside and the inevitable battles ensued. The old fella insisted I come back with him on the coach as he didn't think I'd get out of Sunderland alive the way things were going. One chant I remember from that match, which I now always laugh at, was not from Boro but from Sunderland and they still shout it to this day: 'We hate Boro! We hate Boro!' Not much, I grant you, but it was the way they chanted it with their weird Mackem accents – 'We hate Borra' – especially from a couple of thousand in unison. Mind, I suppose our 'We hate Sunlan' doesn't sound much better to a Mackem.

For the rest of the season, Boro continued to steamroller the opposition and won the title with a record number of points. The last home game was against Sheffield Wednesday and Jack's lads really turned it on for the fans with an 8–0 super show, sending poor old Wednesday down to the Third Division. After what had gone down at Hillsborough earlier in the season, the Wednesday fans had decided to have a go at the Holgate – and we weren't expecting it! It was about 2.30 p.m. and everyone was just getting in the party mood when there was a bit of a commotion at the back of the Holgate. The chant went up: 'WED-NES-DAY, WED-NES-DAY.' Two or three hundred had burst in all at once. At first Boro backed off, then charged at them. A full-scale ruck developed with Wednesday eventually scattering.

As it was well before kick-off the police were not in full attendance, so those who got involved were given licence to do what they wanted. This I enjoyed to the full. I must have punched and kicked more lads that day than I had in my whole life, mind the Wednesday boys weren't all that shy themselves. After what seemed like ages the law finally made their appearance, much to the relief of the Wednesday fans, who were duly escorted round the pitch to the relative safety of the Clive Road corner; I say relative safety because during this season a new mob of boys had been populating other areas of the ground in order to get into the away fans, and sporadic scuffles broke out for a short while until the police managed to segregate both sets. Sheff Wed, like all teams at that time, had a good following of boot boys. They were another giant club who had hit hard times and surely should have been too big for the Third Division but they were to stay there for some time. This was their swansong, and on talking to older lads I found out that they had been expected to come. 'They've always been up for a good ruck, Wednesday,' said Winker. 'Remember going there in '72, fucking hell on, we got well turned over.'

The final game of the season was away to Preston, who were managed by big Jack's brother Bobby. They needed to win to have a chance of staying up. Everyone thought big Jack would do his brother a favour, but no such luck. Boro won 4–2 and 10,000 travelling fans celebrated on the pitch. Oh and we took their end as well. After the game we went to Blackpool to carry on the celebrations throughout the night. Four of us got fixed up with some slags from Liverpool and shagged them on the beach, in fact there was quite a lot of shagging on the beach that night if my memory serves me right. Well that was it, one hell of a season, loads of crack and the big boys to look forward to in the coming season.

CHAPTER THREE

Into The Big Time

DURING THE SUMMER I left school and started my apprenticeship as a welder down at Smith's Dock shipyard. In those days you worked either at the shipyard, the steelworks, ICI or as a labourer somewhere. Office workers were few and far between, especially among the match lads. Smith's Dock was an old shipbuilding yard, the sort of place where men are men – tough, uncompromising blokes who couldn't be arsed training apprentices, as they were all on piece work (paid for what you produce). When you were placed with a welder you had to learn fast or end up getting a slap if he didn't get his 'count' in. We had to work in very trying conditions, freezing cold in the winter and sweltering hot in the summer, there was never any in-between.

There were always taxis coming and going at the dry dock with prostitutes visiting the seamen while their ships were under repair. That was an eye-opener. My mother once told me that Middlesbrough was renowned for having a high percentage of prostitutes due to all the heavy industry, which had attracted workers from all over Britain. Apparently this 'Infant Hercules', as Middlesbrough was once described (by then-Prime Minister William Gladstone) had grown up with people from all quarters of the globe, just like a wild west town (my stepdad's words). I suppose that's what made the place so tough. South Bank, for instance, has a very high Irish Catholic population (South Bank St Peter's FC was a nursery club for the Boro for donkey's years). Redcar has a very high Scottish contingent (there are both Rangers and Celtic supporters' clubs). If you check out the phone directory for Middlesbrough, you'll find a lot of unusual or foreign names from Poland, Italy and nowadays Asia, due to the high influx of people (the population grew from 10,000 to 150,000 in just a couple of decades).

Before the big kick-off, Boro played in some pre-season friendlies, one of which was a testimonial game against Leeds United who were the champions at the time; the game finished 4–4 and a bit of chew occurred with their fans (they brought about 2,000 through) although nothing major.

The season started for real away to Birmingham City, with about 4,000 Boro travelling to St Andrews. If I hadn't known we were in the big time, I was about to learn the hard way. The coach dropped us outside a pub near the ground. It was a warm August afternoon and there were about 100 Boro already drinking outside the pub, so we joined them. Nothing much happened before the game, just the usual pre-match singing ritual and pisstaking of the locals, and at 2.40 p.m. everyone started to stroll up to the ground. Our kid asked a Brummie where our end of the ground was. 'Yow've not got wun, mite,' he said. We had a laugh at his accent but didn't realise the significance of his answer.

Things became apparent when we reached the ground and asked a copper the same question. 'Just go through any turnstile you like lads,' he said, so we did. As I was about to pay at the turnstile, a lad with a Boro scarf came hurdling back over from inside the ground, his face covered in blood. 'No chance of getting in there mate,' he said, 'they're waiting for us as we go in.' We looked at each other and then at the copper, who laughed and said how rough it was here, remarking that if we didn't like it we should fuck off home.

We waited until the Brummies appeared to have gone (and a few more Boro joined us) then paid into the ground, everyone agreeing to wait until we were all through before entering the terraces. When we had about fifty inside the ground the Brummie boys clocked what was going on and came at us – hundreds of the fuckers. We stood our ground for all of ten seconds then beat a hasty retreat back over the turnstiles. Now this was getting ridiculous. I couldn't afford to do this all day, so we tried further round the ground, where we met more Boro in the same predicament. All the Boro decided to get together, 400 or more, and we made another attempt. This time we managed to get in unheeded. As we got onto the terraces, where there was already a sizeable crowd of Boro, we took great delight in leading a charge towards their fans, sparking a full-scale battle back and forth. The Brummies loved it and played a major role in the fun and games.

THIS HAD BEEN my first taste of big-time football violence and it wasn't to be my last. The first few home games didn't live up to expectations, possibly due to the fact that we played the likes of Carlisle and Luton, who we had already taken the previous season. The next big home game involved Manchester City, and they brought a few thousand fans, with a load on the train. A lot of away fans were about to learn that you just don't come to the Boro on the train – the ground is about two miles from the station with a rabbit warren of terraced streets to negotiate – and Man City found this out to their cost. In the Second Division we had got a lot of fans through on the train only when we played Sunderland or in big FA Cup matches. Now we were in the First Division, the crowds were bigger and travelling fans became the norm, especially from the bigger clubs. Ambushes would be a regular feature for some of these unsuspecting fools.

I heard from some of the lads in the Holgate during half-time that City had brought a good mob of boys by rail and that they had managed to march up Linthorpe Road virtually unheeded, so we agreed to wait out the back of the Clive Road

End ten minutes from time to ambush them. It's amazing how quick the rumours go round: when we left the ground to head for the Clive Road there must have been 1,500 to 2,000 in our mob. We could see the City fans looking over the back wall; they must have been deeply worried at what was waiting for them. The Boro had been winning 1–0 when we left the ground and scored another as we reached the corner, prompting the City fans to start leaving the ground. That in turn prompted us to start a charge, which sent them scurrying in all directions.

About 150 of them stuck together and held firm within the confines of the Clive Road corner, and the law moved in to disperse our lot with horses and dogs. We moved on towards Linthorpe Road, knowing that they had to come in that direction. Then we heard another roar and knew there had been another Boro goal. We didn't have to wait long for the City to come down the road: at first we thought they were charging us, then realised that a mob of Boro were chasing them from behind. Well, it was like Christmas. None of them were up to fighting, they just wanted to get away, so the turkey shoot began: tripping them up, smacking fuck out of them, removing their scarves, all the way to the station. I saw one lad whose nose was bleeding so badly you would have thought he had a tap on his head. Someone was about to give him it again but Daller said to leave him alone as he'd had enough, so he was relieved of his silk scarf and told not to come to Boro again. What with a 3–0 win and a good set-to, I enjoyed my Saturday night in the dance palace, showing off my trophy to all and sundry.

MY FIRST VISIT to Anfield came when one of our kid's workmates organised a trip to Liverpool with a night out in Blackpool after the match. We were happily boozing in a pub called The Arkle, right near the ground, with no bother at all, just good banter between the Scousers and ourselves. When it got close to kick-off time, we left the pub and headed for the ground. Whether it was due to the beer I had drunk or just naivety I cannot say, but I didn't notice several scouse wideboys eyeing us up. Nothing happened immediately, probably because we numbered so many, but as all the lads entered the ground and there was only me left to go in, a big lad with a huge shock of ginger hair asked me where I was from. His accent told me he was a scouser. I looked around and all I could see were Liverpool fans. *Oh shit, I'm gonna get it here*, I thought.

'Liverpool,' came my unconvincing, shameful reply.

'Fucking lying Geordie bastard,' snarled the scouser.

I attempted to pay my way into the ground but as I took my money out of my pocket he put the nut smack on the bridge of my nose, removing the £5 note from my hand at the same time and leaving me on my knees holding my face. Five pounds was a lot of money in 1974, when entry to the ground was only 60p. A copper stood no more than ten yards saw the whole thing but didn't lift a finger to help me. When I complained, he pointed to a sign saying 'Beware of Pick-pockets' and told me to fuck off. I wiped the blood from my nose and went in the ground, by now full of fuck and busting for revenge.

Nothing happened in the ground apart from a few skirmishes that the police broke up by wading in with those big sticks they always seem to carry in Liverpool. One chant by the Boro fans, started by the black lads funnily enough, went, 'Oh I'd rather be a n***er than a scouse.' There weren't any laws against racial chanting then and even the Liverpool supporters seemed to find it amusing.

I did get a form of revenge in Blackpool on the night when a scouser asked me the score from the game (2–0 to Liverpool). I gave him the answer with a right-left combination and chased him halfway along the seafront. Fuming I was that night. When I caught up with our kid and the rest of the lads we headed for the Manchester, a pub that is still just as popular today, mind it was the first time I'd ever had to drink out of plastic glasses. Blackpool in those days was a bit less commercialised than now and if you wanted to kick off a bit of chew there were always some locals willing to accommodate you. Nowadays it's different, money appears to rule the roost (doesn't it always?) and everywhere has gone way over the top. There's even mobs of lasses out these days; we never had that back in the Seventies.

I spoke to a Blackpool lad a few years later at an England match and asked him, 'How come your lads never turn out when there's a mob on your turf anymore, 'cos you used to when I was younger?' His answer was simple: 'We used to all the time, but you think about it, fighting every week of the year, slowly but surely the old bill get to know you, you get sick of all the arrests, it just becomes boring after a while.' I had to agree. He went on, 'I go to England matches for my kick-offs, I can't even go to Bloomfield Road any more, all the fucking coppers know me, soon as anything goes off with the Bisons [Blackpool's firm] I'm bang to rights.' I probably saw this same lad hanging around outside the Manchester as we were leaving, along with a small mob of Blackpool youngsters. Nothing happened as the law were in attendance, eyeballing us all the way to our coach.

The Geordies at home that season was an all-ticket affair, with Newcastle getting 7,000. It would have been sacrilege if nothing went off in these circumstances, and so it proved. I left the house and went up the town nice and early and was in the Empire pub at eleven bells, along with quite a few other Boro lads who had the same idea; after all, with 7,000 Geordies coming to town we had to be on duty early doors. Most of the town firm used to occupy the town centre pubs: the Erimus, the Shakespeare, the Wellington and the Masham. By about noon the word came that the Trooper (a pub set back away from Linthorpe Road about halfway between the ground and the town centre) was full of them, so a couple of lads went round to check it out. When confirmation arrived we decided to go in a few at a time so as not to spook them into an early confrontation. When we entered the pub we made for the bar, with the 'Mags' (Magpies is the nickname of Newcastle) occupying the lounge area. As our numbers grew to match theirs, we started singing, 'We hate Geordies and we hate Geordies,' etc. The Mags replied with the usual 'We hate Borra' crap, whereupon the inevitable bottles, tables and bar stools started flying.

As it was all going off, most of the Mags managed to run out into the street save for four hardy souls who took refuge behind the bar. One waved a broom shank about while the others hurled more glasses from the bar top. Bravely (or stupidly) I charged straight into the flying glass to land a punch smack on the jaw of the one waving the broom. He dropped the broom as I dragged him from behind the bar by his hair, throwing him to the floor, where two lads proceeded to kick the living shite out of him. The other three somehow managed to find their way outside pursued by a posse of Boro lads. I managed to stop their mate from taking too much of a beating by shouting to the two Boro lads to let him go. Up he scrambled and headed for the door, blood streaming from his face. Outside, and it was the usual up-and-down-the-road battle as the Mags who had got out re-grouped and launched a token counter-attack. It didn't last too long as more Boro piled out of the pub, filling the road and forcing the Mags to retreat. One or two of them were well into their thirties and quite handy with it but when you are up against superior odds there's only going to be one winner. As usual the law turned up to send everyone scattering in all directions, with odd Mags still getting picked off here and there.

We turned our attention further up Linthorpe Road to the Park Hotel, near to the ground, where more Mags had decided to wet their whistles, with the same results. This time we went in a couple at a time, waiting until we had far superior numbers. A couple of tables under the large bay window had a group of twenty Mags sat drinking and singing their usual Blaydon Races shite. They were totally unaware of what was about to happen as we sidled alongside, eventually surrounding them. A couple of our lads got chatting to them, which made them feel even more comfortable, then Stevo nutted the nearest Geordie to him. He went down like a sack of shite clutching his face. As his mates stood up everyone piled in. They started chucking glasses at us but we returned them two-fold, leaving them stuck in one corner, tables turned on their side to protect themselves as much as possible. The whole pub seemed to join in with the onslaught and they didn't stand a chance. This went on for a good few minutes, then once the missiles stopped some lads got stuck into them, punching the Mags at will. They had lost any fight they had in them and were cowering, holding up their arms in defence.

I could hear the sound of sirens and decided to vacate the scene, as did everyone else. Looking down Linthorpe Road I could see the police vans coming and moved over to the other side to watch what was happening. An ambulance pulled up next and after a few minutes several Mags came out of the pub. Some got in the ambulance, covered in blood, while the rest were escorted towards the ground by the police. One Mag looked over the road at me, smiled and nodded his head as if to say, 'Yeah mate, you got us good style there.' I could tell by the way he had his scarf tied round his wrist and the riding boots with his jeans turned up that he was one of their boot boys. He knew the score and he knew he'd have his chance up their place.

One thing I noticed was that the Geordies were all big fuck-off gadgies with an age range between eighteen and forty, whereas our lads were all between fifteen and twenty. It always seemed to take odds of two or three to one in our favour to get the better of them and this was the way it was going to be for a few more years to come. The game finished 0–0, a usual dour derby in front of the *Match Of The Day* cameras. After the game came the usual kick-offs in the streets, especially down Linthorpe Road towards the station (some fans never learn).

LEEDS UNITED AWAY was the next match and for the first time I decided to go on the train, one of those football special jobs purposely laid on with cheap fares. Now this game should have been designated all-ticket due to the fact it was a derby, Jack Charlton's first return to Elland Road and we had upwards of 15,000 fans travelling through. Anyway we got to Leeds station and similar to Boro it was a two-mile hike up to the ground. There were buses laid on but we walked, not knowing how far it really was. By the time we got to Elland Road it was 2.30 p.m. so a drink was out of the question, especially when we saw the size of the queues to get in. After we had waited twenty minutes the turnstiles were shut, with about 3,000 locked out. Then someone said the Gelderd End (Leeds's kop) was still open. I didn't need asking twice and along with several hundred other Boro made my way round. We joined the queue and after ten minutes, with 200 or so Boro managing to get in, the gates were closed again.

This was beginning to piss everyone off, me included. Someone suggested we knock down a fence – so we did. A copper was on the other side trying to stop us by hitting our hands with his truncheon but to no avail as the fence eventually collapsed. Mr Plod fled for his life as we surged up the grass bank into the ground. When we got to the top of the bank, we were met by another fence and thirty coppers, truncheons in hand. A swift about-turn and back out the way we had come. Talk about being pissed off; all I had seen of Elland Road up to now was queues, turnstiles, coppers and fences.

In the end I settled for watching half the game from a large billboard situated behind the away end. We had to chase a few Leeds fans who were already up there, and as soon as I got settled, Leeds scored to make it 1–0. Soon after, they scored again. *Typical Boro*, I thought. However, just before half-time big Stuey Boam managed to pull one back to set up a cracking second half. This goal also prompted a bit of chew in the ground and I could see a constant stream of fans being frog-marched around the pitch by the police. Early in the second half Boro scored again to make it 2–2. Now it was end-to-end football, one half of which I could see, and the atmosphere was unbelievable. The game ended at that score, which we were obviously happy with.

Thousands of fans poured out of the ground to sheer pandemonium, Leeds and Boro mingled together with fights kicking off everywhere. I wanted to find all the lads off the train but that was nigh-on impossible and it seemed the only people heading towards the station were Leeds, and they weren't friendly. After visiting the likes of Birmingham and Sunderland I had learned my lesson and knew when to keep shtum, so I got my head down, mingled with the crowd and headed for the station. It was some task under the circumstances, as I was in possession of a red and white beanie hat and scarf, which I had secreted about my person, while everyone else was bedecked with Leeds colours, leaving me standing out like a Belisha beacon. Amazingly I made it back to the station unscathed.

There was a bit of a ruckus going on with our lads and theirs, which I gleefully joined. No sooner had I thrown one punch than a copper had me away with my hand up my back, bouncing me all the way to a meat wagon. When I got in the back, a plain-clothed copper said I had two choices: 'If you think you're hard enough I'll feed you to our lot and see how hard you are then, or you can shut your mouth and join your mates and if I see you at it again you're nicked.' Well I'm no mug, so I promised to be on my best behaviour and he let me go, not before punching me in the lug hole and kicking me up the arse. On the train ride out of Leeds it was like being in a shooting gallery with bricks flying through half the windows. Mind, Leeds fans have always been like that.

Boro went on quite a run after the Leeds game, culminating in a 1–0 victory over Sheffield United to put us up to second in the league. However, as I was to learn time and time again Boro always build you up then let you down badly. We went seven games without a win in the league although we fared much better in the FA Cup, knocking out the Mackems in a thriller at Ayresome, another of those days where it was going off all over the place, especially with 10,000 Sunderland fans to have a portion with.

During our bad run we had to travel up to Newcastle. This was daunting to say the least; it was hard enough taking on the Geordies at home, never mind going to St James's. They gave us 7,000 tickets for the Gallowgate end, so I thought well we should be all right with that many. No such luck; the bastards were everywhere, hunting Boro like rabid dogs, and we made it easy for them. We went up totally unorganised, with a sort of 'look after yourself and fuck everyone else' attitude. It was as if everyone thought they could just hide in the crowd, but it's not easy when there's 7,000 all trying to do the same.

I went with my brother and a couple of other lads on the regular bus route, which dropped us off at the Gallowgate bus station. As we got into Newcastle, one of the lads we were with stuck up two fingers at a Mag. He promptly alerted several more Mags, who followed the bus to the terminus. By the time we got there the bus was surrounded. *Shit*, I thought, *we're gonna get it straight away*. Anyway, some coppers had clocked what was occurring and scattered them. Thank fuck for that, I thought, *but where do we go for a drink?* The whole area was crawling with the fuckers. Our kid suggested we go in the Magpie, their supporters' club, as it will just be full of ra-ras and we shouldn't have any bother, so in we went. The doorman suggested we go straight to the ground but being young, gifted and daft we went in. Fuck me, even the barman was a thug, taking the piss and letting all and sundry know we were Boro fans. If we had turned tail and left they'd have followed us out and torn us to shreds, so we ordered four bottles of brown ale and stupidly found the corner furthest from the door to make camp.

At first it was good banter with the Geordies happy to talk to us, saying how brave we were to go in there in the first place and talking about Lord Westwood (their chairman) and how they wanted him out of his job, 'sack the board' and so on. Then they came round with a petition calling for the resignation of Westwood and asked us to sign, which we did, only I wrote, 'The Holgate End rules OK', which none of them noticed at first. By now the club was in full swing, singing 'The Blaydon Races' and all that other Geordie crap, when one Mag noticed what I had wrote. Suddenly the mood turned sour. A few beermats were hurled in our direction followed by ashtrays, then a beer bottle flew over. Our kid ducked and it hit this old Geordie bloke on his head, causing blood to spurt everywhere. In the ensuing pandemonium one Geordie stuck the nut on our kid, giving him a black eye. We managed to open the emergency exit and get out into the street with half the pub chasing us. Me and our kid still had our bottles so we hurled them at the doorway, sending the Mags scurrying back inside. This gave us enough time to get over the road to the ground where good old plod were in large numbers. Our kid was the only one to take a smack and other than that we had escaped pretty much unscathed.

We went into the ground expecting to find our end full of Boro, but the Gallowgate held about 15,000 then so there were just as many Mags and no segregation, causing ninety minutes of mayhem. At the end of the game, which we lost 2–1, the banks at the back of the stand were covered with thousands of Mags waiting for us. *Shit*, I thought, *we're fucking dead here*, so me and our kid calmly picked our way past them, smiling and pretending we were local, our scarves of course safely tucked away out of sight. No one seemed interested in just the two of us, thank fuck, so we made our way to the bus station, which was only a short walk round the corner.

We had half an hour to kill before the bus was due to leave, so we sat on the compound wall waiting for the others to get back, chatting to a few Geordies who thought we were Mags from Yorkshire. As the rest of the lads turned up we continued the pretence, telling the Mags that we had sussed out a busload of Boro and would they fancy getting into them with us. Our kid claimed he had got the black eye fighting them before the game. The Mags shouted over a few more of their mates, making about twenty of them and thirty of us.

'You looking for Boro lads?' said big Stevie.

'Aye,' replied one Mag, 'whoar are they then?'

'Fucking here ya soft Geordie bastard.'

With that he floored one lad where he stood and we set about the rest. A short scuffle ensued and the Mags got on their toes. We could hear our bus revving its engine and we all boarded just in time to see the same lads coming back with about seventy more, armed to the teeth with bricks, lumps of wood and bottles. We told the driver to get his foot down before all the windows came through, which he duly did. We got away, just, and had a good laugh recounting the day's events all the way home. Big Stevie was the perfect example of a Geordie, something like twenty stone and sometimes he was known as Bully (no he wasn't a bully, he was named after that show *Bullseye* with Jim Bowen) because he liked his darts. He wasn't hard but looked the part.

The next big match of note brought Leeds to Ayresome, 7,000 of 'em and another crew who were about to learn not to come on the train. Saturday, February 22, 1975 is a date that will probably live with a lot of Leeds fans for a long time. Why? Because they got one of the most comprehensive hidings it has ever been my pleasure to witness and be part of. There are several ways of gauging the effects of how good a job you have done, but going from 7,000 visiting fans one season to a paltry 1,200 the next (all on coaches under police escort) is some indication, and when you consider they carried on taking thousands all over the rest of the country and gave our ground the nickname 'Suicide Park', it tells its own story.

On the night before the game, I had been out with a load of the G-town lads and we agreed to meet early on the Saturday in the Zetland pub, near the train station, to give Leeds the business. When I got in the pub at 11.20 a.m. there were already seventy lads sat around drinking. By noon you couldn't move; it seemed like every man and his dog were there. The Grand next door was half-full as well. At about 12.30 we heard the sirens of police vans and knew the train was pulling in, so everyone drank up and went outside, glasses and bottles in hand. We filled the road and it wasn't long before the law clocked us and moved in with horses and dogs. Everyone split up, some going back in the pub and myself and others moving further up Linthorpe Road to the Masham, which was already full of Boro lads out for one thing. We must have had seven or more pops at the Leeds escort up Linthorpe Road but they were too well protected by the law. Once we got near the ground we left them to concentrate on the fans who had travelled by coach and car and who did not have the protection afforded the train lot.

Ayresome Park was surrounded by a warren of side streets and back alleys that the police just didn't have the resources to cover, making a visit to Boro a nightmare for away fans. These streets were fully policed by Boro boot boys hunting down the huge travelling support. They had to be somewhere, and they were found several times getting out of minibuses, cars and vans. No mercy was shown; the only ones to get away were women, kids and older blokes. It was not the done thing to 'do' easy prey and I found myself playing fuck with a Boro lad for smacking a young Leeds fan who was with his mam and dad. This almost resulting in me getting smacked as well, although I had Bomber and some other gadgies with me who agreed.

At the time the newspapers seemed to be full of accounts of hooliganism going off all over the country; it was the fashion in a sense, so anyone who went to a match was deemed fair game. Basically if you were a football fan you had to be a hooligan whether you liked it or not. The music around then was mainly skin-style reggae and the fashion was turned-up jeans, DM boots or Riders and Wrangler/Levi jackets, all stuff associated with boot boys. Anyway, right up to kick-off time we had Leeds running scared all over the place.

The Boro had their biggest crowd of the season, 39,500, and the Holgate was bouncing. It's a pity the game never lived up to the hype, fizzling out to a 1–0 defeat for Boro. With ten minutes to go, I had not noticed loads of the main lads leaving the Holgate and going round to the away end. Suddenly a huge gap opened up in their end and there stood Ginger Jimmy, arms out giving it the big come on. Jimmy was easily recognisable with his long ginger locks and distinctive clothing (he always wore a light blue jumper, no coat just a jumper, no matter the weather). For a few moments it looked as though all the Leeds were running from him alone, then hundreds more Boro piled in after him, Leeds were running towards the pitch, swarming out the exits, it was chaos. Watching this prompted the rest of us to leave and get round there ASAP, as no one wanted to miss this. By the time I arrived, all I could see was Boro punching fuck out of anything in a Leeds scarf and removing said offensive woollen appendages to take as trophies.

The police were nowhere to be seen for a good five minutes, as they were trying to sort out the trouble inside the ground.

When they did turn up, we left the area and waited for Leeds to come down Linthorpe Road. As with Man City earlier in the season, the Boro had a mob behind them charging in. The Leeds fans didn't know which way to go, resulting in pure panic by them. They ran into a wooded park just off the road, where we were all waiting. It was already fairly dark, giving us perfect cover. Now it was pure carnage; even I was amazed at what I saw. I am not talking handfuls of lads here, more like hundreds getting the shite kicked out of them. It was a massacre that Cecil B. De Mille would have been hard-pressed to film.

I spoke to some Leeds fans a couple of years later and they were in the park that day. They swore that we came out of the trees and from behind gravestones like ghosts. It was after this game that Leeds gave Ayresome the Suicide Park nickname and they have never come in force since. The police made quite a few arrests, Ginger Jimmy being one, and due to the nature of the carnage that occurred the magistrates came down very heavily on everyone, dishing out fines of £100, which was unheard of at the time. Poor Ginger Jimmy got sent down for twelve months.

The rest of the season panned out as per the norm for those days. Chelsea away was scary, I got chased all over after the game and even when I made it to our coach the fuckers came on board battering the co-driver and smashing the windows as we pulled away. Man City got their own back. We got dumped out of the FA Cup by Birmingham (no chew this time but the song 'Keep Right On To The End Of The Road' was most impressively sung) and in the last match of the season away to Coventry we had probably the only chew we would ever get there, sharing their kop and having a mass brawl in the park near where the coaches were parked. Yep, every club had a firm then.

I was another year older, I had been to a few more grounds, I'd been right in the thick of one hell of a massacre, I hadn't been arrested (phew!) and I had got to know some more of the main gadgies in the Holgate. But I was a long way from being a Frontliner. The next season was to take me further along that road, starting with a London trip to Spurs that I would not forget in a hurry.

CHAPTER FOUR

Friday Night To Sunday Morning

FOR TOTTENHAM AWAY, one of the Eston boys organised a coach travelling down on the Friday and returning Sunday morning. Everyone who was anyone was on it: Bomber, Jacko, Joe (Bugner), Bram, Sharky, Three-fingered Mick, Nailer, in fact half the main lads from the Holgate. Word had it that the main firm from the town had a coach sorted as well. Three-fingered Mick was a small lad who I had seen in a fight locally. He was fast as fuck and not afraid to take on anyone bigger. Bomber was a well-built gadgie who didn't follow Boro much but was very handy all the same. Never one for talking much, he kept himself to himself; I don't think I ever heard him say more than a few words. Bram was one of those well-informed lads, very likeable, always up to date with current trends and talked the talk. He knew his way around London, as he used to live there. Jacko was a nutter, there's no other description for him, small but wild and would fight anything, including his own mates. Fucking mad.

We set off at 11 p.m. on the Friday after last orders. Everyone was full of drink and fired up. As the bus pulled away, one of the lads called for a minute's silence on behalf of Ginger Jimmy, who was banged up for the Leeds trouble last season. It was immaculately observed and promises were made to do the business for him at Tottenham. On the way down we must have had about fifteen piss stops due to the beer that had been consumed, and three halts at service stations that were duly relieved of their goods without payment.

Eventually we arrived in London, the coach dropping us at Kings Cross station and arranging to pick us up there on Sunday morning. It was only 6.30 a.m. and a few of us went to the toilets for a wash and brush up. As we got on the station platform, Three-fingered Mick and Joe clocked a couple of Millwall boys heading down to the toilets. Well, it was like a red rag to a bull and the first good hiding of the day was dished out. I didn't see firsthand what happened but the state of the two Millwall boys told its own story. One or two of our lads had a go at Mick and Joe about it, but they made the point that it was a straightforward two-on-two fight. Enough said, I thought. We vacated the station after that in case the Old Bill turned up, and found somewhere to get breakfast.

By the time we'd all had something to eat it was about 9.30, too early to head for Tottenham, so we got one of those all-day tube tickets and had a bit of a look round the city. Bram knew his way around so we let him take the lead. After an hour or so we were on our way up to the Seven Sisters tube station. Our numbers had gone down a bit from fifty to thirty-five, as some lads decided to visit Soho. Several Spurs fans were waiting when we got to the Seven Sisters, so we immediately charged at them up the stairs and out on to the street. No punches were thrown, as they got on their toes at first sight. Once we were on street level and they saw our numbers, they got a bit braver and mobbed up on the opposite side of the road, numbering about fifty. Bram remarked that we should give them it now before any more of them came, so for the next few minutes it was us going at them and them running off, but they kept hanging around and as their numbers grew we started to get a bit worried.

By the time there were eighty of them, they weren't running any more. We were cut off from going any further down the road towards the ground, so we tried going through an estate with loads of scruffy-looking flats. Bad move! As we entered the estate, loads of black geezers started coming out of the flats at us, baseball bats, the lot. We were in trouble. We made it through one courtyard to the road with half of the estate after us, only to bump into the Spurs fans, who now numbered about 100. As they were only youngish we went at them and luckily they backed off, preferring to chant at us. The black lads caught up but a couple of coppers came to our rescue and escorted us up the road to the ground. It was a relief.

The law left us at the ground, saying we would be okay. The Spurs fans had followed and stood on one corner, although not doing too much, just keeping an eye on us. It was still only 11 a.m. and we didn't fancy hanging around there for ages. Then a couple of coaches of Boro fans pulled up at the other end of the road and they all piled into the White Hart pub, so we joined them. What a pleasure it was to walk into that pub with 100 Boro singing their heads off. The first pint didn't touch the sides and the second didn't even touch my lips, because all hell broke loose as I was getting served. A load of Spurs fans had burst through a side door and without even thinking I threw my (full) pint straight in this lad's face, putting him on his arse. The rest of them beat a hasty retreat into the street. We followed, and the usual up-and-down-the-road ruck took place, with Boro having the upper hand.

The police stopped everyone from going back in the pub and told us we had to go in the ground, but the turnstiles hadn't opened, so they made us wait outside until they did. We entered the ground at 1 p.m. and as I was famished I went to the food bar for a pie. This resulted in me losing the rest of our crew. The end we were in, I later found out, was Spurs' kop, the famous 'Shelf'. I made my way to the front near the halfway line, where there was a TV camera, and sat on the terracing to eat my pie. When I had finished, I started looking for the rest of the lads. I found Bram and five others, so we stayed put and slowly scanned the ground for our mob. Eventually we found a load of Boro gadgies who were game as fuck and up for anything. Behind one of the goals a full-scale fight was going on and I could make out Three-fingered Mick and some of the other lads going for it good style.

'Come on, we're Boro, lets get into them behind the other goal,' said one of the gadgies we were with – so we did. We slowly edged our way to the corner and then charged in, scattering everyone. The punches were flying everywhere. Spurs fans ran on the pitch, leaving a big gap with about forty of us stood in the middle, arms in the air beckoning them to come at us. And come at us they did – fucking hundreds of them from the Shelf. Now we were in the shit. I remember seeing Bram on the pitch followed by a few more as the tables were turned against us. I did a quick side-swerve and ducked into the crowd, becoming anonymous for a while.

I was alone now and, to be honest, a little scared, so I made my way back to the Shelf near the halfway line hoping to bump into some of our lads who might have had the same idea. I stood alone for the whole of the first half, watching the game, and by half-time I was so tired I sat down and almost fell asleep, only to be alerted by a young black lad with a cockney accent who said he used to live in the Boro and that he recognised me from the Holgate. It turned out he was one of the younger brothers of the black family that followed the Boro. I was a little bit suspicious until he mentioned a couple of names, then he said he'd show me where some other Boro lads were. He took me to the top level of the Shelf, where our kid was stood with a few others wearing Tottenham scarves.

'Thank fuck I've found you,' I said.

'Shut your fucking mouth you daft cunt, we're right in the middle of their end,' our lad whispered to me. 'Just stand here with us and don't say fuck-all and you'll be all right.'

I asked where they had got the scarves from. 'Trophies,' came the reply. *I'd better get one as well,* I thought.

Spurs scored to go one-up near the end, so we took the opportunity to leave the ground as their fans were celebrating. There were only six of us as we walked up towards the Seven Sisters but no mobs of Spurs. I was quite happy with this but one lad with us wanted to fight every cockney he saw, the end product being ten or more Spurs fans going home battered and scarfless. I managed to get a scarf from one lad who surrendered it without a struggle.

When we got to the tube station, five Spurs fans were stood with a few coppers pointing at us and saying, 'That's him!' The police grabbed hold of the lad who had been battering everyone and removed all but one of his scarves – apparently he said he had bought that one. Amazingly they let him go, no charges or anything. More of our lads turned up as we waited for the tube, but even more Spurs arrived as well. We numbered about forty when the train pulled in, most of us with Spurs scarves on. Some Boro wearing red and white scarves sat in the same compartment as us, and a few Spurs fans started on them, thinking we were Spurs too. Well, that was all it took; we mashed them. They must have got the shock of their lives and being on the tube there was no escape.

One of the cockneys started it all by punching this poor young Boro lad sat minding his own business. As they weighed into the others, Jacko made his way through the carriage, grabbed the one who had started it and nutted him square on the nose. The lad went straight down and the rest of us piled into his mates. They cowered at one end of the carriage as we traded punches to start with, then just smacked fuck out of them. After a couple of minutes we stopped as they protested. Not Jacko though; he was booting the living shit out of this one lad who was curled up in a tight ball. Every word Jacko shouted at him was followed by a kick: 'You-fuck-ing-cockney-twat-we-are-Boro-don't-fuck-with-Boro-you-wanker.' The lad lay there taking everything, squealing each time Jacko booted him. No-one tried to stop him as he would probably have turned on his own mates, such was his temper. They dived off the tube at the next stop with a few kicks up their arses, minus their scarves and with us lot laughing.

At Kings Cross we got everyone together and set off to a pub in Vauxhall that had strippers on. After the first couple of strippers had done their stuff, we got a bit too boisterous and the landlord called the police, who made us leave. We trawled around London for a couple of hours, getting thrown out of pub after pub and eventually finishing up back at Kings Cross at 10 p.m. We were hanging around the station area when one of the lads rushed over, saying, 'Tottenham are here, fucking loads of them.' I looked over the road and true enough Tottenham were here, about 150 of them. We all ran out of the main entrance straight into them and a toe-to-toe battle ensued, with us eventually backing off into the doorway due to their superior numbers.

A couple of beat bobbies turned up to scatter them and told us we had to go on to the St Pancras side, as a train of Chelsea was due to arrive from Sunderland and they could not afford us any protection. However, they said they had called for back-up. When we got to St Pancras, we met another coachload of Boro who were getting picked up there. Then Spurs came again, about 200 of them this time. We numbered about 100 and had the advantage of being at the top of a flight of stairs. The fighting lasted only a few minutes but it was full-scale, hands-on battling which halted mid-stairway when one of our lads rolled a mail trolley down the steps into them. There was a lull as they regrouped, then five vans full of police came screaming up the ramp. Suddenly there were coppers everywhere, pinning us up against the wall and searching everyone. Five lads got lifted for carrying offensive weapons (sticks and stones picked up to use during the battle) and the rest of us were herded together in the middle of the car park and surrounded by police.

After what seemed like ages, we heard a loud roar and we were attacked by hundreds of what we thought were Tottenham, but the police informed us they were Chelsea fans just back from Sunderland. I couldn't believe my eyes at what I saw: they were literally fighting the police to get at us, and as soon as we retaliated it was our lads who were getting locked up. When they backed off to regroup, the head police officer asked what time we were being picked up. 'Tomorrow morning' was not the reply he wanted to hear. Somehow he managed to find both coach drivers and we were put on the coaches at about 1 a.m. As we drove out under police escort I saw what must have been 700 or more boys lining the streets. If that lot had got hold of us, we'd have been dead meat. It was a very impressive mob if ever I saw one.

THE NEXT GAME was away to the Geordies on a Wednesday night. I'm ashamed to say I missed it due to being skint. By all accounts I didn't miss anything except the usual slip into the ground, keep shtum, incognito, back to the car/bus/train and home again. Newcastle was always a dodgy place to go to, especially at night. The streets near the ground were dimly lit, dark and narrow. Every pub looked unwelcoming and always seemed to be full of gadgies. On the other side of their ground you had Leazes Park, which led up to the Royal Victoria Infirmary; it was fitting, I suppose, to have a hospital so close (I know of a few lads who ended up in there) and this was similar to the area surrounding Ayresome in many ways. St James's Park was another of those grounds without the safety of a sectioned-off terrace for away fans, meaning you would spend half the game keeping one eye on the Mags. It wasn't just the young Mags you had to take on either; half their firm consisted of big fuck-off gadgies over thirty.

Middlesbrough's trophy cabinet hasn't exactly been bulging over the years but we did see cup success that year– of a sort. The 1975/76 season had actually begun during pre-season with a competition called the Anglo-Scottish Cup, involving a local group stage with Carlisle, Sunderland and Newcastle. We won through and were 'rewarded' with a two-legged quarter-final with Aberdeen. Boro won the first leg 2–0 at home and the second leg at Pittodrie 5–2, which I went to. I missed the coach after the game and had to hitch back home, something I wouldn't recommend to anyone – have you seen how far Aberdeen is from Boro? The semi-final draw put us against Mansfield Town, those giants from the Midlands. A tough two-legged tie that saw us scrape through by the close margin of 5–0. So on to the final, another two-legged affair against those West London behemoths Fulham! The first leg was at home. We pounded them into a 1–0 submission courtesy of an own goal by a guy named Strong. It set up a thriller of a second leg, which I had to go to. Now, we had just played Manchester United at home on the Saturday and had the usual kick-off with them, so Fulham on a cold Tuesday night wasn't going to be a problem – or so I thought.

Getting time off from the shipyard was not easy, especially when you needed half a day followed by a full day and your gaffer was known as 'The Bungalow' because he was short in the upstairs department. He also hated football, football fans and especially Boro but I somehow managed to convince him I needed the time off for a doctor's appointment in the afternoon and then phoned in the next day with a sicky. So to Fulham. I travelled down with the Boro ra-ras, even though I swore I would never go with the supporters' club coaches again following Birmingham in the cup the previous season. I mean, they are such a boring bunch of wankers, run by a load of tosspot jobsworths, but cheap travel and convenience won the day.

When we arrived at Craven Cottage – all FOUR coach-loads of us (for a fucking final as well) – the 'organisers' said they had arranged for us to be allowed in their supporters' club. It was bad enough having to travel all the way down listening to these wankers without being told we had to drink with London's finest tosspots as well, so myself and a few lads who were okay decided to miss out on this wonderful invitation and set off to find some decent pub action. Not too far from the ground we found a pub which was populated by a couple of dozen Boro boys who had travelled down by car. I had twenty or so lads with me, so we made this our gaff until it was time to enter that mighty stadium.

Southerners have always held us northerners in low regard, slagging off our industrial heritage, claiming we live in little, Coronation Street-style housing, saying how cold it is up north and all that shite. Well London can't claim to be all that smart (didn't it used to be called 'the smoke'?), especially in the Seventies. There always seemed to be some construction work going on, no matter where you went; maybe they were still rebuilding the place after the Second World War. 'Up-market' Fulham was a right dump, still is really. Chelsea next door, their ground backed on to a gasworks. West Ham was set in the middle of a scruffy terraced housing estate. Millwall was near the docks while Tottenham was situated near tenement blocks full of impoverished ethnic minorities. I don't wish to slag off my capital city, but when it comes to defending my town, well these southerners ask for it.

While in the pub we joked and had a bit of crack with the locals and even managed to outsing the Fulham fans, who looked about as rough as a bunch of carol singers (maybe they were; it was pretty close to Christmas after all). Then we left and went up to the ground. Boro had been sent tickets for the seats but we weren't having that and went onto the terraced

end behind the goal. Having met the Fulham fans in the pub
we didn't envisage much chew on the terraces. How wrong
can you be, eh? We all took position roughly centrally behind
the goal and when the teams came out we started chanting,
'We love you Boro, we do.'

Suddenly there was a big surge from behind and a few
punches were thrown before I heard the words, 'Come on
then Boro, Chelsea's here.' When I looked round, all I could
see were these big gadgies in sheepskin coats and donkey
jackets giving it the big come-on. A load of coppers moved in,
trying to separate both factions. The Chelsea mob just moved
back away as if to encourage us to get together, also giving the
police a false sense of achievement. This appeared to work, as
the fighting stopped, everyone calmed down and the law
moved away. Job done, or so they thought. Everyone appeared
to be watching the game and nothing happened for the rest of
the half. Even the two coppers left in close attendance
eventually decided to move away.

During half-time a cockney wideboy came over and started
talking to me. I asked how he knew I was Boro. He told me my
clothes were a dead giveaway. 'Londoners don't wear all that
DM shite and Wrangler jeans halfway up their arses,' he told
me. I noticed he had a smart sheepskin coat on with flared
'bags', a pair of black riding boots and a checked scarf around
his shoulders, neatly tucked into his coat. His hair was long
but immaculately styled, with a centre parting. He went on to
tell me he was one of those Chelsea fans who had been at
St Pancras station earlier in the season and that's why they
were all here tonight, to finish the job so to speak.

'Youse 'ad a good firm out at St Pancras, we woz well
impressed. Stood your ground as well. Were you there then?'
he asked in a strong cockney drawl.

'Yeah. It went off for fucking ages. Anyway, what were you
doing with Spurs? I thought you hated each other?' I was
goading him a little.

'When you've just 'ad it in facking Sunderland and you 'ear of more Geordies in London going for it, you get togevva, doncha.'

'Geordies? We aren't Geordies mate, no way. We hate the fuckers more than you, and we'd never team up with them either.' I went on to explain that we were no more Geordie than Luton were cockney.

'Who's the top firm in the Norf then?' the wideboy enquired.

'Don't really know,' I bluffed. 'We do them at our place, they do us at theirs.' I was using the tactful answers.

We continued chatting for a while, then he asked if we were up for it with them. I informed him that most of our main boys weren't there but assured him the lads would make a show if they went for it. To be honest, looking around at the lads who were there, I thought our lot would run like fuck, but pride wouldn't allow me to slag off our own fans, so I agreed to organise our lot for a set-to at the end of the game. This was to give me a bit of time to tell everyone the score. Another lad had been out the back for a pie and had had a similar conversation with one of their lads, so we decided to move to the bottom corner nearest to where the rest of the Boro were sat in the seats, right near that cottage house thing.

As we moved over, about 100 of us, the Old Bill clocked us and moved in to separate us from the rest of the crowd, forming a line between them and us. This made me feel a whole lot better. The Chelsea boys weren't best pleased, as we had robbed them of a surefire ruck, a bit shitty-arsed on our part I grant you but safety first was our intent that night. At the end of the game, which was a 0–0 draw, meaning we won the cup, all hell broke loose, with Chelsea and Fulham trying everything to get into us, throwing coins and fighting with the police. Only a couple of them managed to get through and were handled easily. So Boro had won their first trophy (it was more of an egg cup really) and I had survived another test with the capital's finest.

There was another cup competition we fared quite well in, the League Cup, reaching the semi-final stage. We won the first leg 1–0 against Manchester City. The second leg was a nightmare away at Maine Road, for the team and for us. First of all our coach arrived late due to too many piss stops. When I got in the ground, the first thing I saw was a goal smash into the back of our net, followed by another to put City 2–1 up on aggregate. Although we had 6,000 fans only 1,500 were in the Kippax, with the rest in the seats. We were separated by a waist-high fence, which was regularly breached throughout the game. The City fans were throwing all sorts of things, including those six-pointed 'kung fu' stars, one of which embedded itself in the wooden fence behind me. I even had to duck to avoid a thin plastic bag full of broken glass.

The second half saw another two goals for City, prompting us to leave (even if just for our own safety). Outside there were all forms of mayhem down those dark narrow streets and back alleys that surround Maine Road. One lad from G-town was put in hospital with a fractured skull (he was smashed over the head with a cricket bat, I mean who takes a cricket bat to the match, for fuck's sake) and several others made it home with bust noses, black eyes or severe bruising. One lad chased our kid through a packed pub with a knife. He left only when I stood facing him with a broken bottle and a dozen mates backing me up. I suppose they remembered the spanking we gave them the season before and this was their revenge. It was one night I don't enjoy looking back on. Although I didn't get turned over myself, I could so easily have been one of the many recipients of the violence dished out on that cold January night. Boro lost 4–0 and came a poor second best on the streets. Maybe this is one of the reasons we still have a bit of history with City.

The rest of the season in the league threw up several interesting *tête-à-têtes*. We drew 3–3 at home to Newcastle in a fascinating encounter both on and off the pitch. Boro were 3–1 up with a few minutes to go when the Mags hit two late goals to steal a point. As half of their fans were leaving the ground when the goals were scored, this caused them to run back in. Our lot, who were waiting outside for the annual kick-off, thought they were shitting out and charged in after them, resulting in a superb toe-to-toe battle in the Clive Road compound which the local plod had no chance of sorting.

Then on to Leeds away. We won 2–0 thanks to goals by big John Hickton in front of 5,000 travelling Boro fans. When we left the ground I spotted some Leeds fans taxing a young Boro kid of his scarf. I must have been the only Boro fan to see it because when I went over I was alone. Knowing there were 5,000 or so Boro fans a matter of yards away, I confronted the Leeds boys and relieved the thief of his booty, only to be set upon by all his mates. There I was, fighting like fuck with a dozen or so boys and no fucker on the other side of the road knew what was going on (apparently they thought I was Leeds and my attackers were Boro). I was saved from a mauling by a copper on horseback who got hold of one of the Leeds lads by his scarf and galloped off, bouncing him down the road. When I got back with our kid and the rest of the lads I had a bloody nose, half a dozen lumps all over my head and my hat was missing. I had been taxed. The lad who swiped it made a mistake though and tried to slip in with Boro's fans. Our lad spotted him and took the hat back, sending said tosser home with a thick ear.

Liverpool was the next away and we won 2–0. However, while stood in the Anfield Road End we were sussed out by the local scallies, who followed us out at the end. There were only four of us in a car and when we walked back to it, twenty or more Scousers jumped us. I received a smack in the face for the second time in Liverpool (two out of two now), however two of the lads I was with were hard as nails, Piper and Acko, and they were knocking these guys out for the fun of it. The law eventually showed face and the Scousers tried to get us locked up, saying we started it. The rest of the season panned out to mid-table obscurity as usual, apart from that wonderful, ahem, cup win.

The next couple of seasons were to throw up more similar confrontations and epic cup battles but things were slowly changing. The Government was starting to introduce laws to combat soccer hooliganism, giving the police and courts more powers to try to halt what was becoming known as the English Disease.

DURING THE SEVENTIES it was pretty much hit and miss whether you did the business away or copped for a good kicking. As I have already mentioned, every town had its firm, no matter which league they were in. One place we always seemed to do the business was Derby County. Now don't get me wrong, they had a decent enough crew of lads (I'm sure even Forest would agree with that) but from the first time we went there, we turned them over good style, and after that it became an annual pilgrimage for all Boro's kick-off merchants. They had the dodgy terraced estate surrounding the ground, always loads of lads out looking for away fans, a tight, compact ground, dark dingy boozers, the lot, but for some reason we always had Derby down as the one to go to. Even our tosspots jumped on the bandwagon.

After a few seasons of this, it got to the stage where the Boro fans would chant at opposition fans that they were worse than Derby County, thus implying that they were soft as fuck. There have been seasons where we took more fans to Derby than we did to Sunderland or Newcastle. Apart from being a huge insult to Derby, it used to piss me off that we appeared to be more wary of our hated rivals, leaving them to regard us as a minor derby match. Mackems and Geordies that I knew used to ask why we took so many all the way to Derby, yet were scared to travel thirty or forty miles up the road. I had no answer other than to say that their ground was shite and that we got a better kick-off there. Even Derby got carried away with the rivalry to the extent of spray-painting the walls around the Baseball Ground with slogans such as 'We hate Boro' and 'Boro die' (not Forest as you would expect).

One season about thirty of us went into Derby town centre and had a drink in a pub called Jimmy's. Yes we were getting a bit too sure of ourselves, as anyone who knows that pub will tell you. I had gone to the match with a firm from Redcar, known as the Redcar Reds, all big lads who could handle themselves. When we got in Jimmy's bar I knew it was the wrong move, but hey what the fuck, we're Boro and this was Derby, we always have them. After we had all ordered a drink we had a look round. All you could see was wall-to-wall black guys, and I mean the nasty six-foot-plus variety. One lad with us called Crow professed to hate black people and he was pissed. No sooner had he clocked them than he started singing, 'There ain't no black in the Union Jack, so pack your bags and fuck off back.' Well, red rag to a bull and all that; there was fucking hell on. Bottles, glasses, tables, chairs, you name it, came flying at us. To make matters worse we were nowhere near the door, so we had to run the gauntlet and literally fight our way out. By the time everyone was outside there wasn't one of us without blood dripping from somewhere and a couple of lads had to go to hospital for treatment.

When we got up to the ground we were stupid enough to go in their end as well. This resulted in another set-to, which was rather mild in comparison. Our battling in their end prompted the rest of the Boro to start fighting with the law. Eventually we were taken out and marched round the pitch to the end with our fans in.

I got to know the Redcar lads a lot more after that, especially when I moved down to that area of Teesside. Redcar is a smart seaside town on the east coast about ten miles from Middlesbrough. Most of the lads there support Boro. There are one or two Leeds fans, who always get the piss taken out of them, but they are tolerated and there is very rarely any trouble. I always used to go to Redcar for my nights out, as I found it a lot friendlier than the Boro, some good pubs and clubs and the women weren't too bad either. It didn't matter how many match lads you knew in Middlesbrough, there always seemed to be some townie who didn't go to the match who wanted trouble. Redcar was different; everyone seemed to know or be related to everyone else, a very close-knit community. I enjoyed going to the Starlight or the Top Deck, two clubs that always had a nice selection of ladies on tap. The Deck was harder to get in and would normally be everyone's first choice, while the Starlight was usually where you would end up if you failed elsewhere. The music scene at the time was mainly Motown, reggae and soul music, especially downstairs in the Deck, with chart stuff in the disco areas. I preferred ska and reggae. The last song in both clubs would be a smoochy number and was almost a cue that 'if you're not tapped up now, you've blown it'. The Starlight would have either 'You'll Never Walk Alone' or 'The Air That I Breathe'. In the Deck it was always 'This Guy's In Love With You'. Funny how you remember these things.

One thing I had now seen was a crew of lads who stuck together and were organised, something Boro had never been able to do. Chelsea, Millwall and West Ham had always been well organised, that's why even with small numbers they were capable of doing the biz. I always advocated that we needed to be organised and well drilled to compete with the likes of the big firms from London, but no one would ever listen. However I was now a bit older and a bit bigger and I had seen the beginnings in this crew of lads who were all mates from

Redcar, all loyal to Boro and game as fuck when it came to standing and fighting. There was the General, Fred, Shell, Tommy, Big Ted, Chunky, to name but a few. They went everywhere. Even the younger lads who often travelled with them were brought up on the same principle: no fucker ever runs. If you did shit out you got worse off your mates, so it was better to be done than run.

The General was a tall, well-built lad, grammar school educated, and got his name through being good at organising the lads. He was very astute and quick-witted. Fred, or Custer as he was known, was a doorman covered in tattoos. He was a bit shorter than the General but built like a brick outhouse. He was one of the first lads I got to know from Redcar; sound as a pound old Custer was. Shell was another six-footer who liked his ale and loved his football (they all did). Chunky I knew from school when he lived in Eston. He was mad as fuck, always doing silly things, a real joker in the pack. Tommy was a huge guy who only ever seemed to need one punch to put someone away, another doorman with massive fists that resembled a football when clenched. Big and handy though Tommy was, he was well respected as a gentleman; he was a very heavy drinker though. Big Ted was a good negotiator, always willing to talk first, didn't go steaming in like a lunatic, very diplomatic. Younger lads that travelled with the Redcar lads included Hobnail, Seggsy and the Shadow, who would become well known in their own time.

I met one of the younger members of the Redcar firm at an FA Cup match at Liverpool in 1977. I had travelled through with a load of younger lads from G-town, we arrived late and only about thirty off our coach got in the ground. The rest were locked out as the turnstiles were shut with 56,000 shoe-horned inside. An estimated 10,000 were from Boro. Everton were playing Derby on the same day, so the Boro fans who were locked out went to that game instead. Boro lost the match 2–0 (robbed more like) but throughout the game there was a constant battle going on with the Scousers in the Anfield Road End. When I came out of the ground at the end, I could see pitched battles going off all over the place. Now I'm not one for missing free-for-alls but the main thing on my mind was to find where our coach was. In my search I found the rest of the lads from our coach plus a few other stragglers, making thirty-five of us. One lad said the coach was parked with some others at the bottom of this long road, so we set off down the road into a very dodgy-looking estate.

After 100 yards I looked back and realised we weren't alone. A mob of fifty or more Scousers was following behind. Up ahead were about fifteen coming towards us. I surveyed the lads I was with. Most were around the sixteen-year-old mark and all were looking to me for a decision. 'Right, everyone stick together,' I said, but I didn't feel too confident.

As we came to the smaller crew in front of us, we weighed into them, sending them scattering all over. This prompted the ones behind to charge down the road at us. 'STAND,' I shouted, to no avail. Everyone started running, me included. As we got to the end of the road thinking the buses were just around the corner, I turned round to see some poor fucker getting the shit beaten out of him, and as I looked down the next road there were no buses to be seen. *This is it*, I thought, *we're gonna fucking die here*. Another mob of Scousers came from out of a side road and now we were surrounded. Everyone started jumping over fences into gardens and banging on doors. Either some local must have seen what was occurring and phoned the law or we were just lucky, because a pig wagon turned up in the nick of time to save us from a massacre. We explained to one copper that we had been left behind. He agreed to call us some taxis and offered us protection until they arrived. The taxis were to take us to the motorway so we could hitch a lift home.

As we were waiting, a young lad of no more than fifteen came staggering round the corner, drenched in blood and having obviously had one hell of a kicking. He had a Union Jack draped around his shoulders with 'BORO' emblazoned across the middle. I asked him if he was all right. 'You said stand,' he replied. Fuck me, he was the only one who had stood. I felt like shit; this poor little lad had taken the lot while we ran off. I told him he was a game little fucker and asked him where he was from. 'Redcar,' he replied. The same lad was to later go down in Boro Frontline folklore. I never forgot his piece of bravado, and as he got to know me better in later years he never forgot to remind me of the day when I left him to the mercy of Liverpool's worst. I was only eighteen myself but I was the oldest one there and should have set an example. This lad grew up to become a well-known face within Boro's tight-knit firm. I'll just call him the Shadow. As for Derby County, well they were there that day, but the Everton fans joined up with Liverpool to 'do' the Boro because 'Derby don't offer as much sport as you do,' as one talkative Evertonian put it. The learning process carried on, and the organisation side of things was improving.

An Arsenal fan wrote a book called *Steaming In* in which he recalled what happened during a visit to Boro during that same season in the FA Cup. Most of his account is fairly accurate, e.g. the fact that the 'Gooners' got a fair old kicking on and off the pitch. To the writer it was one of the worst away experiences of his life. I was there and I suppose it will have been a bit hairy for them, but to us it was just another bunch of Cockneys being stupid enough to come on the train and we dished out the same as we had done on several previous occasions to the Mackems, Geordies, Scousers and especially Leeds. What made this match most noticeable was the fact that most of the violence took place in the stadium, and several national tabloids showed a photo of an Arsenal fan being led round the pitch with a dart lodged in the corner of his eye. A pitched battle also took place in the hospital where several injured fans had been taken for treatment. Apparently both Arsenal and Boro fans fought each other in the corridors, even using crutches as weapons. When you add that to the beatings dished out all the way to the station, along with loads of arrests, it does look worse than it actually was.

CHAPTER FIVE

Get Organised

SEASON 1978/79 SAW Big Jack leave and John Neal come in to take the Ayresome Park hotseat. The football side of things had stagnated into mid-table mediocrity and gates had started dropping, due to the increase of soccer hooliganism according to the powers that be (mind you it's funny how there was always an increase on the gate when a big kick-off was on the cards!). This season was one where we were going to be taught a few lessons in how to get organised. I was twenty now and regularly attending matches with the Redcar lads. A lot of Boro lads had also become friendly with the Redcar crew. In the past there had been this us-and-them mentality, where lads from other areas of Teesside had not got on, but now something new was emerging.

In the early Seventies most lads just stayed with their own mates from whichever estate they were from. Sometimes this led to in-house fighting. I recall Eston and Redcar having a few set-tos in the Holgate, mainly when a fight that had occurred in a nightclub in Redcar carried on at a match. Eston also had a bit of a war going with Stockton, which went off sporadically for three years. Middlesbrough and Stockton had their own war or two which resulted in more bad feeling for a few years, even into the Eighties. Often the rivalry came about when two top gadgies from an area wanted to find out who was 'Bull Goose', 'King of the Holgate' or if someone copped for a bit of friendly fire during a skirmish with away fans. I have taken many a punch from a Boro lad by mistake and just lived with it, shit happens, however some people don't think that way. Rival areas also used to fight with each other away from football. For example Teesville had a war going on for a long time with the NTP (initials of Netherfields, Thorntree and Park End, areas that were close to each other). This would also carry on to the match.

Early in the season we played QPR at home and some late arrivals from London were ambushed by a Boro firm known as 'Block Two, the Bob End Crew', leaving two of the cockneys in hospital with stab wounds. Although I didn't agree with anyone using a knife, I was impressed by the way this particular crew organised themselves, to the point of missing the beginning of the match so as to collar their mob. Apparently the Bob End Crew had been done by the QPR firm in Shepherds Bush the season before, so it was a sort of revenge mission, and it was planned.

One gadgie, who later became a leading referee, used to be always saying 'get organised'. He didn't even look the type to be a football hooligan but he rumbled just like everyone else. Our kid and I used to laugh at him but he was right, we did need to get our act together, especially away from home (even against Derby). And when we played against Chelsea at home that December, we were taught just how much damage a small, well-organised firm could do.

I was in the Westminster pub in a side street near the ground, having a beer and enjoying some general chitchat with some of the lads. Funnily enough, we were talking about Chelsea and how they never seemed to bring a big firm to the Boro, when this young lad came flying in to the pub, puffing and panting.

'Lads, lads, there's loads of Chelsea in the Holgate.'

'Fuck off you daft little cunt,' came the response. I agreed; after all, it was only 2.15 p.m. Then some more came in with the same message. An older lad relayed the crack.

'Here, fucking loads of Chelsea have just come up boot boy alley and gone in the Holgate. No bull, fucking loads of 'em.'

It must be true, we all thought, so we piled out and made haste to the ground. As I entered, the first thing I noticed was 'CHELSEA' sprayed on the back of the Holgate fence. Entering the terraces, I could just see the last few Chelsea fans being escorted by police into the away enclosure. Fucking hell, they'd done it, it was true. I couldn't believe it; Chelsea had been in and done the biz. I asked some of the lads who had been in at the time what had happened. The word was that they came in all quiet like and waited until they were fully mobbed up, then gathered at the back, let out with a chant and weighed into everyone. The Boro that were in mostly consisted of young kids and old codgers, who legged it onto the pitch. Some of the old school – Lou, Winker and co. – held firm and eventually sent them packing but the damage was done. You had to hand it to them, it was an excellent piece of organised violence.

Lou was about thirty-five and was one of the original Ayresome Angels, a handy lad by all accounts. Apparently he had one Chelsea boy in a headlock and was punching him repeatedly asking him, 'What are you doing in here, you naughty boy? No-one comes in scaring little kids like that, nobody tries to take the Holgate when Lou's around. All right? All fucking right?' A copper actually asked Lou to let him go, even using his first name and saying please. One of Lou's mates had told me what he had done but Lou was more modest and shrugged his shoulders, saying, 'Well, I just did what youse fuckers should've been doing, mind you it took me back a bit, think I might get back into the crack again.' Then he laughed again and turned round to view the away section of the ground. 'Those fuckers will claim a big result here today, you need to have that sort of organisation to shake anyone up these days.' Lou was right, Chelsea would claim a big result, but for me it was all part of the learning process. Boro actually won the game 7–2, quite a cracker to watch as well, but the big talking point after the game was Chelsea's mob.

Although we should have learned from this, we were still novices when it came to getting ourselves organised, and Chelsea were to prove that again a few years later. Another crew who were well organised were West Ham. Though they were in the Second Division, having been relegated, they always gave a good account of themselves, showing no fear and sticking together even if they were short on numbers. I remember once in the early Seventies they brought a firm up numbering no more than eighty lads. All were huge and stuck together; even with hundreds of Boro trying to get at them they held firm, and we couldn't get them on the run. They came by train and walked all the way to the station from the ground with Boro trying unsuccessfully to get at them. They were solid.

One encouraging note was that we were starting to arrange meeting places at away grounds, such as pubs known from previous visits, and rather than an unorganised mob of a few thousand, we were sticking in more close-knit mobs of forty to fifty, where everyone knew each other, thus preventing infiltration. Of course each mob knew the others; there'd be Stevo's firm (the Bob End Crew), the Redcar Reds, the Farm posse, the Eston Boys, Stockton's Wrecking Crew, the Townies and several other groups. Sometimes I would travel with other firms to a game and other lads would travel with our firm, forging better links. This was the start of Boro becoming a well-disciplined and much envied firm that would eventually gain the respect of every mob in the country.

One place where we managed to meet up successfully was Southampton. Due to the length of the journey, everyone set off the night before, most straight from a nightclub. Many a lad has gone to a club in the Boro with no thoughts of going to a game, only to jump in the back of a Transit van and find himself waking up in a south coast town (oh the perils of too much drink). Even his missus wouldn't know where he had got to until he got home the following Sunday and many a marriage has broken down because of this.

To get to this game I actually set off at 10 p.m. with Bully to hitchhike down to the Dell. We comfortably made it to Wetherby roundabout for 11 p.m. but ended up stuck there for the next two and a half hours, until a coach came along full of Park End lads. What a godsend that was. They let us on and took us all the way there and back. We arrived at a service station in the middle of the night and had to cross over on a footbridge to the other side for the cafe. When we got there we saw a dozen Boro lads having it big style with a coach load of Mackems, who I believe were travelling to London. I recognised Spanka, a well-known Boro lad, who was hemmed in with his mates to one corner of the café, where the food counters were. As we trooped in and saw what was happening, everyone got straight into the Mackems and the tables were turned.

One big fat Mackem was jumping about waving his arms around shouting, 'Howay then ya Borra bastards.' I caught him right in the nether region with a beauty, sending him to the floor where he was subjected to a good kicking. Spanka had another lad pinned over a table, punching fuck out of him. The rest of the Mackems were now the ones hemmed into a corner taking all the flak, tea cups chairs and tables were flying at them from all quarters as the carnage continued. Then another three coachloads of Mackems arrived to put the odds well in their favour. We didn't hang around, as we were well outnumbered, and beat a hasty retreat back across the bridge, onto the coach and away. Spanka and the other Boro lads managed to make their escape as well.

Spanka was one of the top lads in Boro. I had met him on a coach in 1975 when we played away to Ipswich. He was only about sixteen years old but looked a lot older. As the coach entered the street leading up to Portman Road, he took the opportunity to jump off at a red light, chase after a home fan, spark him, steal his scarf and return on board before the lights changed to green. He was quite good-looking in a rugged, Charles Bronson sort of way and scored with a local lass at half-time, slipping out of the ground to her place, doing the necessary and returning in time for a kick-off at the final whistle. He was famous also for holding up a game at Derby for a good five minutes by running on the pitch with Big Billy and fighting several stewards and police. They locked up the pair of them in a top-security jail in Leicester. Arrested more times than any lad I know, he recently counted up his tally: sixty-two arrests. In the past few years Spanka has kept fairly quiet, although he was arrested against Leeds in 2002 for smacking a lad who referred to him as a 'child molester'! These days he enjoys going to the local bingo club (as I do myself) with his long-suffering wife, although I do enjoy having a chat with him about the old days during the break.

We arrived in Southampton at about 7.30 a.m. The coach driver dropped us in the estate near the ground and went off to get his head down. Well there we were, forty-five Boro fans wandering around at half seven in the morning. Someone suggested we go apple raiding, as all the houses seemed to have their own orchards. Anything for a laugh, so apple raiding it was. Before long we bumped into loads more Boro fans who had arrived early and they joined us to make 100 or more rampaging through this quaint little estate. I borrowed a postman's bike and this lad jumped on the front basket, so there we were riding along with this postman looking on in astonishment as we made off on his bike throwing apples at him. The lad on the front of the bike was called Bri and was to become my best mate to this day.

Without really planning anything, we had met up hundreds of miles away and organised ourselves into a tasty firm of over 100 boys. For the rest of the day we were in complete control, taking over pubs, chasing Saints fans from outside their own end and covering the walls round the ground with Boro graffiti. It was the perfect away sortie, apart from the result (2–1 to them) and me getting a bottle on the head during the match. I also spoke with a few lads who were of the same opinion as me.

'How is it we can get ourselves organised all this way from home, yet can't go to places like Sunderland or Newcastle without ending up split all over?'

Stevo chipped in, 'Chelsea, Millwall, West Ham, they all keep their numbers to a minimum, quality lads who stick together. When we go long distances like this there's usually only a few of us and we stick together. When we go up the road everyone goes in their own little clique.'

Spud, another Boro lad, said, 'We should get a mob of lads from all the areas, we all know each other, and regardless of who we're playing, stick in the same crowd. That way you won't have all these shithouses running and panicking everyone. You know what it's like, as soon as one runs every fucker follows.'

He was right, though getting lads to do this was another thing. At least it was a start and we were talking about it but we still had a lot to do to catch up with the likes of Millwall, Chelsea and co. I remember watching a documentary about Millwall on TV about their firms; I say this in the plural because they had more than one. There was the main crew, led by Harry the Dog, which was known as 'F-Troop', the middle order, known as 'Treatment', and another outfit known as the 'Halfway Line'. They were few in numbers but effective due to their close loyalty. No one was accepted into their firm without first proving themselves, usually by having it with the opposition on your own. That was not something I would have suggested for us but there were things we could still learn from them.

AFTER THE 1978/79 season, I had decided to get married and start a family (actually the family was already well on the way with my daughter, and my first son newly planted in the womb). A lot of my mates thought this was the end of my soccer away days with the lads. Far from it. I was now twenty-one and in my prime. The Boro were starting to head in the right direction as far as organising themselves was concerned, and I was deeply involved with the main boys. In fact on my twenty-first birthday I celebrated by getting mortal drunk and going to the match at home to Liverpool in the away enclosure, fighting like fuck with the Scousers and getting arrested. It must have been my lucky night, as the copper who arrested me took off the handcuffs to pass me over to another copper outside the turnstile, saying, 'This one in the van, section five.' The other copper can't have heard him and asked what I was doing. I told him I had been thrown out, so he just said, 'Well, fuck off then!' Huh? I didn't need telling twice.

So there I was getting married, buying my own house, good job, raising a family and yet I still couldn't go without my football fix. What a lot of people don't realise about football fans is that they are carrying out a natural inbred instinct towards tribal rivalry. You see it everywhere not just at football matches, in the discos, on holiday abroad, at work, even out in the street among children. The older generation were always saying bring back National Service, well sorry, but a great proportion of the lads I know at football matches are ex-soldiers and some of them are amongst the top boys! During the two world wars the tribal rivalry couldn't have been more evident, and the fact that we won on both occasions made us even more aware of our status within the world. The young generation today are just living out their own tribal culture, be it with another town or football team, or just another estate or even the next street, there will always be this rivalry one way or another. The very fact that we give names to everything and encourage competition between ourselves means that there will always be conflict between us, and thus there will always be soccer hooliganism.

So that was the end of the Seventies and a new era was beginning to dawn, but I cant help looking back on those great days with fond memories, the big derby match battles, the away day outings, the football songs and chants, and even some of the football played. Some of the lads I'd knocked about with had 'retired' from the crack, some had got married and settled down, others had just drifted off to do other things with their Saturday afternoons, but the majority of the hardcore lads were still there week in week out, rain or shine, home or away. One regular event from the Seventies I haven't mentioned was the pre-match Stripperamas that were put on by a local venue known as the Rock Garden, one lass in particular was a favourite of the lads, she was called Lola (most probably not her real name). She had a massive pair of 44 DD jugs prompting the song:

> Oh, oh Lola, Lola
> I'd walk a million miles
> Just to look at your tits
> Oh Lo-ola

If you can imagine 400 lads singing that to a stripper while she set fire to a Newcastle scarf, it was enough to get any red-blooded fan's emotions into a frenzy. Add to that someone announcing that there was a load of Geordies in the boozer just down the road, and it was the signal for unbridled carnage as 400 boys charged out and into a pub full of Geordies taking no prisoners. Yes, they were great days and far too many events happened during that era to be put down on paper; suffice to say they were probably the best of my life. Now a new age was dawning with the advent of the 'casuals', and the organisation of Boro into one of the most respected firms in the country.

BY THE END of the 1979/80 season, Boro were not only showing signs of improvement on the pitch under John Neal's leadership but were also top dogs in the North East, due to Sunderland and Newcastle being in the Second Division. Things were looking quite rosy. Young lads had started to come through the ranks of the firm and with them they brought a new style of fashion. This was the start of the casual era. Some of these lads were game as fuck, even to the extent of embarrassing some of the more seasoned veterans who they regarded as the 'Bellies' or the BBC (Beer Belly Crew). They took a great pride in their appearance: smart wedge haircuts, tight faded denims, Pringle jumpers, hooded jackets and expensive training shoes. They used to laugh and take the piss out of our gear, calling us 'fossils'. We in turn called them 'Joeys' in reference to their appearance and age, or 'flickheads' due to their hairstyle.

One big difference they brought was the idea of not wearing colours. Where once it was regarded as cowardice not to wear your colours, it was now quite the opposite. I even used to pull up these youngsters asking why they didn't wear their scarves. The reply was always the same: 'It don't complement the gear I'm wearing.' What I noticed, though, was that without a scarf they seemed invisible to the police, therefore able to travel where they liked and get in the local bars easier. Walking around without being rounded up by the local plod had its uses, especially as they used to escort you into the ground at 2 p.m. on occasions.

The 1980/81 season was to be marred by a shocking event at the start of the season. Boro began with a win, a draw and two defeats. Then we played Nottingham Forest at home. I went to the game with my mate Bri, the guy I had met at

Southampton when I nicked the postman's bike. We'd had chew with Forest on a couple of occasions in the past so everyone was up for this one. There wasn't a big crowd up from Nottingham, although they did have plenty of boys out, which we made note of. Nothing happened in the ground, the game petered out to a 0–0 draw, and five minutes from the end a crew of us left the ground, waiting down a side street for the Forest firm to come out. When they walked down the road towards their coaches escorted by police, a small but game crew of their lads broke away to confront us. We had about the same in numbers and a battle took place. It did not last too long, no more than a couple of minutes, but this one big Forest lad was as game as fuck, taking on everyone. A lad called Craig took a smack on the side of his head and went down like a sack of spuds. As he fell, he hit his head on the kerb and went out like a light. The big Forest lad who put him down was still dishing it out when a Boro lad caught him on the side of his face with his belt, at which the Forest lads backed off and the police came piling in, sending everyone scampering in different directions.

It was not until I got home later that night that I heard Craig had died. I didn't know him too well but I felt sad that one of our lads had been killed in what could only be described as a minor scuffle, the kind that happened all over the country week in, week out. The police were asking for witnesses to come forward and guaranteed immunity from prosecution for anyone who did. However, the first couple of lads who offered information were immediately arrested and charged with affray. This prompted everyone else who was there to keep quiet. Bri said it was pointless coming forward, as we couldn't identify the lad responsible and we would probably end up being charged as well. The ones who did come forward were hammered in court: one lad was sent down for two years and the Forest lad got done for manslaughter and got four years. Craig was buried with full honours.

For a while things went a bit stale. Everyone was talking about dawn raids by the police and some lads left the scene altogether. Personally, I put the tragedy down as one of those things. I was extremely sorry that someone had lost his life and his family must have been devastated; I know I would be if it was my son. I took time to reflect and made a promise to myself to be very careful, but life goes on for the rest of us and there was not a lot of time to think about it too much, not with Sunderland around the corner. I have always had this belief that I would know when it was time to meet my maker. The fix I got from football and the lifestyle that went hand-in-hand with it were such that this tragic incident did not put me off. Even a drug addict who knows he is taking his life in his hands every time he takes heroin, still does it. I suppose that's what it was like for me.

Our next match was away at Sunderland and emotions were running high. There was not much chew due to the massive police presence but we beat the bastards thanks to a superb strike from Bosco Jankovic. I do remember one particular chant from that game, which went, 'You'll get a boot wrapped round your head', sung to the tune of 'Oops upside your head'. What I found funny was my mate Bri; he was joining in with the chant when a copper grabbed him and asked what he was singing. He told him he didn't know the words and was just humming along. The copper let him go with a kick up the arse. We tortured him all day with, 'How does it go again Bri? How does it go?' But that was Bri, forever the diplomat when the occasion warranted it.

Mind, he could be very tasty when anyone upset him. On the train coming back from the match he recognised a lad who was a Sunderland fan living on Teesside. Bri knew him from when he went to school in Billingham, where Sunderland have a large following. The same lad had been a bit of a bully and Bri had once told him he would catch up with him one day. Well, today was the day. Bri waited until the lad went to the toilet and followed him in, then gave it to him good style, leaving him with his head hanging over the bowl, dripping with blood. Fair play to the lad, he didn't do a thing about it even though there were coppers on board.

Although we did not set the First Division alight, we had our moments. One was Sunderland at home. They brought about 10,000 fans down, mostly boys, and they were everywhere: in the Holgate (they got battered), in the side terrace (they got battered eventually) and in the Bob End, where Bri and I were. Most of the Bob End firm went in the Holgate for this one because they heard that the Mackems were planning to go in there, leaving about forty of us in the Bob End. When we entered the ground we could hear Mackems singing their heads off; mind they weren't lads, so we barged through them telling them to shut their mouths. When we got to our usual spot, there were only a handful of Boro trying to hold off a huge surge from several hundred Mackems heaving their way up the back stairs. These were their boys, led by a big fat fucker known as 'the Bear'. Being full of beer I had no sense of danger and made my way to the crux of the matter, eventually finding myself leading the charge towards the Mackems, with fists flying everywhere. After a few minutes of this their superior numbers forced us back. I could see this big fat fucker coming at me and threw my right boot at him, catching him square in the balls. He crumpled into a heap on the floor. Bri pulled me through a gap in the wall to the other side of the Bob End, informing me I had just put the Bear on his arse.

We did not have many in our mob but all were game and the Mackems seemed content to stay on the other side of the wall, shouting obscenities at us throughout the rest of the game. That included the Bear, who spent most of the game talking to 'Chal', one of our lads, who was quite diplomatic himself. At the end of the game the Mackems made a charge, forcing us out through the corner exit. We held them off at the narrow gateway and I noticed one swinging his leg over the wall, shouting and calling us wankers. I jumped up, hooked his leg and pulled him over. His taunts turned to screams as he landed and was set upon by half a dozen boys, who kicked the shit out of him.

Fighting continued all the way down Linthorpe Road. We were in front of them with thousands of Boro behind them. Our group did not have enough numbers so we let them have it with bricks, bottles and anything we could lay our hands on. I was collared by a copper but managed to get away because he was too fat to catch me, mind he ripped a jumper off my back which had been given to me as a Christmas present by my mother-in-law. The same copper grabbed me again later but I had dumped my jumper and denied all knowledge of being involved. He knew it was me but told me to fuck off home and not to let him see my face again that day. I thought, fair comment, and did just that. Why spoil a good day? I had to tell my wife what had occurred so as to explain my missing jumper, but my daughter was listening in and spilled the beans to my mother-in-law on the Sunday lunchtime, much to my embarrassment, as she was totally unaware of the antics I got up to at the matches.

Fair play to the Mackems though, they came and had their share of what was a full-on battle. These days it would be classed as a victory to them. Oh to dream of Boro taking 10,000 to Sunderland in all areas of Roker Park.

NOT A LOT more happened in the league for the rest of that season and Boro finished in a less than impressive fourteenth place, but it was a different story in the FA Cup. We were drawn away to Swansea in the third round. They were flying high at the top of the Second Division with John Toshack at the helm, making us the underdogs; well that's how the press saw it anyway. With it being a long journey we set off straight from a nightclub in a battered old minibus, meeting another couple of minibuses en route. We arrived in Swansea at about seven o'clock in the morning, parked the bus up and had a wander about, meeting a few other early arrivals. By half past ten there were about sixty-odd lads roaming around waiting for the pubs to open. Then we heard a mob of Boro singing their heads off, so we headed towards them and found them near Swansea jail. There must have been about 100 lads, all shouting up to some prisoners and having a good bit of banter with them.

A pub nearby was due to open so we gathered outside. Some police had got wind of us and turned up to make sure there was no bother. They left after we convinced them we were all right. Once the pub opened its doors, we made it our base. Eventually the Boro fans packed the place out, making it a no-go zone for Swansea fans. At about 2 p.m., a crew of Swansea tried to have a pop at the pub, so we charged outside, sending them running down the road. We chased them for a few yards, then returned to the pub – all except Chal. He'd had a few too many beers and carried on running after them with a bottle in his hand, making himself a nice easy arrest for the local plod. Bri had stayed outside the pub and saw him being frogmarched to a police van; anyone but him, we all thought, as he had only just been released from jail for stabbing QPR fans a month previously. He was still on licence so was facing a long stretch this time.

When we got to the ground they put us in this shitty side terrace and only opened the bigger end behind the goal once we had filled the side. I was quite surprised at our following, which must have numbered at least 1,400. The game was a cracker with Boro winning 5–0 and Terry Cochrane scoring a spectacular overhead kick for the goal of the game. I tried to run on the pitch to congratulate him but Bri pulled me back to save me from a certain arrest. Chal was released from the cells in time to catch the last few minutes of the game, thinking we were losing as the police had been winding him up with the score. When he went to court he got a one-way rail ticket, as he thought he was sure to be sent down. To his and everyone else's amazement, the magistrates fined him £50. This apparently was due to the fact that they did not have his previous record to hand. He offered to pay at £1 per week and even had the cheek to ask for a sub so he could get back home.

The next round put us against West Bromwich Albion at home. We expected nothing from them as they had shown their true colours a couple of years previously, leaving the ground at half-time (talk about Derby County!). It was the most humiliating sight I have ever seen: 1,500 fans leaving a ground because of what *might* happen. I wouldn't care but they are pretty tasty at home. The unusual event during this game came when David Hodgson, a fans' favourite who was out injured, decided to stand in the Holgate to watch the game with the fans. He even stood on the barrier with a scarf round his wrist leading the singing. Yes, he was a top bloke 'Hodgy'. We won the game 1–0 and were drawn against Barnsley in the fifth round, again at home.

Now Barnsley is not a name that you would associate with the major firms but don't be fooled; they have quite a tasty following, as they proved in this visit. West Bromwich from the First Division had brought a miserly 800. Barnsley from the Third Division brought a 12,000 or more and their support was absolutely magnificent. They were in the pubs, all over the ground and they were well up for any chew we threw at them, especially those big fuck-off Yorkshire miners. We had them running all over the shop in the end, but credit where it's due, they were game.

We won the match 2–1, just, setting us up nicely for a sixth-round cracker with Wolves at home. I had just secured a job working near Hamburg in Germany and had to miss this one. I was working in a shipbuilding yard, welding up barges on the River Elbe. This was where I found out I hated Turks!

They seemed to have the run of the yard and did their best to let us know it. Seven times in the three months I was there they attacked my workmates, twice with knives. Hated the bastards we did; they always carried knives and weren't afraid to use them. They were horrible and sly, always going behind your back and trying to get you into trouble with the German bosses.

I had to content myself with listening to the cup match on radio. We drew but lost the replay 3–1 after extra time. My mate Bri filled me in with all the details when I returned home and by all accounts it was one hell of an emotional night down at Molineux. Hodgy was crying his eyes out at the final whistle and was joined by several thousand Boro fans, me included in my hotel room in Germany as I listened on the radio. Most Boro fans had had enough of being under-achievers year after year, and this told in the gates for the rest of that season and for many to come. We were constantly selling our best players. That season alone saw the beginning of the end for quite a few, starting with Armstrong closely followed by Johnston. As for our firm, they were getting smaller in numbers as well but the main lads were always there. Maybe this was the catalyst we needed, as all the loyal lads became even closer and started going to away and home matches together more regularly.

The next season saw our biggest disaster: we were relegated. This had a catastrophic effect on Boro, as you would expect. The only saving grace was that we beat the Mackems at Joker Park, had a good kick-off with them before the game and had them scurrying all over after. Normally when a team goes down there is some point in the season where the team puts a run together to give the fans a bit of hope, but we didn't even get that; quite the opposite, as the Boro went on a run of nineteen games without a win, stretching from October 1981 to March 1982. We tried all the 'sack the board' crap and some of the lads even organised a funeral procession up to the ground, which the police put a stop to. Eventually we went down with a whimper. The only bright spot was the thought of going to some of the grounds we had not been to in a long time.

Off the field things had got worse, to the point of fences being put up to keep fans off the pitch. Our fences, like Millwall's, had horrendous barbed spikes on top. It was also the law to keep rival fans segregated, which meant being crammed into the worst part of the ground, usually without cover, when you went away.

CHAPTER SIX

The Wilderness Years

THE START OF another season and everyone was optimistic as usual. Back in the Second Division, things can only get better – or can they? We started away to Sheffield Wednesday and lost, home to Burnley and lost, then carried on for nine matches without a win until we finally clocked up our first success, 1–0 against fellow strugglers Bolton. Boro were rock bottom and the chairman had fucked off.

The new guy, Mike McCullagh, showed some bottle when he sacked Bobby Murdoch and brought in Malcolm Allison. This had an immediate impact, as we beat QPR 2–1 to bring renewed optimism to the players and fans. The next game was away to Rotherham and suddenly we had found ourselves again. Boro's firm had stuck by the team, unlike the fair-weather fans. We made our way down to South Yorkshire, about 3,500 of us. Most of us now travelled by minibuses and cars, however quite a few lads decided to go on the train. Word went round to meet at the nearest pub to the station and about 400 boys turned up. What a firm! There were the Joeys, the Redcar Casuals and the BBC and everyone was of the same mind: let's go in their end. As none of us had any colours on, it was easy; the law didn't take a second glance as we queued up and went in.

A few of us made our way to the front right behind the goal while about 150 went up the back. As we took up position I noticed that a lot of their younger fans were next to us, so I suggested we make our way up to the middle where their main boys were. As we moved up, the lads who were at the back of the end surged down. Rotherham did not know which way to run. The skirmish lasted all of two minutes, by which time we had done the business, the law were in attendance and it was time to leave. As the police took us round the pitch, Malcolm Allison looked at us as if to say fuck me, where have all these come from? Some lads shook his hand, then a high-ranking police officer stopped everyone and told the other coppers to take us back and through the side paddock, right through a crew of their lads who had been giving us the verbals as we passed. Another minor scuffle erupted as we went through the paddock but we saw them off in two shakes.

The restoration had started on the field, and the Boro crew were becoming one of the best close-knit outfits in the country. We showed this two weeks later when we went to Charlton. They had just signed a top player called Alan Simmonsen, and though they normally had crowds of 5,000 they were expecting to double that, which they did with a little help from us. I travelled down by coach with a mixture of firms from Redcar and the Boro. On board was the young lad who had received a good hiding at Liverpool a few years back – the Shadow. He was a lot older now and had started carving out a bit of a reputation.

On the way I noticed a few Transit vans with lads in going down to the game, one of which ended up having some chew with a coachload of Leeds. Apparently the van left a service station and waited on the hard shoulder for the Leeds bus to go past, then one lad threw a brick through one of the windows. The coach pulled up further up the motorway and when the van passed they forced it off the road, resulting in the van turning over onto its side. When the police arrived a couple of lads from the van were nicked. One was a postman who lost his job yet none of the Leeds fans were nicked either.

When we arrived in Charlton, most of the main firm were there. We met up in a pub not far from the Valley and Bri and I got talking to a few locals.

One tall skinny lad informed us, 'Millwall have a firm out for your lads today.'

Bri laughed and said, 'Are we supposed to shit ourselves, like? Why do you cockneys always think the name Millwall is going to scare every fucker off?' Bri was stood looking at this lad, shaking his head and laughing.

Stevo came over after hearing what the lad had said. 'I hope Millwall are here,' he said, 'cos youse fuckers haven't got a fucking firm, have ya? Now fuck off and go play fantasy games somewhere else, ya skinny dying bastard.'

After the match (which Boro won 3–2), we all walked up towards the station where the coaches were parked. The street was very dimly lit (I think half the lights were out) and both Boro and home fans merged in the darkness. I was on one side of the road and had lost most of my mates in the crowd. All I could hear were cockney accents. Suddenly the crowd in front of me stopped and turned to face us.

'Come on then Barra, facking Millwall's here, lets 'ave it, come on you Geordie barstards.'

Thirty cockneys were coming towards us. Fighting started, then a group of Boro lads came in from the middle of the road, catching them from the side. It was hard to tell who was who for a short while due to the lack of light. Punches were flying all over. I kept my eye on one guy who kicked a Boro lad in the back then pretended to be with us.

'Can't tell who's who here,' I said to him.

He just shrugged his shoulders – he didn't dare speak.

'I know who you are though,' I said. Bang. I smacked him right on the side of his face and again on the back of the head as he tried to cover up. He started protesting, saying he didn't want any trouble. 'Nah mate, saw you kick that Boro lad, ya fucking cockney shite,' I said. He backed up against a wall, shitting himself, and another Boro lad came alongside and punched him full belt, putting the lad clean out.

I moved away and looked around to see what was going on. I could make out Bri on the other side of the road with a group of Boro going at it with a dozen or more lads. They had them pinned against a small garden wall, lacing into them. As soon as I got over a horse came charging in to break it all up. I got covered in horse saliva as the animal's face nudged into mine. I felt like throwing up; it's horrible, that frothy stuff. It seemed to be calming down, with the cockneys on the other side and us being held back by two police horses and a few more coppers on foot.

The shout went up again, 'We are Millwall, we are Millwall.' There were sixty or more lads on the other side but some Boro lads who had slipped away and got behind them were straight in, fighting like fuck. As the police tried to break it up, that was our cue to pile in and it was going off again. After a minute at the most they were off, running like fuck, job done, sorted. I found Bri and we told of each other's contributions to what we claimed as a victory. We stood, they ran, end of story. If they were Millwall, and I say if, then they were soon dispatched by our firm. If they were, I would say they were not Millwall's main firm, probably some of their younger charges.

On the way home we stopped off in Rugby, a nice little market town near Leicester (and allegedly the place where rugby was invented by some chap who picked up a football and ran with it) for a few beers. Big Billy had a broken ankle and decided to get his head down on the bus while we sampled the local ale. We had split up into smaller groups spread over three or four pubs when a younger lad came into our pub to announce that Billy and the driver were having some chew with a group of locals. We told the lad to go and find the rest of our lot while we headed for the coach. There was Billy, hopping on one leg and waving his crutches around with a crowd of a dozen lads surrounding him. In we went, scattering the mob across the coach park, except for one lad who ended up going one-on-one with Bri. They traded a few punches before the local ran off to catch up with his mates.

The lads came back with more of their mates and now we had a fight on our hands. A police car arrived but couldn't control the situation as fights were erupting all over the coach park. Then more of our lads came back from the pubs to even up the odds. All the police wanted to do was get us on the coach and away, but we refused to go until all our lads were found and safely on. The longer we hung around, the more the local mob grew in numbers. Eventually, with only a handful of lads missing, more police arrived and made us board the coach. However, as they put us on at the front, lads were jumping out of the back door to join in the fighting, which had started again.

The police were getting pissed off with all this and told the driver to get moving whether we were all aboard or not. As the coach slowly reversed down a one-way alley, one of the lads took a sweeping brush and started putting windows through as we edged past what we found out was the rear of a pub. Inside the pub, as luck would have it, were the remaining lads from our coach. They had been oblivious to the events of the past hour. When the windows went through they thought they were under attack and came rushing out, bottles and glasses in hand. They saw the coach surrounded by locals and moved towards them. Once again lads jumped out the back door and another fight started. Finally the police managed to split everyone up and get the coach, with the full complement on board, on its way home. What a night and no arrests either. I can recommend Rugby for a night of chew anytime, fucking class.

THINGS WERE LOOKING quite good for Boro. I started to enjoy my football again and the crack at the away games was excellent. We didn't set the season alight but we finished in a comfortable fifteenth place. Off the pitch we had established our firm as up with the top mobs in the country and I was in the thick of the action, regarded by most as a Frontliner. Personally, I was daft more than brave, but not so daft as to know when to keep out the way when Mr Plod was around. Unlike my mate Bri, who had a nasty habit of getting lifted for the daftest of things, especially when he'd had a drink.

One away trip springs to mind: when we went to Ipswich. It was Bri's twenty-first birthday so he was well up for a drink. The game had been called off by the time we got there, so we went to watch Colchester versus Oxford. On the way back we dropped off for a drink in Cambridge and decided to make a night of it to celebrate Bri's birthday. As we had been drinking all day, it didn't take long to get to that stage when you know you've had enough. Not Bri though; he was fucking mortal, insisting on wandering off all the time.

I was sat in one pub and a couple of the lads came in to inform me that 'your mate has been fighting with a bouncer'. I went looking for him and there he was, laid in a gutter with blood dripping out of his hand (apparently he had tried to punch the bouncer through the pub window). He could hardly walk, let alone stand up and fight a gadgie twice his size. The police turned up, looked at his hand and arrested him on the spot, despite my protestations that he hadn't done anything. When he sobered up he blamed me for not keeping a better eye on him! I suppose he was right in a way, as he always seemed to look after me when I got in a state.

So Boro had managed to survive the threat of relegation and our firm had done the business at several grounds, including Rotherham, Charlton, Carlisle (chased their end all over), Oldham and Blackburn, to name but a few. One firm we didn't have the same success against though was Chelsea. We played them last match of the season at Stamford Bridge.

They had to win to be sure of staying up so a big crowd of around 20,000 (they'd only been getting around the 13,000 mark) turned up, with the majority of them boys.

We went down on a bus full of most of our top lads: Stevo's mob, Jonka's crew from the park, the Redcar Casuals and the G-town crew, all tasty gadgies in their own right. One lad from Redcar had previously been one of Chelsea's boys, but he was with us for this one. The game was shite, ending in a 0–0 draw. This was just enough to keep Chelsea from going down but not enough to stop their fans invading the pitch and heading straight for us. We held firm, protected by several hundred police and an eight-foot-high fence. It took thirty minutes to clear the pitch and another thirty before the police would dare let us out of the ground. Although we all got away unscathed, I knew we would have been mashed had they got close to us. We still had a long way to go to think of competing with a mob like that.

The trip home after the game was eventful. The driver agreed to let us have a night out in Leicester, who had just secured promotion to the First Division. The whole city was celebrating, and it must have seemed like Christmas when a coachload of Boro's finest turned up. No sooner had the coach stopped and half of us had got off than we were at it with a mob of Leicester's 'under-fives', as they were known. We did the business quick-style but they started coming from all over. One of the lads said to get back on the coach, as we had no chance of getting a drink in this climate. We had to fight a rearguard action with gadgies coming at us from everywhere. The coach pulled away with Stevo running alongside with a broom shank in his hands, fighting off a dozen lads. We stopped when a window went through, giving Stevo time to get on board. Soon enough the police turned up to put a stop to what was becoming a really ugly situation. A Leicester lad was arrested for breaking the window; it probably wasn't even him, just a case of wrong place, wrong time. The police escorted the coach to the police station and held us there for two hours, threatening to arrest anyone who got off. That didn't last long as half the lads left the bus and went for a drink in a nearby pub. There was no more chew and eventually the police let us carry on our journey home. That was the end of that season and the bonding between Boro's firm had grown stronger.

THE NEXT SEASON was more of the same. We started with a long trip to newly promoted Portsmouth, whose firm were well noted and had been shaking a few big names along the way. They were known as the 6.57 squad (something to do with the train they took to matches). As with all south coast matches, we set off straight after a nightclub, arriving in Southsea, which is on the coast a couple of miles from the ground, at 8 a.m. Pompey obviously were not expecting us that early and we had the run of the place until opening time, when our numbers had grown to eighty or so. There was a funfair nearby with a pub backing onto it, so in we went, making it ours for the day. A few of the younger lads were having a lark about on the fair and one even dived into the sea for a dip. There was no trouble or even any sign of it.

At 2 p.m. some of the lads came into the pub to announce there was a firm outside looking for it. We supped our pints and moved outside to confront them. There were only a few coppers trying to separate us from them, with us being in the majority, as they had only about thirty though they were all big gadgies. There was a stand-off, with the police trying to get us to move towards the ground. One copper remarked that they weren't Pompey's firm but local fair lads looking after their own patch. Slowly we moved away to our vehicles and drove up towards the ground.

Once we had parked up, we had a short walk to the ground. Then we saw our first Pompey boys: fucking hundreds of them. This was a firm we had not bargained on meeting. All looked very tasty and didn't give a fuck about the law, doing all they could to get at us. The fact that we were thinly dispersed didn't help. Bri had stopped to buy a match programme and ended up losing the rest of us. By the time I got to our turnstile, I realised he'd gone missing. He'd had a few to drink and I got a bit worried about him. A copper told me to make my way into the ground. When I explained why I was waiting around, he said, 'Just wait here. What's your mate's name?'

'Brian.'

Next salute, the copper's talking to a motorcycle cop, who roars off.

'He'll find him for you, you're okay.'

What a nice copper, I thought. Within a few minutes I saw something I had never seen before in my life: Bri was on the back of this cop bike getting a ride up to the ground. The copper stood with me turned and said, 'There you are mate, told you he'd be all right.'

Bri, still a bit the worse for wear was laughing his head off. 'I don't believe that,' he said. 'There I am, surrounded by Pompey boys who had sussed me out, when in rides this copper on a motorbike and says, "Are you Brian? Jump on the back, I'll take you up to the ground." Fucking unreal.'

The away end at Pompey was on one corner of the open terrace. As we basked in the sunshine watching the game, I surveyed the rest of the ground. From what I could make out they seemed to have a mob in all sections of every end. 'By fuck these look a tasty mob, Bri,' I remarked. 'I think we're gonna have a bit of chew at the end of this, mate.' He agreed.

Suddenly Boro scored. As we celebrated, Bri went tumbling, and after the cheering died down I found him laid on the floor, his ankle up like a balloon. A few Boro fans had run on the pitch to celebrate and this was the cue for hundreds of

Pompey to run on to confront them. Our brave handful retreated back to our end with Pompey in hot pursuit. One or two Pompey jumped into Boro's end but were quickly dealt with by those at the front and arrested by the law, silly buggers. Bri had disappeared down to the medical staff and was taken to hospital with a broken ankle. I agreed to pick him up there later after the game.

The Pompey fans were now in very high spirits and just wanted to do anything to get at us. They looked to be capable of doing it as well. At the end of the game we were held back for our own protection, fucking good job too, they would have murdered us. It had been a long time since I'd seen that many boys at a match, a very tidy mob I have to say. After we got back to the car, I went to the hospital to pick Bri up but he wasn't there. He had somehow managed to get a taxi to Littlehampton, where he knew some Redcar lads were having a night out, and came back with them. Due note was made of the 6.57 for future reference.

The 1983/84 season had started well with three wins and three draws, taking us up to fourth in the league, but five defeats on the trot saw us slip down to mid-table and that's how things would stay for most of the campaign. Off the pitch our firm was carrying on where we left off the previous season – until we played Chelsea on January 2. None of us expected Chelsea to bring a firm up, and personally I hoped they wouldn't because I had just had an operation on my leg and was trussed up with bandages from my groin down to my ankle, forcing me to limp around tentatively. I still went to the match with Bri and couldn't believe my eyes as a tasty firm of about 300 hardcore boys came out of Middlesbrough train station. There was not even anyone about to confront them.

At the ground we managed to get a crew together and went into the Bob End. Some of our firm who lived in London had been in contact with Chelsea and they had assured them they were coming with the intention of doing the biz. The Chelsea firm went in the seats above the South Terrace, so we spent the rest of the match watching and waiting for them to make a move. With five minutes remaining and the score locked at 1–1, Currie scored for Boro. Amid the cheering, nobody seemed to notice the Chelsea boys leaving the ground, but when we saw their empty seats everyone started making for the exit. This was it; the big kick-off with Chelsea was about to happen.

It happened all right, only not on the streets as we expected. No, they had done it again! They invaded the Holgate, sending them streaming onto the pitch. The main gadgies held firm and got weighed into them, sending them running back out into the path of the Bob End boys, who had a good ruck by all accounts. I was gutted that I couldn't join in, but once again that well-oiled Chelsea firm had done the business. After the police had restored order and collared the Headhunters to escort them to the station, I set off down Linthorpe Road with Bri, reflecting on the events that had just happened. I could only limp along at a slow pace with Bri holding my arm giving me support. Then from behind we heard the Chelsea firm coming down the road and before we knew it they had caught up.

'Fucking hell Bri, we're right in with their main firm,' I said under my breath.

'Shh, I know, just keep walking,' said Bri.

One lad pulled us up, saying, 'Don't try putting the limp on, you're facking Barra firm, aintcha?'

'Ow lads he's genuine man,' said Bri. 'He's just had an op on his leg. We don't want any trouble, all right?'

'Fack off to the other side of the road then,' the Headhunter advised. Nice of him I suppose; we could have copped for a couple of smacks there.

As we were moving over to the other side, I noticed Boyo's firm moving across the road in front of their mob to confront them. The Chelsea crew started, letting off CS gas that sent everyone scattering holding their eyes, including the police. I stood on the other side of the road watching. Boyo was dressed similar to the cockneys, with a long trenchcoat and carrying a brolly (no, it wasn't raining). With Boyo's group now dispersed and the police at sixes and sevens, Chelsea took the opportunity to slip their escort and head towards the bus station. I had no chance of keeping up with them but our kid, who was waiting for a bus, told me they came steaming through, smacking anyone and scattering people all over before continuing on to the train station unmolested. Now that was Chelsea at their menacing best. We still had a lot of catching up to do.

As if we hadn't learned from Chelsea, the very next match was home to Arsenal in the FA Cup and they also did the biz at the train station. They had not brought many up except a tasty firm of boys, mostly big black gadgies, chanting, 'GOONE-ERS, GOONE-ERS.' Nothing went off before or after the match and as I was still limping I went straight to the station to get the train back to Redcar. As I sat there reading the local evening paper, I heard the rumbling of feet coming up the stairs to the platform. Suddenly all these women, kids and some lads I knew ran past, closely followed by about seventy Gooners. I stood up to see what was going on, only to be surrounded by a dozen Arsenal fans, some of whom had blades on them.

'Do ya want some then, Barra?' said one of them.

I stood transfixed, as if I was dreaming, then they all gave chase down the platform towards some Redcar lads who had stood their ground. One lad who was minding his own business got stabbed; that could have been me, I thought. When the police came they just calmly boarded the train as if nothing had happened, except for one big black guy who prowled up and down the platform asking if anyone wanted to have a go. No thanks, he was fucking huge.

The season ended after that with nothing more exciting other than a bit of crack up at Newcastle. The Boro finished in seventeenth position and Malcolm Allison left the club, with Willie Maddren taking over the hot seat.

A TRIP TO Portsmouth started the 1984/85 season. We did the usual thing and set off straight from Rumours nightclub in the Boro. We regularly went there as it was easy to get in; most of the up-market places like Maddison wouldn't entertain us due to the way we dressed and because we didn't have any women with us. The bouncers on the doors at Rumours were mainly match lads themselves so we could usually get in for free. One lad knew the DJ and he'd play mostly ska and reggae music for us. I liked 'Skinhead Moonstomp', which used to get all the lads up on the floor bouncing all over the place. It was never much fun for whoever was driving so we took this in turns, although not everyone had a licence and myself and Bri usually ended up doing more than our fair share. This was to be Bri's turn.

We arrived in Pompey at about 8.30 a.m. At first we were going to head straight for Southsea but one of the lads told us of a pub that was ideal for a meeting place and was sure to fill up with Boro, as it was on the main dual carriageway into the city. We parked the van and I went to look for a cafe with another lad as driver Bri tried to get his head down for a couple of hours. As I was crossing the central reservation a car pulled up and a lad got out. He came straight to me and asked the time. I could tell he was Pompey so I shrugged my shoulders in reply. He looked past me and saw the van parked up, then ran back to the car, announcing that they had found us. The car sped off towards the roundabout further down the road. I knew what was going to happen next so I ran back to the van to tell the lads.

'Come on,' I said, 'let's get away from here. There's a firm of Pompey on their way in the next few minutes.'

'You're just seeing ghosts John, calm down,' said one of the lads.

I had seen Pompey in action before and spent the next few minutes trying to convince them to leave. Suddenly it was too late: they were here, about forty of them. Panic set in. We had a dozen lads, half of whom weren't Boro firm. Bri started the van and told everyone to get in so we could make a break for it. One lad was in the toilet so we had to leave him. A brick came through the windscreen, causing Bri to lose control and ram into a fence, which the van axle lodged on to. Now we could not go backwards or forwards, we were stuck. The Pompey lads surrounded the van, putting all the windows through and systematically wrecking it with us inside.

One lad, who appeared to be their leader and was the one who had asked me the time, shouted into the van through the rear window, 'Come on Barra, you facking wankers, come on.' I picked up a battery from a radio that one of the lads had brought and threw it, twisting my body to get as much power in it as I could. It just bounced off his chest and he laughed.

'Is that the best you can do? Facking wankers, get out 'ere an' fight.'

I looked at the rest of the lads in the van. Fear was written across most of their faces and I must admit I was shitting myself as well. Get out of the van and fight? He must have thought I was daft. At least staying where I was meant he'd have to come in to get me, something I don't think he fancied too much either.

After a while they moved away and this gave us a chance to get out. I turned to Sean and Bri, asking, 'What do we do, fight or what?' Young Gary had a log in his hands and charged towards them shouting, 'Come on then Pompey, ya tossers.' All that did was bring them charging back. I turned to see the rest of our lads running for their lives. Gary and I had no choice but to join them. A little humour crept in as we legged it towards the docks area. This Boro lad running alongside me said, 'What are we running for?' Before I could reply, he ran straight into a lamppost. I had to laugh (maybe it was my nerves). As I picked him up the Pompey boys were getting closer and we sprinted into this loading area, looking for something to use as weapons. All we found was piles of sand and gravel. 'We're fucking dead,' I said to all the rest, who were just stood staring at the entrance, waiting for them to rush through at any moment. But they didn't come. They had given up chasing us and vacated the area.

As we made our way back to the now wrecked van, we saw why. The police had arrived. Bri had managed to get into a RAC cabin, from where the police had been called. They asked what had happened, then took us and our van to the local cop shop, informing us that the van was a write-off. We had hired it on the pretext of moving some equipment from Middlesbrough to London because the local hire firm wouldn't let you use them for football matches. The police told us we were in deep shit and that we would have to cough up £12,000 to pay for the van unless we co-operated with them and identified some of the Pompey firm. They took us round some pubs near Fratton Park, where one of their lads was picked out. He admitted being there but said he didn't do anything. That was enough for the law, they got their man and we got away with not having to pay for the van.

At the game, we were in the away end with two CID coppers when a radio message came through asking them to be on the lookout for a known Boro fan who had escaped from jail and was thought to be heading for the match. It was my mate from years ago when we played Liverpool; he had been sent down for football violence offences this time. The coppers asked if I knew him. I said, 'Yes, but you won't find him in here, he's more likely to be in the home end doing the biz.' They were straight on the radio to their colleagues, telling them to concentrate their efforts on Pompey's end of the ground. Funny thing was he was stood next to me all the time, laughing like fuck. He was later to become known as 'the Silver Shadow'. We lost the game and it was to be another six matches before we registered our first win, heralding another relegation dogfight, which we only survived by the skin of our teeth on the last day of the season with a win at Shrewsbury. Some day out that was; we took over the place.

The FA Cup threw up a derby match with Darlington. We drew at home, setting up a juicy return at their gaff. Darlo had brought a decent enough following to our ground but there was no sign of their firm. However, things were different in the replay. Darlo's firm, the Bank Top 200, are a handy, well-organised little mob, ably led by a couple of lads who are known to one or two Boro lads. This was a massive game for them and a chance to take the scalp of a big club and a respected firm. I didn't know many Darlo lads except the odd one or two I had worked with in the past, but the word had got round that we would need to be at our best for this one. As they are only seventeen miles down the road, we took every man and his dog through, and they had every man and his dog out for us.

The battles were kicking off in the town centre from the lunchtime onwards. Some of our lads copped for it in isolated incidents but in the main we had them all over the place before the game. There had not been time to make the game ticket-only, so it was pay at the gate. This led to Boro being all over the ground and battles with Darlo going off all the time. There had been a lot of snow during the days leading up to the game and at the end of the game there was a mass free-for-all on the cricket pitch next to the ground. It was quite a sight to see two mobs charging across the white snow towards each other and was funny as fuck when half of them were poleaxed by the wire fence surrounding the batting square. Even funnier was the fact that they beat us as well,

2–1. The local rags were full of the violence that had occurred and the usual witchhunt followed. Questions were asked of both clubs' fans, although I would guess the Boro would be more interested in asking questions of the players following this humiliation.

That was as good as it got that season, one to be consigned to the history books. Could it get any worse? I asked myself. Yes it could, with dire consequences.

THE 1985/86 SEASON started poorly and got worse. I don't think we got out of the bottom six all season. Anyway, we somehow managed to give ourselves a glimmer of hope by beating Millwall at home to set us up with another last-day showdown – at Shrewsbury again. It was one of those us-or-them situations and we had to win, so 4,000 Boro, mostly boys, invaded Shrewsbury for the day. This was not what that quaint little town wanted after the previous season, when we half-wrecked the place to celebrate staying up.

I travelled down with Bri in a minibus. After we had parked up and hit the town centre, all you could see everywhere were Boro fans roaming the streets. Most of the pubs shut their doors to us following the damage caused the previous season, so we had to settle for carry-outs from supermarkets. By the time we got up to the ground you could cut the atmosphere with a knife. Everyone was tense. I took up position behind the goal, which was packed with Boro, all boys. One conversation I overheard was from two Boro lads: 'I hope they score here, because we'll go fucking mental.' I was quite shocked at this; personally I wanted the team to stay up, but these lads were hoping we would lose so they could have a riot.

Sure enough, Shrewsbury scored early on and they got their wish. All hell broke loose. At first everyone tried to get over the fence to invade the pitch, but dozens of police formed a line in front of the fence and those that got over were promptly arrested. Then Shrewsbury scored again. This was the signal to make things worse and the police had to use all their resources to stop the fans from invading. Then the tuck shop at the back of the stand was attacked. Without any police protection, the occupants were powerless and ran off, leaving the place to the mercy of the rioters. The whole shack was demolished and the sheets were used as missiles hurled in the direction of the police, some of them landing on the heads of our own fans stood in front, leading to a procession of injured people seeking the aid of the ambulance staff. This wanton violence continued up to half-time with a continuous to-and-fro battle going on between the police and the Boro supporters.

Just after the re-start, Boro scored to ease things down a bit. Then about 100 fully togged-up riot police marched into the ground. I noticed they were from Birmingham by their badges. The riot cops formed a line and advanced towards us with their shields deflecting missiles and long batons swinging at anyone in their way. This tactic proved most effective as everyone calmed down and eventually settled into a more orderly behaviour. The game finished 2–1 to Shrewsbury, meaning we were relegated to the Third Division for only the second time in our history. But that wasn't the end of the trouble. As everyone piled out, they headed for the Shrewsbury fans' end of the ground. The police kept them in for their own protection, so the Boro fans made for the town centre, wrecking anything and everything in their path. Myself and Bri were hungry, so we went to a fish and chip shop for some grub. As we waited in the queue, some locals came in saying that a minibus from Boro had driven into a crowd of Shrewsbury fans as they left the ground. This was never confirmed, though with the mood our fans were in that day I wouldn't have put it past them.

It was the first and, as far as I am aware, only time that full riot police have been deployed at a football match in Britain, certainly in Shropshire. The witch-hunt continued back on

Teesside, with the local paper producing photos of persons wanted in connection with the riot, resulting in several arrests throughout Teesside. So that was it: relegated, branded scum of the earth, and a team unworthy of such passionate supporters. Personally I had had enough and seriously considered calling it a day. That is until news broke that the club had gone bankrupt and was in grave danger of going out of existence altogether.

CHAPTER SEVEN

Boro Bounce Back

DURING THE SUMMER of 1986, the Official Receiver was called in by the Inland Revenue and several other creditors with a demand to wind up the club, due to debts of over £1,000,000. At first I, along with others, thought it would never happen, we were just too big for that. But when they locked the gates and started repossessing items, and shitbags like Peter Beagrie deserted the ship, I started to believe it. I didn't really comprehend what was happening on the legal and monetary side, all I knew was that my beloved Boro were in danger of disappearing from existence. The team I had supported all my life, the crack with all the lads, travelling all over the country, the rivalry with other fans; Saturdays would never be the same.

Throughout the summer we waited while local businesses and the council tried to draw up a rescue package, holding collections and fund-raising events to do our little bit. The fixtures for the following season were out and time was running short yet still there was no agreement; we didn't even figure on the Pools coupons. Then, in the last week before the start of the season, a compromise was reached between the consortium and the creditors. For now we were saved and Middlesbrough Football Club 1986 Ltd was born. We had only been given a reprieve and still had a long way to go but it was a something, and turned out to be the start of one hell of a rollercoaster ride that is still rolling along to this day.

Our first game had to be played at Hartlepool's ground because we still had not regained possession of Ayresome. We drew with Port Vale 2–2. I had almost knocked football on the head after the previous season but the events of the summer had made me realise just how much I would miss it. We went ten matches before losing our first game, giving us a great start and putting us in the driving seat at the top of the Third Division. At home we were virtually untouchable both on and off the pitch, and away from home our firm dominated every club we went to.

Gillingham was good crack early in the season, one of those straight-after-a-nightclub jobs. Two vanloads of us left the Starlight club in Redcar at 2 a.m. – our van from Redcar and another with a crew from Stockton. One of the Redcar lads, Ally, had been out in fancy dress, asked where we were going and just jumped in the back pissed as a fart. He fell asleep for a few hours and woke up as we were approaching London. I laughed like fuck when he suddenly realised where he was, especially as he was dressed as a woman in make-up and a wig.

We arrived bright and early and parked near the ground. With no-one about, we went in and had a game of footy on their pitch until the groundsman chased us off. From the pubs opening to kick-off time we got as drunk as skunks. More Boro fans kept turning up and joining in the binge. Everyone decided to go in their end as it was pissing down and the away end was uncovered. Bri and I were first through the turnstile, then the police sussed out the rest of our lads and stopped them entering. We decided to stay quiet and took up position on the corner. Bri was reading the programme nonchalantly as I surveyed the scene. Then I noticed a few familiar faces behind the goal. Before we knew it a fracas had developed, so we both made our way to where the action was. I often wonder what the Gillingham fans must have thought as Ally tore into them dressed as a woman. After a few more punches had been exchanged the local plod moved in and escorted us out. It was not on the same scale as Chelsea at Boro but the same result was gained nonetheless, and from little acorns great oaks grow.

We managed to take over most places that season, however one or two firms did give us pause for thought. Bristol City turned out their mob impressively at Ashton Gate, though disappointed at our gaff after sending word that they were going to do the biz – we had every man and his dog out for that one. Darlo promised much but failed to deliver as we ran them ragged, mind I ended up in the wrong place at the wrong time and copped for a clip. I always seem to get caught in the least expected of places, I mean Darlo, you wouldn't expect anyone to end up getting slapped there, but as I have already said, it can be a naughty place.

I had gone to the match with our kid, Bri and Mark, who was on crutches after breaking his leg playing football. I knew there would be trouble in the town, as all our lads had gone through and Darlo had promised them a reception. We went late on and walked into the ground well after 3 p.m. Something had gone off, which was obvious, as the kick-off had been delayed; apparently Boro had invaded the pitch to get at Darlo, resulting in a mass brawl on the pitch. Unknowingly we had gone in the end where most of the Darlo lads were gathered, known as the Tin Shed. As we made our way to the front due to Mark's condition, one young Darlo fan asked me where I was from. I looked him up and down and thought, *what the fuck are you gonna do, like?* 'Boro, why?' I snarled at him and off he went, melting back into the crowd. Within a couple of minutes a few lads came over and surrounded me. Bri climbed over the wall onto the side of the pitch and I was about to do the same when this lad of Asian appearance stuck one on me. As I struggled with him, a copper pulled me out of the crowd, telling me I was under arrest. I protested and pointed out it was me who was attacked.

'We're sick of you Boro bastards today,' he rapped.

'Yeah but I'm here with a couple of friends, one has a broken leg, do we look like troublecausers?' I protested.

'Go on then, I'll give you the benefit of the doubt. Come with me, I'll take you to another area of the ground.'

My protest worked and we ended up in some seats on the side of the ground. At the end of the game, which Boro won, there was trouble all over Darlo but as I'd had my warning I decided to stay out of it. The next day's papers described the scenes as a riot. Once again there was a local witchhunt, resulting in over 100 arrests. It went on for months, with pictures of 'hooligans' displayed in the papers for snitches to identify.

Even Newport looked promising as they had a pop at us before the game, but we saw them off at a canter (this one was a case of men against boys). Blackpool threatened briefly but failed and went the same as the rest. I believe their mob were known as the Bisons; aren't they almost extinct now? Blackpool always brings out all the lads, even those who have not been for a while, and true to form thousands of Boro descended on the west coast seaside resort, some as early as the Friday night. I travelled down with Bri in his dad's car (Bri's dad, Ron, was a sound bloke who had followed the Boro since his childhood days continuing right up to the day he died), arriving in time for the pubs opening. We went into a pub not far from the ground, which rapidly filled up with some of the many fans descending on the resort. Some who had arrived the night before told us of battling that had already taken place on the Friday.

After a couple of pints we decided to leave Ron and find some of the lads (Bri didn't want his dad involved in anything that might go off). We ended up in another pub full of Boro, which was being systematically wrecked, for want of a better description. The cigarette machine had been robbed along with the fruit machine, young Joeys were helping themselves to booze from the bar, the landlord was helpless and his doormen had long given up the fight and left the mob to it. Word came that Blackpool's boys were just up the road in another pub, so half the place emptied and the pub was laid siege to, with most windows going through and a running battle outside, eventually cut short by the police, who were obviously getting stretched as reports came in of fighting at several other locations. The police tactics were of a zero tolerance nature with some lads getting locked up for the smallest misdemeanour. I saw one lad get arrested for shouting over the road to his mate, then his mate get nicked for trying to explain to the copper that no offence had been committed. He did grab hold of the cop so I suppose in the loosest sense that constituted assault.

On the way to the ground I clocked a group of Boro lads chatting to some Blackpool. They told me they had arranged a kick-off for after the game with the Bisons in the car park outside the ground. Inside the ground there was fighting in the South Stand even before a ball was kicked, as a mob of Boro lads invaded the home ranks. This continued as a running battle for quite some time and the law struggled to contain it. There was more trouble once the match started as Boro fans spilled onto the pitch fighting with police. This in turn sparked more disorder in other areas of the ground. Basically it was going off all over.

The match turned out to be a walkover for the Boro, who won 4–1. We lost Bri's dad and took advantage of the opportunity to head for the car park, where most of the lads were going. As we turned the corner, true to their word they were there: 150 or more Blackpool lads. Both mobs piled into one another, setting off a full-scale ruck which went on for a few minutes. Even when the police moved in they couldn't contain the mayhem. Eventually Boro gained the upper hand and Blackpool's boys backed off and ran towards the seafront.

As we left this area to find Ron's car, I spotted Sean, my brother-in-law, being frogmarched by a copper into the back of a police van. He saw me and smiled, then shouted, 'See you on Monday, I won't need a lift.' Sean ended up jumping the train to get home after appearing in a special court on the Monday, where he received a £100 fine for his labours.

ANOTHER FIRM THAT did have a creditable go were Bolton. A magazine called *Bulldog*, which used to print a hooligan league table, had put Boro's firm top and had offered Bolton five points to do us, so the stage was set. I don't know how the points system worked but it was something like three points for doing a rival firm and bonus points for pitch invasions, doing it away from home, number of arrests, etc. Chelsea had apparently always been in the top three places, mind I think the mag was edited by a Headhunter. We arrived early and arranged to meet at the nearest pub to the station, as usual. At about half past one Bolton's mob turned up, a good couple of hundred. The windows went through and we piled outside for a kick-off that lasted about a couple of minutes before they got on their toes. All good stuff and credit to Bolton as they played their part to the full. Inside the ground there were a couple of smaller-scale set-tos and some lads ended up fighting on the pitch. Bolton didn't get their five points; I think our firm even strengthened our lead at the top.

So that was it. We bullied our way through the Third, culminating in a never-to-be-forgotten night at Ayresome when we got the point we needed against Wigan that took us back up to the Second Division. The last game was a party day out at Doncaster, where we took over the whole ground (Doncaster fans were warned not to even think about going to the game). The inevitable pitch invasion took place, the goals were converted into the letter M and a good day out was had by all.

It was at this time that my marriage was going downhill fast. I was working away from home and during the summer of 1987 I parted from my wife, or rather she parted from me. For the next few years I stayed away from Teesside most of the time, returning only to see my family and to watch the Boro, the only two loves in my life. I lived where I worked, including Cambridgeshire (boring hole), Kent, Liverpool and various locations in London. Mind you I was earning good money, a lot of which was wasted on booze and women.

NOW WE WERE back in the Second Division for the 1987/88 season but we didn't start too well, winning only one of the first five matches. Then we took off again on a run that had us top of the league by the end of November, led by Captain Marvel Tony 'Mogga' Mowbray and goal machine Bernie 'Offside' Slaven. Off the pitch things were just plodding along, we had no chew off anyone until we went to Sheffield United, where we had another eventful away day.

The trip to Sheffield began in a pub in Redcar at 9 a.m. The landlord was a keen Boro fan who was going to the game and he opened the doors early so we could have a few drinks before we set off. When we got to Sheffield we parked our arses in a pub right in the city centre, thirty-six of us from two vans and a couple of cars. Although we were few in number, the quality was top drawer. Our crew consisted of the General, Big Tommy, Fred (Custer), Doddsy, Hobnail, Mossy, Fazza, Dooza, Snapper, Turtle, Burger and several other well-respected members of the Redcar firm, all game lads who didn't know the word run. Doddsy, Hobnail, Mossy, Burger, Turtle and Snapper were the younger members of the firm, dressing in smart designer gear and into the new wave music going around at the time. Doddsy was regarded as a sort of leader. Short and stocky, he loved the buzz of fighting and inevitably did a lot more than most. Mossy was taller and slimmer, very fast and game as fuck. He had a dry wit, always coming out with stinging one-liners that would put you in your place. Snapper (*aka* Broken Nose) wasn't quite as handy as most but willing to have a go just the same, regularly coming off second best, hence his distorted features. Hobnail was a huge lad, very nice-natured, a bit of a gentle giant although rather naïve at times. Burger was good at organising trips and was very diplomatic, while Turtle was fairly quiet although very funny. Talking of funny, Fazza was the ultimate comedian, along with another lad known as Spasky, although sometimes he could be too much. One thing all these lads had was an excellent camaraderie, always sticking together. Any inhouse rivalry would always be put to one side at the match.

We had been in this pub for about an hour, playing cards and having a chat with one or two locals, when one of the lads noticed a mob on the other side of the road. 'Here they come lads, get on the doors,' ordered the General. Sure enough, seventy or eighty boys came at the pub, throwing bricks at the windows. We held firm as they did their best. One big Sheffield lad managed to get through one door and stood shouting at us to come outside but someone threw a chair at him and he backed away. They moved off when the police turned up but that wasn't the end of it.

The barman told the police we had done no wrong, and as nothing was happening they let us leave the pub. When we got outside there was only one police car there with two coppers. They told us to stay outside the pub while they called for back-up. Then the Sheffield mob came back, so we went at them across a footbridge. Big Tommy, Custer and the General led the charge into them. Now these lads were all one-punch knockout merchants and so it proved. Six of seven of them must have gone down straight away, with the rest of them running off into the shopping area and us in hot pursuit. A couple of their lads who tried to stand and fight were totally wasted, with Custer getting arrested as the police arrived in large numbers. It took four coppers to drag him off as he pummelled one gadgie.

Fearing more for the locals than us, the police commandeered a bus to take us to the ground. The driver demanded payment but we refused, saying we would rather walk. The police made him take us free of charge. The game? Oh we won that as well 2–0. Now I knew we had arrived as a force, and a well-organised one at that.

We had a few more tasty little set-tos that season, including one at Leeds where we took over 6,000 fans. Millwall would have been good if we'd got there but our local police stopped the coach from travelling. The lads who did make it assured me we had a good mob out but the law won the day by keeping them well apart from the Millwall firm. Ipswich was a nightmare as we lost 4–0. I was rather drunk and almost got nicked for running along the roof and jumping into the stand below. The police didn't bother with me because a crew of Boro had invaded the Ipswich end, sending home fans scurrying all over. We rounded off that trip with a top night out in Great Yarmouth. Some of the lads were picked up by the law a few days later in Redcar after they had studied video footage of the attack on the home fans' enclosure. New police tactics were being used now; I mean, fancy getting lifted ages after the event.

We were lying third with two games to play: away to Barnsley and home to Leicester. We won at Barnsley 3–0, had a bit of chew as well (we normally do there) and the scene was set for the final match, which if we won would guarantee promotion. In the build-up to the Leicester game everyone was already talking about the next season and how well we were going to do. Nobody envisaged us losing. Leicester, however, had not read the script and spoiled the party by winning 2–1, leaving us having to go through the play-offs in order to enter the Promised Land.

After the game I stayed down the town for a few drinks; we had intended to celebrate but as it turned out we ended up commiserating instead. As the night wore on and the beer flowed, a lot of the lads I was with started to get a little over-boisterous, and when we left a pub called the Wellington there was a bit of trouble going on over the road outside another pub involving the police. A Boro lad was on the floor with four coppers trying to arrest him. One of our lads shouted over, 'Fucking leave him alone, you black bastards.' Two of the coppers pulled their truncheons out. 'Stand back, move away now!' one of them ordered. You could see he was worried as more people came into the street. Then a couple of lads managed to pull the one being arrested away from the police. He had handcuffs on one wrist already but once he was free he disappeared down a street shouting, 'Cheers lads.' He must have spent the rest of the night sawing those handcuffs off. More police arrived, things started to get ugly and a full-scale confrontation took place. A police car was wrecked and it was becoming a riot. All the pubs were now emptying, most of onlookers, and the police sealed off the roads to prevent any more people getting involved. The law tried a baton charge at us but nobody moved, in fact it was the police who retreated when we went at them. Eventually things did calm down and I ended up back in Redcar in the Starlight, drunk as a skunk and fixed up with some slapper.

The first match in the play-offs was away to Bradford. We took our full allocation of tickets and filled the away end. We were losing 2–0 when Trevor Senior scored a vital away goal for us to set the return up nicely. I didn't see any trouble at Bradford but a couple of mates who had travelled separately had a right old kick-off in one of their pubs with a load of black lads. In the second leg at home, Slaven scored in the first half to put us level on aggregate, but we couldn't find that killer second goal to see them off, so the game went into extra time. With only one minute of extra time played, Gary

Hamilton scored to send the crowd into raptures. The atmosphere now was electric, but those last twenty-nine minutes seemed like twenty-nine hours. To everyone's relief the ref finally blew his whistle, and we knew who we were playing in the final: Chelsea. I suppose Bradford could count themselves unlucky; they had played us four times that season, winning on three occasions.

We expected Chelsea to turn up for this one but they brought only a couple of hundred, a shameful turnout by anyone's standards let alone the famous Headhunters. Boro breezed through the game, winning 2–0 to set us up nicely for the return in London – and what a day that was! Although Chelsea's firm had given the first leg a miss, you could bet your last penny that they would be out in force for the home leg. Our boys all got their heads together to arrange a meeting place for the away trip and agreed to meet in a pub called The Pride of Paddington near the station. I was working down south with a bunch of other Boro lads and we were first there. By half past eleven you couldn't move for Boro gadgies. Eventually there were three pubs full of boys, all up for it, no scarves or colours. When we left to start our journey to the Bridge, all the other pubs emptied and joined us. What a firm; there must have been at least 1,000 or more in the mob. As we got nearer to Chelsea's ground I looked up ahead and there was Boro as far up the road as you could see. The scene was the same when I looked back. Nobody could live with this.

Chelsea's boys tried to come out of some pubs near the ground to have a go but soon disappeared when they saw the size of our mob. The law forced us straight into the ground on arrival, and when I entered the terracing I was taken aback by the size of our support: there were at least 10,000 Boro singing their heads off. This brilliant support must have made Chelsea ashamed of what they had brought to Boro, and when the teams came out you could hear only one set of fans. On the pitch Chelsea made it hard for us by scoring early in the first half. This led to one of the best rearguard displays I have ever witnessed from a Boro team. They fought like the true lions they were. At the final whistle, with the score still 2–1 to us on aggregate, our end erupted. Half a dozen Boro fans scaled the fence and ran over to congratulate the players. The Chelsea stewards (who all seemed to be Headhunters by the look of them) tore into them and this in turn prompted a pitch invasion by Chelsea fans. They came charging towards us, fucking hundreds of them, stopping short of the fence but throwing bottles and whatever they could get their hands on. We stood in our end goading them and taking the piss. I loved every minute of it. The police took ages to clear the pitch and wouldn't let us out of the ground until all of their mob had disappeared.

Chelsea's fans got all the bad publicity and even claimed a victory over us, but we know different. As I was working down the south I got to know quite a few of Chelsea's boys and they freely admitted they would have been hard pressed to take on the firm we had before the game, and stated that they had the utmost respect for our firm.

ALTHOUGH THE PLAY-OFFS with Chelsea got most of the media coverage, it was in the FA Cup against Everton where we would have our biggest kick-off of the season. We were drawn away at Goodison in the fourth round and as we'd had some chew there in the past, we got our heads together to organise a meeting place in Liverpool away from the ground where the police would not think of looking. As usual it was nearest pub to the station, which turned out to be the Crown, situated right near the bus station on the corner of Lime Street railway station. Most of us travelled by car and minibus, with some coming through on the train. I was with Bri and three other lads in a car. We got to the pub just after opening time and were the first ones in. There were some Everton fans already in when we entered and they asked if we were bringing a mob across, as they'd heard we had been doing the biz all over. We played daft and said we didn't know what they were on about. Soon more of our lads arrived, putting our numbers at about thirty, and the Scousers realised the score and left. We knew they would be back with their mob and things looked better for us as another fifty Boro came in off the train.

By about half past one we had filled the pub with 130 boys. Then one of the side doors burst open. There stood an Everton gadgie with a knife in his hand, shouting at us to get outside. It took no more than twenty seconds for us to empty the pub and pile into the street, where a sizeable mob of Scousers were waiting, all tooled-up with either blades or bottles. We charged straight into them and a full-scale, toe-to-toe battle raged, with the Scousers eventually backing off up the road. One scouser was thrown through a shop window, four or five more were left lying in the road and then before we could get back in the pub the law arrived.

We had them on the run and didn't want to give them the opportunity to regroup, so we tried going round the back of the pub and cutting them off from a different direction. The police followed and made a line across the road, preventing us from getting any further. Bri was absolutely mortal drunk and had missed most of what had been going on. He came staggering out of the pub and shouted across the road to me. As I looked to see where he was, a copper grabbed him and arrested him, shoving him in the van face down with his hands handcuffed behind his back. After what had just gone down he was the only one to get lifted, and probably the only one not involved. That's the perils of drink, I suppose. Once the police had got us all together one of our crew noticed he had been slashed across his back; luckily it was not too deep as he was wearing a leather coat. The police marched us all the way through some hideous inner-city areas up to the ground. I was intrigued to observe how scruffy and dilapidated the city of Liverpool was.

The game was quite the classic cup tie, with Everton taking the lead in the first half and Boro coming back to equalise and force a replay. We had to make our way back to Lime Street, which we did on buses (no-one fancied that walk again). When I got there, the first person I saw was Bri, who had been let out by the police. He was getting abuse from some local scallies who soon fucked off when we arrived. Some of our firm had parked in the multi-storey and told us of some grief they encountered on the way to their cars, which resulted in them having to take refuge in a hotel lobby. When I arrived back home I was not surprised to read in the papers of several slashing incidents before and after the match. This was typical of Scousers: brave with a knife in their hands. Most Boro fans abhorred the use of knives, especially our firm. Although one or two had been known to use them on remote occasions in the past, with the Scousers it seemed like part of their scene, and whenever we had a do with either Liverpool or Everton I was always wary of 'Stanleys' being used. They had it off to such a fine art they even used two blades separated by a match stick to make the wounds harder to stitch. I know some readers from Barnsley may well disagree with our view of carrying blades following an incident in the Eighties when several of their firm were subjected to a brutal attack in Boro town centre, which resulted in some lads receiving emergency hospital treatment for slash wounds, but I stress this was a one-off incident that I neither saw nor was party to. The guilty have served their time and paid the penalties they deserved for what can only be described as a heinous offence totally against the unwritten rules of engagement, end of.

In the replay at Boro another classic encounter unfolded, with Everton scoring first, Boro equalising in the last minute to force extra time, then we scored to put us 2–1 up. With time ticking away, Everton snatched a last-gasp equaliser in injury time of extra time. So 2–2 and another replay, this time back at Goodison. They had not brought a mob to Boro so nothing happened, but sure enough 5,000 Boro made the trip back across the Pennines for the second replay. This time we kept clear of the city centre and concentrated on drinking near the ground, but Everton did themselves no favours again by slashing more Boro fans, mainly young kids. The total over the two games amounted to 15 Boro fans slashed – shithouses! We lost 2–1 in a close, hard-fought game but we had done ourselves proud both on and off the pitch.

That was it, another season over, now the First Division to look forward to. As the song on the terraces went:

First Division here we come
Right back where we started from
We've been away far too long
First Division here we come.

We were back in the top flight and with us we brought a togetherness akin to the old Dunkirk spirit. Boro started poorly, winning only one of the first five matches, but we were not getting hammered, only losing by the odd goal. We were playing some pretty attractive football as well. We were to remain in the lower half of the league all season, constantly battling against the dreaded drop. A lot of Boro fans felt the same as me, that maybe we had come up too soon and we should have had another season in the Second Division to prepare better for the top flight. Once again we were to be relegated, but there was no finger-pointing or blame bestowed upon anyone. We had given it our best shot and went down with honour. Bruce Rioch had showed himself to be a magician with the resources at his disposal and is still held in high esteem in Middlesbrough to this day.

Off the pitch our fans proved themselves more than a match for anyone, both in terms of loyal support for the team and taking on the best that other firms could throw at us. A couple of away trips are worth mentioning, starting with Tottenham early in the season. I was still living and working in London, as were quite a lot of Boro fans at the time, so most games in the capital were guaranteed a healthy following. Boro have one of the biggest fan bases in the capital, mostly brought about by the closure of a lot of the traditional industries on Teesside. For example there were no longer any shipyards, the steelworks which once employed 20,000 had been reduced to 5,000, the chemical giant ICI had gone from 16,000 down to about 3,000, and not enough new industries had replaced these giants, meaning a lot of workers had to travel further afield. Some areas of Teesside had pockets of unemployed standing at forty per cent or more. The police had started to target known Frontline boys and two Middlesbrough coppers travelled away with the Boro to spot ringleaders in a bid to prevent any trouble. However with so many of us already living down London, their task was made all the harder, as we arranged for the lads to come down on the Friday night and did our drinking away from the usual places.

For the Spurs match we met at a pub in Highbury, near the tube station, called the Cock, only a couple of stops from the Seven Sisters. Once we had met up there were 150-plus boys and little chance of getting any chew off the 'Yids' with this firm before the game. So it proved, as we marched up to White Hart Lane totally unheeded. Boro lost the game 3–2 in a thrilling encounter. As we walked back to the tube station, there was a firm of Yids in front giving it the big come-on, so we accommodated them good style. The actual fighting lasted only a couple of minutes with the Yids on the back foot throughout. It was hard to estimate numbers as the road was filled with a mix of boys and scarfheads from both sides. To our advantage was the fact that we all knew one another, while Tottenham were totally disorganised.

One place we had never had much return from was Newcastle. For one reason or another we had always failed to really organise ourselves, but this season was to be the start of Boro becoming the top firm in the North East. Newcastle away was a night match, and as we had not done much in the past, the police were not expecting a lot of trouble. I went up on the train with about 100 of our firm and the police escorted us straight to the ground. Boro were hammered 3–0 but when we came out of the ground the police were not interested in us, so we got together and marched down the road towards the station. We had moved only 100 yards away from the ground when a crew of Geordies came piling out of a pub throwing bottles. They probably expected us to get on our toes but we stood firm and counter-charged, sending them running all over. Some big gadgies stood and fought but they had no chance as we steamed in. One Geordie went down and took a hell of a kicking before the police arrived to calm things down.

While we were on the station platform a group of Geordies were shouting the usual obscenities from the other side. 'How man, yez ar aal shite, yeez Borra fuckas, ah'll tak any one o' yez on,' came one comment from a large Geordie in his late thirties, a proper old-schooler from the Seventies. One Boro lad took him up on his offer, shouting back, 'Howay then, you come over here, one to one, just me and you, ya fat Geordie twat.' Well that was all it took, the fat Geordie came charging straight over the tracks, only to be met by several coppers who pounced on him dragging him to the floor. He struggled like mad, with four coppers needed to hold him down and get the cuffs on, the lunatic. 'That's what they used to be like in the Seventies, mad as fuck, the fucking idiot,' I informed the young lad, who looked quite shocked at the fact that this nutter was prepared to do all he could in order to get at him.

Towards the end of the season we played West Ham in a relegation battle at Upton Park, another night match that was to be remembered for one or two notable reasons. This was another place we had not fared too well in the past, and another acid test was to be passed with flying colours. Once again the police weren't expecting anything. We met in the famous Blind Beggar pub in Whitechapel, the place where Ronnie Kray gunned down George Cornell, and had about 80–100 in numbers. Boyo, like me, lived in London and had all his mates down: Jonka, Stevie Mac, Stevo, Ernie Ragbo, Napper, Sean, Ged, Lenny, the Spark brothers, everyone was there. I had met up with the Redcar firm earlier. Now a mob like that doesn't like to get together without coming away with some form of result. Where once we would have been happy to go to West Ham and get away without a caning, this time we wanted some sport.

As we walked to the ground Boyo suggested going in the Queens pub to have it with their firm. We were not sure if this was their main pub but I had been in there before and left sharpish as it was full of big fuck-off Hammers. As it is so close to the tube it was also the most convenient boozer. So in we went, all quiet like, then once most of us were inside we announced our arrival. You should have seen them fighting each other to get through the doors. As we were giving them it inside, the ones who got out were met by the rest of our firm who had stayed outside. This all lasted no more than a couple of minutes, then we moved on to the next pub. The West Ham inside it were trying to get out to have a go but we held them inside the doorway. The police turned up and got us all together to escort us up to the ground. The Hammers boys managed to get themselves organised but it was too late, we had done the biz. It was great to see the looks on their faces and hear the comments that they had been done. We won the match 2–1 as well, a good night's work by all.

The next match was also in London, at Queens Park Rangers. Boyo and his now well-established London-based firm lived in West Kensington, which is QPR turf, and he had organised a kick-off with their firm. Bri had won a load of money on the Pools and paid for a coach to bring the lads down, and yet again we had a big firm out. The kick-off with the 'Bushers' had been arranged well away from the ground, and true to their word they turned up with a decent-sized firm. As we went at them they hurled dozens of milk bottles at us, forcing us to back off, but once they had exhausted their arsenal we counter charged. Some of them stood, most notably their black lads, but the rest ran like fuck, leaving their mates to take a beating. As there were no coppers in attendance the battle went on for quite a long time, with us forcing the issue all the way up to Loftus Road itself.

The season ended with a match at Sheffield Wednesday that Boro needed to win to stay up. Our ticket allocation was reduced to 2,000 due to the terrible events that had occurred between Liverpool and Forest earlier in the season, when ninety-six Liverpool fans were crushed to death. This resulted in Boro fans buying tickets for all ends of the ground, including their kop, which I though was a recipe for disaster. But Sheff Wed did not have the firm they used to and the day passed off peacefully enough. Boro lost and we were sent back to the Second Division.

CHAPTER EIGHT

Wembley At Last

SEASON 1989/90 TURNED out to be quite memorable for two reasons: we stayed up on the last day by beating the Geordies, which also prevented them gaining promotion, and we made our first visit to Wembley.

The season started with a 4–2 home win against Wolves but the rot set in early and we were to remain in the bottom five for most of the season. There were a couple of notable days out away to Leeds, Sunderland and especially Newcastle. We had to play Newcastle away on a Wednesday night for the second season running. This time we gave the train a miss and all arranged to travel up by cars and minibuses. We met in a pub in the Metro Centre in Gateshead, which has a Metro station nearby. I estimated we would have about fifty boys but was amazed to see a good 150 turn up. We thought we would be spotted by the law as we boarded the train but we were not even given a second glance; then we thought they would pick us up when we got to the monument, but once again no law. So there we were, 150 Boro Frontline marching through the streets of Newcastle unchallenged. The law eventually picked us up as we neared the stadium and made sure nothing untoward occurred.

The game finished 2–2 and was quite good as it happens, but we were a bit more interested in what was going to happen outside. Once again we mobbed up after the game and marched down towards the station. As had happened the previous season, the Geordies came charging out of the pubs at us, and as before we held firm and sent them running off in different directions. We all got back unscathed and even a little bit pissed off that we had not had a better kick-off with the scum.

Doing the biz twice in a row at Newcastle was the icing on the cake; we had finally arrived as a respected firm and our reputation was second to none. You know how heavy your reputation is when you talk to other boys from the likes of Chelsea and Millwall, especially when you meet on holiday, and I have taken great delight in basking in some of the praise dished out while sat in a bar in Spain. Our notoriety was also evident at England matches, but more of that later. At home we were totally untouchable, so most of our home games went off without the slightest hint of trouble. In the FA Cup we had another marathon tussle with Everton, going out in the second replay, and the knife-wielding Scousers managed to extend their unenviable rate of referrals to the plastic surgeons (I wish I had a pound for every stitch they have put in our fans' faces).

There was one cup competition we did rather well in: the Zenith Data Systems Cup. So well that we made it to the final at Wembley. I mean Wembley, you know twin towers and all that! What a weekend that turned out to be. For years and years it had been every Boro fan's dream to march down Wembley Way, a dream that burned even brighter every time a Mackem or Magpie taunted us with the chant that we had never been there. The competition was not the most popular by any means, but the prize at the end was. Boro had won their way through to the semi-finals by beating Port Vale, Wednesday and Newcastle. We were drawn away in the first leg to Aston Villa. They did not seem all that interested which told in the attendance of 16,000. Seven thousand were from Boro.

It was absolutely pissing down, but we didn't care as Bernie Slaven and Mark Brennan scored to set us off dancing in the rain. Villa pulled one back to make the second leg more than interesting but it did not stop one lad running the length of the pitch in celebration at the final whistle with his betting slip in hand, as he had put £100 on at nine-to-one. The second leg saw a tense affair come to life when Villa scored to even up the tie and send the game into extra time, but Slaven and then Paul Kerr banged two in to settle it and set off scenes never before witnessed in Middlesbrough. The town centre was bouncing all night as we celebrated. Due to my passionate nature I burst into tears at the emotion of it all.

Our opponents in the final were none other than Chelsea. This alone guaranteed a sell-out, mind we'd have sold out even if it was Torquay. Also guaranteed was the coming together of two of the most notorious firms in the country, and I kid you not when I say it was going off from the start of the day to the end. Boro received around 38,000 tickets for the game, and half of those arrived in London on the Friday night. Most of our firm travelled down on the train but I went with Bri on a minibus from G-town, meeting up in Paddington with the rest of them. The game was due to be played on Sunday so we had the whole of Saturday in London drinking ourselves silly. Doddsy and Lancey got themselves arrested on the Saturday night fighting some foreigners in a kebab shop and missed Boro's finest taking over Trafalgar Square.

During the Saturday afternoon Bri and I spent our time wandering around Covent Garden and the West End getting drunk, eventually making our way to the Three Kings pub to meet up with the firm right in the heart of Chelsea territory. Rumours went round all day that their mob was going to come and have a go, but by four o'clock most of us got fed up and left to make our way up to the West End for the night. Some of the lads who stayed told us later that Chelsea came just after we left, throwing a CS canister into the pub but not doing much more.

When it got to 11 p.m. Bri suggested we make our way to Trafalgar Square so as not to miss all the crack. On our way we spotted some young Boro kids getting done off some Chelsea tossers. Well we were having none of that, so along with another lad Bri and I chased after them down the Underground. We caught up with them on a tube train. Bri went to one door and I went to the other to block their escape. There were six of them sat singing, 'Wembley, Wembley, here we come,' scarfheads for sure but too big to be going round hitting little kids. Bri and the other lad weighed into them while I smacked one who tried to get through the doorway. Then I heard the hissing noise of the doors closing so I pulled back. Bri shouted the other lad to get off but he was enjoying himself too much and the doors closed, trapping him on board. As we stood on the platform watching the train pull away all we could see was this Boro lad still going for it good style with these Chelsea lads. We thought he would be a goner for sure but the next time we saw him he said nothing happened; apparently he ended up sat talking to them and just got off at the next stop.

Feeling slightly sorry for the other lad and knowing there was nothing we could do, we set off to Trafalgar Square. We did not have to ask where to go as you could hear Boro voices echoing all over the West End, so we just followed the noise. What a pleasure that sight was as we turned the corner to be greeted by thousands of Boro fans adorning the fountains and lions, singing all the old Boro songs. We stayed long into the night and literally sang ourselves hoarse.

When we got up in the morning we made our way to the Hospitality Inn, where the Redcar firm were staying. We had a bit of a chat and agreed to meet them on Wembley Way later in the afternoon. We jumped into the minibus and drove up to the north end of London and parked near the last stop on the tube, so as to get away from the traffic after the game. Well, we only picked a pub full of Chelsea to booze in, didn't

we. It was a good job they were all scarfheads or we would
have walked into a right pasting. Bri and myself decided to go
to Wembley to meet up with the Redcar firm as arranged and
when we got there all you could see were Boro fans, especially
on Wembley Way. I heard from some lads that there had been
a fair old kick-off near the Greyhound pub, with first Chelsea
then Boro having the upper hand. Seeing as it was our first
time at the twin towers we decided to get in the ground early
to soak up the atmosphere. Most of Boro's firm had decided
to do the same, which turned out to be a bad move, as Chelsea
steamed through all the Boro fans outside the stadium just
before kick-off: big brave Chelsea chasing women and kids
who were only down to enjoy the day out, mind we should
have known better.

The first half of the match was notable for one thing:
Chelsea scored a goal. Half-time was notable for the toe-to-
toe battle in the concourse between hundreds of boys from
both sides, which must have raged for a good ten minutes.
The police were powerless to stop it. I noticed that a lot of
Chelsea's boys were wearing T-shirts with the words 'No
fences this time Boro' in reference to the play-off game at
Stamford Bridge in 1988. Sharky had come out of retirement
for this one and collared a couple of Chelsea fans in the
toilets, leaving them both laid out face down in the piss
trough. The match plodded on to finish 1–0 to Chelsea,
hardly a classic, in fact I think it was the only shot Chelsea had
during the whole game. The one lasting memory was of the
ovation we gave to our defeated team, one that even Chelsea
fans complimented us on.

I lost Bri in the crowd so I stayed with the Redcar firm,
who were all hanging back trying to get a mob together for the
inevitable battle with the Headhunters. We managed to get
about 100 boys together, then we made our way to the tube
station. Suddenly hundreds of Chelsea's firm came from all
over. Fuck me, I thought, this is where it's going to happen,

on Wembley Way itself. We were totally outnumbered so we slipped through a gap in the fence, where we managed to hold them off, like nobody wanted to come through that gap first. The police made the gap secure so we made our way through the car park and attempted to head up the road to the tube station. As I looked up the road there must have been several hundred Chelsea boys at the top waiting. A lot of them looked to be scarfheads so we just charged towards them. They in turn charged at us, then the mounted police arrived, sending us scurrying back down the hill. The police got us together in an escort and took us up to the tube station, holding the Chelsea fans back to give us a free passage to the trains. Thank fuck, we would have got mashed otherwise.

No sooner had we boarded the train than hundreds of their lads appeared on the platform. The doors had not closed but nothing happened, just verbal threats. The tube pulled out and we waved bye-bye to the Chelsea, thinking we had got away with it – if only that were true. We had to change at Baker Street, which resulted in a fifteen-minute delay and giving the pursuing Headhunters the time to catch us up. At Baker Street we lost more than half our firm, reducing us to about forty-five, and the train following ours pulled in with Chelsea's finest on board and in far superior numbers.

We managed to hold them off as they crossed the foot-bridge, then our train came in. Once we had boarded we managed to occupy only one carriage while they piled onto the others, hundreds of them. When the train stopped at Paddington, where we had to get off, a game of cat-and-mouse developed. As we went to get off, they did, so we got back on again, so did they. This went on for a few minutes with the doors opening and shutting several times before some coppers came along. The coppers agreed to keep their doors shut while we got off and told us we had five minutes to get away before they would let them off. One Chelsea boy asked where we were staying. Someone said the Hospitality

Inn, another lad said, 'Yes, in fucking Glasgow,' before rebuking the big mouth for giving away our location.

I should have been heading home on the minibus instead of running the gauntlet in London, and I must admit I feared the worst. It was not funny at the time but I can laugh at it now. We spent the night boozing round Paddington and apparently just missed bumping into Chelsea's main mob. I got my head down on the floor of one of the lads' rooms. My old mate the Shadow stayed in the same hotel. He had just been released from prison (again) in time for Wembley but he was sharing with Mad Lance, who took a dislike to the TV, fridge and coffee-maker and dispatched them out of the window five storeys to the street below. He said the bed would have gone as well but he couldn't fit it through the window. The Shadow got nicked for it and when Mad Lance was asked why he did it, he just replied, 'For the crack.' (The Shadow got his nickname following an incident at Notts County when he was nicked for going into their side terrace alone but tooled-up, lashing out with a blade and sending the whole end running on to the pitch. He put several lads in hospital with nasty slash wounds. When he appeared in court he claimed the act was revenge for the murder of Craig by Forest fans in 1980, described earlier in this book. In court he was described as the 'Silver Shadow'.)

SIR BRUCE RIOCH had been sacked just before Wembley, not the most popular decision at the time as the fans had come to regard him as a bit of a god. The man left in charge was his number two, Colin Todd, who was to have the narrowest of escapes at the end of the season. A poor run of results saw Boro drop into the relegation places and we were left with the last game of the season against Newcastle to save our Second Division status. They needed a win to get promotion, which made the game all the more spicey. The little matter of it being a local derby helped as well. The first half was a bit cagey with both teams sizing each other up, then after the break the fireworks started. Slaven scored swiftly followed by Ian 'Dicky' Baird to make it 2–0 to Boro. Then they both scored another each, with the Mags getting a consolation to make the final score 4–1. What a pleasure it was to see the miserable faces on all those Geordies at the end of the game. They were not even interested in the traditional after-match set-to. It was a fitting finale to end the season, one that will always be remembered for that first Wembley appearance.

During the summer I left London and returned to Teesside to live at my mother's (where do all wayward sons end up?) but not for long, as I left England altogether to work in Holland. For the first few months of the new season I could not get to any games but I had a good crack following Feyenoord in Holland.

I was working in a place called Dordtrecht, which is close to Rotterdam and houses some of Feyenoord's most notorious boys. It was a bit like going back in time, as the Dutch fans were about ten years behind us in terms of fan culture. I got to know some of their boys and one huge guy called Martin took a liking to me and arranged to take me to some of their matches. The first game was at home to Sparta Rotterdam, which Feyenoord comfortably won 6–0. I was amazed to see that there were no Sparta fans at all at the game. I asked Martin why, as this was a derby match after all, and he told me that nobody other than Ajax or Den Haag would dare to come to their ground; maybe PSV if they were doing well would bring a few hundred. I asked how many Feyenoord took away, and was assured they had a healthy following everywhere. I told him we had to go to some away games.

Big lad though he was, Martin wouldn't go to Den Haag, remarking that it was far too dangerous and that there were often people killed at that fixture. He did take me to the away match at Arnhem against Vitesse, which allowed me to get a firsthand view of their boys in action. Vitesse had a small ground with a capacity of about 12,000. Feyenoord took about 1,500 through, most of them on the train though we went by car. Martin refused to go for a drink in the bars near the ground saying it would be too dangerous, as Vitesse had their boys out looking for Feyenoord fans. He also insisted on talking English for fear of giving himself away as we walked up to the ground with the home supporters (yeah, the Dutch have accents as well). At the ground we were met by scores of police who insisted on searching everyone as they went in. On the terraces I made conversation with several other Feyenoord fans, who looked a tidy firm it has to be said. I discovered that quite a lot of them followed well-known English teams including Leeds, Man United and most of the London clubs. I was proud to hear them praise Boro and acknowledge our firm as being one of the top outfits in England. They then provided me with the evidence of their loyalties by displaying tattoos declaring their allegiance to Feyenoord, all written in English.

The game was shite, finishing in a goalless draw, but one thing that amused me was that they all sang their songs in English, obviously picked up from watching the TV. The police kept us back for five minutes and when we got outside there were about 1,000 Vitesse fans waiting at the bottom of the road. The Feyenoord boys got together and charged down straight into them. I stood back and observed as they went for it up and down the road for several minutes until the police moved in to make arrests. Martin was looking fairly concerned because we had to make our way to the car, which was parked in the opposite direction. He told me to remove the hat that had been given to me by one of the lads in the ground and to keep my head down. We had to walk half a mile to the car along a road full of Vitesse fans who were looking for any Feyenoord boys. Martin was absolutely shitting himself, desperately pretending to be English. We made it to the car unchallenged and set off back to Dordtrecht. On the radio we heard there had been 52 arrests, all Feyenoord fans. Martin explained that the home police only arrested away followers, which gave the home crew a licence to do what they liked.

I fancied going to the away game with Ajax, but it was an all-ticket affair and we had no chance of getting one. By all accounts, and from what I saw on the Dutch TV, it was on the same lines as an Old Firm game. At this time Boro had been plodding away in the league at home and I had managed to follow most of what was occurring by way of TV, newspapers and phoning Bri. By November I decided to call an end to my self-imposed exile in Holland. Martin had become obsessed with my stories of the Boro and I agreed to let him come over to attend a Boro match. He chose to come when we played Millwall, having heard so much about them. I tried to tell him not to expect too much as Millwall never really do it up north and I was proved right as Boro beat them 2–1 and nothing untoward occurred. Mind you he loved the songs that were dished out by the Holgate and could not get enough of Newcastle Brown Ale, with which he drank himself silly over the weekend. I also brought a Dutch girl over who I had been seeing, she was a right fucking lunatic as well. I tried to ditch her when I left Holland but she kept coming over, begging me to go back to Dordtrecht to live with her. I thought I would never get rid of her but eventually after three visits and 200 phone calls she got the message and left me alone. Take it from me, if you ever get fixed up with a Dutch bird don't let her know where you live, they're a bastard to get rid of.

A LOT OF the bigger firms, such as Chelsea's Headhunters, West Ham's ICF, Millwall's Bushwhackers and Leeds's Service Crew had gone to the wall, following dawn raids and changing football cultures. Boro's firm, which had become well known as the Frontline, had continued and even got stronger. Several factors contributed to this. One was that the police had not launched any raids on the main lads, possibly due to the collapse of so many of the other trials involving the Headhunters and others. Another reason no raids were carried out was that the Frontline lads never did any of their 'stuff' inside the stadiums (unlike, for example, Millwall at Luton). We were not known for attacking the police with bricks and actually had quite a good relationship with some of them. All these factors contributed in some way, but the main one, I believe, was the fact that Boro were now regarded as being one of the top firms in the country and this was a status most of our lads wanted to keep. As a football team we had never won a thing in our entire history, so why not be noted for being one of the top firms? It's not a great claim to fame, I admit, but it's all we had.

So I was back in Middlesbrough, living at me mam's and following the Reds once again. The 1990–91 season had got off to an average start while I was in Holland, and Boro were sitting in the top half of the league. By the time we had beaten Ipswich 1–0 on Boxing Day we were in third position and looking well equipped to get ourselves promoted again, but years of following the Boro had taught me never to count chickens. The rest of the season panned out without much to write home about but we managed to secure a place in the play-offs by finishing seventh before our last match away to Barnsley. This was another place where we always seemed to get a bit of a kick-off. It was my birthday and I was in the mood to get totally smashed, so Bri organised a minibus to take us to Oakwell with a night out in Ripon thrown in.

We had a good drink outside Barnsley and parked in the car park near the ground. Walking up to our end, we saw a firm of Barnsley boys and had a quick skirmish in the street, sending them running off towards their end. In the ground we had the usual healthy following of 4,000 or so, and as Barnsley were hoping to get in the play-offs themselves, they had quite a decent crowd by their standards. The game was a non-event for Boro as we had already secured our place, and most of our fans were there for the crack, none more so than Bri who ended up demolishing a toilet at the back of the stand. The police were not too pleased with him but they let him off with a caution.

At the end of the game, which Barnsley won, the home fans invaded the pitch thinking they had made the play-offs but in fact they had finished eighth. The eventual realisation of this resulted in them coming towards us looking for a fight on the pitch. A few Boro got over the fence, including Doddsy, and confronted them, resulting in a bit of a scuffle but the police did too good a job and prevented anything major occurring. The night out in Ripon ended with me getting us thrown out of most pubs after I drank a pint of spirits, which left me totally mortal and barely able to stand. As for the play-offs, we were knocked out in the first round by Notts County.

CHAPTER NINE

Lenny's Lions

COLIN TODD GOT the sack at the end of the season and Boro had a new chairman, Steve Gibson, who brought in Lenny Lawrence. Lenny was a nice enough chap, probably too nice, an excellent tactician who built a team good enough to give anyone a game, he just seemed to lack that little bit of charisma which all top managers need. Steve Gibson was a young, dynamic chairman with a huge ambition to take Boro into the elite brigade, regularly competing for trophies and European football. He is a genuine fan and brought up on a rough council estate on Teesside – local boy makes good type of stuff. Around the same age as myself, he had also started out as a welder, then branched out into the bulk transportation of chemicals and waste products through a haulage firm that he started by buying a couple of trucks. He built the company into a worldwide organisation. The man is an icon on Teesside and if someone like Bobby Robson should get a knighthood, then Mr Gibson certainly deserves one; he not only champions our football team but also anything to do with the town. He loves Teesside as much as we do. Arise Sir Steve; come on your Maj, do the right thing and honour the bloke.

In his first season, Lenny did us proud. He took us to the top of the league by September, the run starting with a 3–0 demolition of the Mags and including a 2–1 win over the Mackems, but it was the cup games that held most of the interest throughout the season. The Rumbelows Cup saw us march past Bournemouth, Barnsley, Man City and Peterborough before we came up against Man United in the semi-finals. We were at home in the first leg, where we absolutely tortured them but only managed a 0–0 draw. The United fans were shite and didn't want to know before or after the match, so it was up to us to do the biz down at Old Trafford, which we did taking, 9,000 fans (even Alex Ferguson complimented us on our backing). Talk about being unlucky: if Gary Pallister had not been so keen to clear off the line we would have made Wembley for the second time in two years, and him an ex-Boro stalwart as well. We went down 2–1 after extra time and left the ground expecting a few fireworks from the United fans, but their days of ruling the roost were long gone and we had to go out of our way to find some action, which was only sporadic and not worthy of much mention.

In the FA Cup we were drawn against Man City (again) in the third round and once again beat them. We followed that with a brilliant victory over Sheff Wed at Hillsborough, where Boro fans celebrated the winning goal by dancing on the pitch. Then we were drawn away to Portsmouth in the fifth round. Now Pompey do have a firm to be proud of and they were out in force. Doddsy and a sizeable crew of 150 boys made their way down on the train. Bri and I contented ourselves with the car, arranging to meet up in Pompey. On arrival, and mindful of previous trips, we decided to make for a pub in the Fratton area near the ground, which was well populated by Boro fans. Soon enough all the lads off the train arrived and we had a nice healthy mob of about 150 boys.

On the way to the ground a few Pompey boys, no more than fifty, tried to have a pop at us. We saw them off but it was a warning of what was to come after the game. The match was hardly a classic, ending in a 1–1 draw, and outside we had a brief but heavy set-to with some of their lads, resulting in some of ours getting arrested, one of whom (Chunky) had travelled down with us. We couldn't leave him behind so we got in the car and headed for the police station to wait for him. As we drove down the road we could see the Boro mob heading for the train station with a good-sized firm of Pompey accompanying them. Sure enough the inevitable happened, with fists flying all over. We had an excellent view of it all as both sets of boys went for it in the middle of the road until the law managed to regain control.

Chunky was not due to be released until 7.30 p.m. so I went for a couple of pints in a bar near the train station. It was heaving with Pompey's boys; boy did I have to keep my mouth shut in there. I listened intently to their stories of what had happened as I sipped away on my pint, and most of what they said was complimentary.

One young lad stood a few feet away from me excitedly told his mate, 'Fucking good firm those Boro boys, they were well up for it, all fucking big ugly fuckers.'

'Always have been,' said another lad. 'I remember having it with them years ago, fucking quality.'

Another lad came in sneaking up on these two, grabbing one of them in a mock arrest. 'You're nicked, Simmo. I saw you fighting the Geordies, you fucking hooligan.'

This Simmo fella laughed and started wrestling playfully with his mate, knocking into me. Then this Simmo guy asked if anyone fancied going to the replay.

'Fucking all the way to the North East on a Wednesday night, you've got to be having a laugh haven't you?' responded one big lad.

The play fight was now getting a little over-exuberant and I got up and moved away before things got any worse. I was dying to correct him on calling us Geordies but it was wiser for me to keep quiet. As the mob grew in the pub and one or two stares were passed in my direction, I thought it would be better to sup up and leave before I was rumbled and in case Bri came trundling in. I found him near the police station and told him not to even bother going for a pint as, knowing him,

The author (front of picture with arms outstretched) flies the flag for Boro at an England game in Slovakia.

A Boro mob in Brussels for Euro 2000 before the inevitable police lock-ups.

A police officer is stretchered off the pitch at Stamford Bridge by colleagues and St John Ambulance staff after violence at a Chelsea v Middlesbrough game. We have had a few ding-dongs with the wideboys from West London.

Boro fans (left) in scuffles with members of Sheffield United's Blades Business Crew, who had invaded the seats in a game at Ayresome Park in March 1985.

Boro's firm outside the Globe (Chelsea's manor) before the Wembley Coca Cola Cup final against Leicester.

The author in between Boro manager Lennie Lawrence (left) and owner Steve Gibson (right) outside a bar in Pisa in 1993. Gibson is a really nice bloke and his money revolutionalised the club.

The Frontline marching through Hyde Park before a play-off game against Chelsea.
At least one Chelsea fan has claimed we didn't bring a firm. Well here they are.

The Boro army on the terraces at that famous victory at Stamford Bridge in May 1988.
What a sight it was.

A fence separates the rival fans baiting each other and throwing coins after the Chelsea lads came across the pitch to us at the end of the game.

The lads on Stevo's stag do outside the Sam Dodd's boozer in Liverpool before our game against terrace rivals Everton. We have had some ferocious clashes with the Blue half of Merseyside over the years.

Two sides of Middlesbrough: the 35,000 capacity Riverside Stadium, opened in 1995, and the docks on the River Tees, where many of the club's supporters once worked.

Boro character Lee 'Oathead' Owens, one of the Stockton lads, being arrested by Belgian police at the Euro 2000 championships in Brussels. This picture appeared in all over the world as a symbol of British fans abroad.

Chris from Redcar being led from the Wembley pitch after his spectacular streak at the Coca Cola Cup final against Leicester. A Leicester streaker kept his undies on - shame on you.

© Cleva/Offside

© Press Association

The windscreen of the Sunderland players' coach after it was bricked by Boro fans on the A19 after a Wednesday night Coca Cola Cup match at the Riverside in 1997. The rivalry between both sets of fans often means that anything goes when they meet.

Police and stewards tried to quell a disturbance during the Sunderland v Middlesbrough match at the Stadium Of Light in February 2003.

My best mate Bri (second from left) and me (fourth from left) on a night out with some of the meatheads in Den Haag.

he would end up either getting a good hiding or joining Chunky in the cells. We lost the replay 4–2 after extra time but only a handful of Pompey turned up at our patch, mind it is a hell of a journey for a night match.

In the league Boro were going along quite nicely. We did the double over the Mags, winning on Boxing Day thanks to a goal from Paul Wilkinson. No mobs came to our ground, as usual, so we had to be content with satisfying our lust away from Ayresome. We had a little portion at Bristol City and Leicester had their boys out in force, but it was Sunderland who provided our big test of the season up at Joker Park. We had a good healthy following with most of the firm on the train but all the Mackems seemed to come from nowhere, emerging out of side streets. Most of our firm gave chase after one group, leaving the back markers to fight a rearguard action against a bigger firm attacking from behind. One lad, Marty, went down and got left on the floor as we tried to catch up with the rest of the mob. A group of Mackems kicked the shit out of him. One lad stamped on his head repeatedly. Even the Mackem fans were horrified and grabbed the lad off him. Marty was out cold, totally unconscious and had to be taken to hospital, where it was found he had a fractured skull. The Mackem in question was arrested and charged. Marty, however, discharged himself from hospital and made it in the ground for the end of the game. It was quite obvious he was suffering from internal damages as he kept spewing blood and lapsed in and out of consciousness. He ended up in Middlesbrough General when he got back after he suffered a temporary stroke, which left one side of his face paralysed. With the police having arrested the perpetrator, he was charged with GBH and Marty received a tidy sum in compensation. Boro lost the game 1–0 to make the end of season run-in more than a little bit interesting.

With three games to go, Boro were in fourth position and in with a shout of automatic promotion as long as we won them all. We put ourselves right into the picture with wins against Bristol Rovers and Grimsby, leaving us needing to win our last match of the season away to Wolves. The Wolves game had every conceivable element of drama. A few days before the match, one of the stands had burnt down, restricting the gate to 20,000. Then the night before the game, someone apparently broke into the ground and planted some detonators under the playing surface, leading to a big doubt over whether the match would go ahead or not. This only served to build it up even more, and with 5,000 Boro fans making the journey down to Molineux, the stage was set.

Bri and myself travelled down by train with all the main faces. As I surveyed the firm it was like watching a who's who of lads dating back through the years to 1970. There must have been 4-500 gadgies on that train, most of them right up for anything you could throw at them. When we arrived in Wolverhampton we couldn't believe our luck; there was not a copper in sight. We got ourselves into a pub and started to get the liquid refreshment that these occasions deserve. At about 2 p.m. some dickhead Wolves fans tried to have a go, which resulted in the law turning up and turfing us all out of the pub. The police tried to get us all together to march us up to the ground but as they set off half of us went in the opposite direction and into the heart of the town centre, where the Wolves fans were packing the pubs. Sure enough they came out to confront us and it kicked off good style, with us having the upper hand all the way until PC Plod arrived to put a halt to proceedings, mind we had a good fifteen minutes of up-and-down-the-road action first. Then for the second time the police got us into an escort and marched us up to the ground. This time they made sure nobody slipped away.

Tickets for the game were like gold dust and some Boro wideboys had knocked a load of forgeries out for a fiver a time. Most of the early punters who bought them managed to get in the ground, then some bright spark noticed they weren't genuine and a rigorous check was made before you could even get near the turnstile. I went in the ground just before kick-off and due to our enormous following had to be content with a crap view from the top corner of that massive end they used to have.

What a game it was. The first half was dead cagey but the second half exploded when we had a player sent off. Shortly after, they scored to go one up. I was not too despondent, as we were playing quite well, but we had to score twice and only had ten men. Then one of our lesser players called Gittens forced the ball home for the equalizer. This had us roaring the lads on. About five minutes later, Paul Wilkinson scored another goal, which went in off his shoulder I think, to put us ahead. We were in ecstasy. I could not believe what was happening and for the last fifteen minutes or so I reverted back to being a scarfhead, ra-ra, chant freak, whatever, I just didn't care, I was enjoying the moment too much to worry what other people thought (whatever street cred I had built up over twenty-five years disappeared in those moments). The ref blew the final whistle and everyone went absolutely mental. We had done it, we were promoted, the Boro were to be founder members of the new Premier League.

After the celebrations died down we made our way back to the station. Everyone had forgotten about the Wolves fans but they had not forgotten us. As soon as we were in the city centre they made a show, coming round a corner about eighty-handed. Although we outnumbered them we were straggled out in dribs and drabs. Snapper, myself, Doddsy and the General fired straight into them with the rest of the lads close behind. Most of them backed off but a few really game lads stood and fought with us until they realised we had too many for them and they were forced to back off.

We stopped off in York to change trains, and as we had an hour to wait, we went for a celebratory drink. On the way back to the station to get the train home some cheeky Leeds fuckers thought they'd have a pop at us. A handful of our lads chased them off but they returned when we were at the station. As they were on the opposite platform they thought they could safely give us all the verbal abuse, but with there being no police around a few of our lads ran straight across the tracks and got into them ending in the usual result with Leeds, yes they ran. Had these lads been Service Crew we might have had a better showing.

DURING THIS SUCCESSFUL season we had not met many firms who could match us, however that's not to say that everything had been plain sailing for yours truly. One away trip ended with me getting my face slashed and Doddsy losing two front teeth, at Brighton of all places. We had all arranged to stay at Hobnail's brother's gaff so we could have a night out after the match, several other Boro lads arranging to do the same. The game was a doddle in that Boro tanked Brighton 5–1, with no chew before or after. When we got back to the digs to get changed, Nail's brother informed us it was hard to get in the pubs mob-handed and suggested we split into smaller groups. I went with Snapper, Doddsy and Shorty, moving from pub to pub towards the seafront.

Although the weather had been okay during the day it was now pissing down with torrential rain. We had taken shelter in an amusement arcade before deciding where to go next when Spasky turned up with a few more lads from Stockton. They had obviously been running and told us that a crew of locals had started on them. 'Away then, there's a few of us now, let's get the rest of the lads if they want some,' Doddsy ordered. He was in his element; action at last. We started walking towards where we thought the rest of our lads were. All told we had about twenty in our group. Snapper looked down an alley and noticed some local lads.

'Here, Doddsy, down here, there's some lads who want to know,' he said.

Doddsy, myself and Shorty walked down the alley thinking that everyone else was coming with us, but the rest had not heard Snapper and had carried on up the road, leaving four of us to take on thirty lads. Snapper punched the first lad who didn't flinch, then Doddsy followed up with a haymaker that put him on his arse. The rest of them backed out of the alley into the street, where we followed. Once in the street we noticed we were alone and outnumbered but we couldn't back off now. One lad came swinging at me, just brushing my face. I punched him, sending him to the floor and followed up with a boot to the stomach. He got to his feet and scampered away but another lad tried to drop-kick me from behind, which sent me staggering to the other side of the road.

Everything was happening quickly now and we were all at it. Doddsy was trading punches with another lad while Snapper and Shorty were both fighting like fuck. Another lad ran past me, taking a swipe which only just caught me. He kept on running. Snapper shouted to me, 'John, he had a knife, you've been slashed.' I put my hand to my face and saw to my disbelief that blood was pissing out the side of my left cheek. 'Come on Snapper, I'm off, my face is fucking covered in claret,' I shouted. I was worried; I needed to get out of this and quick. Doddsy was still going at it hammer and tongs with this big lad while Shorty had already disappeared. I shouted Doddsy but he was still fighting. I calmly walked towards Snapper, holding my face. None of these lads challenged me, preferring to move in on Doddsy, who by now was taking a fair old beating. I moved about fifty yards up the road where I caught up with Snapper, who was breaking off a piece of garden fence.

'Fucking hell, look at the state of your face John,' he said, with an air of concern.

I looked in a shop window and to my horror there was blood streaming down one side of my face. Now I was angry. I ripped myself a piece of fence off.

'Away Snapper, let's just charge into the fuckers, hit everything.'

A we ran back towards where we had been fighting, it was all over. There was no sign of anyone, not even Doddsy.

'Away John,' Snapper said, 'let's go find the rest of them, we're gonna need more lads.'

We both looked around for ages before we found Doddsy, who looked quite well considering he'd just had a good kicking. We also found Spasky and the Stockton lads, some of whom apologised, thinking they had left us in the shit. Well, they had. A Boro lad came over to report that the set of lads we had been fighting were queuing up outside a club just up the road. There were now about twenty of us so we all agreed to get some payback. Sure enough the same lads were there. Immediately we piled into them, no warning, just straight in punching anyone who wanted to know. They were off on their toes in seconds. As we were stood congratulating ourselves, they were back, this time armed with long thin iron bars picked up from some roadworks. These iron bars were whistling through the air coming at us from all angles. One flew just over my head another skipped off the road, clattering into my shin. A third smashed straight into Doddsy's face, sending him to his knees.

'John, my teeth, find my teeth,' he spluttered.

I looked down. The rain was bouncing three feet off the surface and I could not see anything other than a river of blood coming from Doddsy's mouth. A young couple, from the Boro funnily enough, came over to help, taking Doddsy to one side to look after him. By now most of the lads were in retreat, maybe because Doddsy had gone down, I don't know, but they were on their toes with this mob after them. The Boro couple told me they would call an ambulance to take Doddsy to the hospital. I was now in danger as our lads had done one and the Brighton lads were in the ascendancy. I slipped away into a restaurant, taking some funny looks from the customers. I went into the toilet and saw the reason: my face was still bleeding profusely. I washed most of the blood away and a waiter gave me a cloth to hold over the cut, advising me to visit the hospital. Instead I went back to the digs to get my head down.

A couple of hours later, Hobnail and the rest of the lads came in, not even knowing that we had been battling away half the night, in fact Bri and Hobnail had been talking to the same mob of lads we had fought with, who told them they had just turned over some Boro lads. Bri had laughed at them, thinking they were telling porkies. Now they knew. At first I thought the worst and feared I would be horrendously scarred for life, but luckily the cut was not too deep and didn't require stitches. In fact it was Doddsy I was more worried about. He was in the hospital half the night having emergency dental treatment and his lips and gums stitched up. At the end of the day as long as you're alive and well these mishaps become secondary and are soon forgotten, though the scars never go away and are there as a reminder of your sacrifice to the cause of your football club. My scar stayed with me for quite a long time but is now so faded that it is hardly noticeable. I told my mother I had fallen while drunk into a thorny rose bush. I don't think she believed me somehow.

So the end of another successful Boro promotion campaign, and we were back where we belonged. The inaugural Premier League awaited us, but first there was the little matter of a 'friendly' game against Celtic at the beginning of the season for Tony Mowbray's testimonial. He had left us earlier in the season to play for them and had come back bringing 10,000 green and white clad arseholes with him.

As you would expect the Celtic fans came down in their thousands and made a weekend of it. I went out in Redcar on the Saturday afternoon making for my usual haunt, the Hydro, and was a bit pissed off to say the least when I entered the pub to be greeted by loads of Jocks in Celtic shirts singing Irish rebel songs. I was quite heartened to notice a few of the Redcar firm sat at one end looking none too pleased, especially Kenny, who is a diehard Rangers follower. After a while a few more of our firm arrived to even up the numbers a bit, then one of the Celtic boys asked why we weren't singing and tried to get us involved in a singing ritual. This resulted in a slight confrontation between him and Col, who he was slobbering over.

Col showed him a spray canister.

'Seen one of these before mate?'

'No, what is it wee man?' the Jock replied in his Glaswegian twang.

'If you don't fuck off I'll show ya, ya thick Scottish twat.' Col's tone had become serious. The Celt was too ignorant (or daft) to understand what he was getting into, so Col just sprayed him in the eyes from point blank range and, as he was blinded, landed two blows to his face. As all hell broke out I could feel my eyes starting to tingle so I headed for the door, closely followed by everyone else. I had not seen the effects of tear gas close up before and after such a small squirt cleared a whole pub I could see why some firms used it, mind it affects everyone equally so it won't win you any battles. As we had to leave the Hydro we went around the town and there seemed to be Celtic fans all over the place. Sure enough it kicked off again in several other pubs throughout the rest of the day and the night.

On the Sunday I gave Bri a ring and arranged to meet him for a few pints before the game. Once again the Jocks were all over the place. We went into the football club bar, which had a healthy Celtic presence, and took up our usual seats. Stevo, Ash and all the Boro lads were there along with most of the Redcar firm. After eyeballing the Celts for a while we decided enough was enough and gave them the bum's rush, sending them scarpering out of the door. One lad left his jacket and an Irish tricolour behind. He came back for it only to find we had torn his flag up and someone was the proud owner of a new leather jacket. He gracefully gave up the ghost and beat a retreat to find his mates.

The game was pretty average pre-season fare, but with 10,000 or so Celtic fans adding to the atmosphere it made things a little special. When half-time arrived some Celtic fans were stupid enough to get onto the pitch with an Irish tricolour and started marching towards us. It was like a red rag to a bull. Suddenly about 100 or so of us invaded the pitch and charged straight towards them, and a full-on battle took place with the police taking several minutes to clear the pitch. The game finished 1–1 and the fighting went on throughout the night in various locations throughout Teesside, wherever the Celtic fans happened to be staying.

It was around this time that I started going out with a bit of stuff from Redcar called Karen. She was just the right sort of girlfriend for me in that she didn't mind me disappearing here there and everywhere following the Boro. I really took advantage of Karen's easy-going nature and used to turn up at all hours of the night, sometimes worse for drink, but she loved me and usually forgot about it the next day.

THE 1992/93 SEASON started with mixed fortunes in the first couple of weeks; we could not win away but we were superb at home, especially when we dispatched champions Leeds, Cantona, et al, 4–1. We got our first away win at Man City, albeit courtesy of an own goal, and we were sitting pretty in sixth place when, typical of Boro, we came off the rails and went into freefall. Just like a Russian sub we went down, down, down. We did not even have anything to get excited about in the cups. In the League Cup we were drawn to play a certain team from up the road managed by a Mr Keegan, who had saved them the previous year from going into the Second Division. Piece of cake, we thought, I mean we're Premier League and we're away in the first leg. Newcastle

were now calling themselves the 'Toon Army', I don't know
why; toon is Geordiespeak for town and they happen to be a
city. Maybe it's short for cartoon, because they've all got a
head full of them. Their firm also had a daft name, 'the
Gremlins'; little green men, aren't they? Fuck knows where
they got that one from either.

The Gremlins' main enemies were the Seaburn Casuals
from Sunderland, a bunch of young lads who dressed similar
to the Redcar Casuals. They had a lot of history between
them, even arranging kick-offs away from football and out of
season in the summer. Although most Geordies did not regard
Boro as 'the big one', the Gremlins were certainly aware of
our status as far as firms go. It always bugs me that both
Sunderland and Newcastle refer to 'the big two-and-a-half',
calling us a small town in Yorkshire and more seriously, child
molesters (following revelations of child abuse by a Cleveland
doctor) and smog monsters (due to the so-called pollution
cloud that hangs over Teesside). All right they both have a bit
of history, but for a small town in Yorkshire we don't do too
badly thanks very much.

So for the umpteenth time in recent seasons we had to
travel up to play the Mags on a night match. Could we do it
again and turn the Gremlins over? You bet your sorry little
arses we could. Once again we met up at a pub near the
Heworth Metro station. We numbered 150-plus and all the
main players were there: Jonka, Stevo, Ash, Doddsy, the
Spark brothers and some lads from Stockton who had followed
the Boro regularly but who I didn't know too well. One of
them was a huge guy known as Burner. He had a loyal crew of
lads who always seemed to be in attendance whenever he was
around.

I had travelled up with Bri, Doddsy, Hobnail and Segsy in
Bri's car, following a convoy of several other Boro cars and
vans. Heworth is a part of Gateshead just off the motorway,
easy to get to and handily placed with the Metro nearby. We

left the pub at about 7 p.m. and made our way to the Metro, one really tasty-looking mob. I could not believe that we weren't clocked by the law and fully expected a welcome committee when we arrived at the Monument. Yet there was not one copper to be seen when we came out of the station, so we marched up the road towards the ground, passing all the Geordie drinking haunts. All they did was look out the windows at us, amazed that Boro had brought a firm to their fortress.

Having got such a formidable firm together, we were a bit pissed off that the Mags had not made a show, so Burner and his crew took the lead and attacked a big pub that was teeming with Mags. We followed suit but two bouncers managed to shut the doors before we could get in. Then someone threw a bin through the window and Burner jumped through after it, closely followed by a few of his mates. It was hilarious to see all the Geordies inside panicking and fighting each other to get away from Burner and his mates. When the police turned up we moved off towards the ground, passing the Strawberry pub on the way. We could see the Geordies looking out at us and beckoned them to have a go but they were not having any of it.

So 1–0 to us and on to the match. The game was the pits but we got away with a draw and now it was time to face the Mags outside, where we were sure they would have a firm up for it. A fat Geordie copper remarked that we were going to 'get it' on the way to the station. 'I fucking hope so, we haven't seen your mob all night,' a lad replied. Sure enough as we got so far down the road without the presence of the Old Bill, a mob of Geordies came charging at us, lobbing bottles and glasses. 'Come on Boro,' said one of our lads, encouraging everyone to get into them, and sure enough as we counter-charged they stood for all of fifteen seconds before getting on their toes.

Suddenly the police were everywhere, hemming us together and trying to march us to the station. We told them we were not on the train. They asked where our coaches were and we told them we were not on coaches either, which had them totally confused. 'Well you're not going to the Bigg Market,' said the fat sergeant, with a worried look on his face. Eventually we led the police to the Metro station at the Monument where we boarded the train back to Heworth, nobody paying of course.

Back at Heworth most lads got in their cars and headed off home, but four carloads of us stayed for a pint. As we were leaving, a crew of Mags turned up to have an off with us. Doddsy thought he had been sprayed with acid as we beat a retreat to the cars, and one car had its windscreen put through, but we managed to withdraw relatively safely. This put a bit of a dampener on the night but it was of our own making I suppose. Boro lost the second leg and the Geordies failed to turn up on our patch. The rest of the season was a bag of shite and we ended up relegated yet again. A lot of Boro fans started to turn their backs on the team, which was reflected in gates that had gone down to around the 16,000 mark. Although I was also a bit disillusioned, I remained loyal along with my best mate Bri and the hardcore Boro firm.

ONE DREAM MOST of us had was to travel to Europe with Boro. I had been abroad with England but yearned to taste it with Boro. One route was through the Anglo-Italian Cup, and the competition was open to First Division clubs, which we now were. The 1993/94 season started with four straight wins in the league and Boro visiting Pisa away in the Anglo-Italian. If past events were anything to go by this was about as close as we were ever going to get to a European away match. The football club put on a trip for the ra-ras; this meant travelling by coach all the way to Pisa with all the jobsworths sticking their two pence worth in all the time. No 'Jack Pallance' of that for us. We organised our own trip, flying out of Heathrow on the Sunday and coming back on the Friday in good time for our derby match with the Mackems.

We had a decent enough firm of thirty-plus on the plane, which turned out to be a right old boneshaker, reminiscent of a Second World War transport plane. We were accompanied on our flight by two Southend fans (they were playing Fiorentina) who were almost tempted to join us as they enjoyed our crack. Most of our firm consisted of Redcar lads led by the ever-game Doddsy, ably accompanied by Mossy, Browny, Ted, Snapper, Shell and the Glenbo, who is actually a Mackem but a sound lad all the same. Stevo and several other Boro lads were meeting us over there, which made our firm up to about fifty. With the club's two official coaches and other independent travellers we had a total following of a couple of hundred.

At Pisa airport we were greeted by some Italian police who asked if we were there for the football. We told them we were holidaymakers and managed to give them the slip. After lots of deliberating, most of us decided to head for a coastal resort to look for a hotel, while a dozen or so went straight to Pisa. Browny went to Pisa and apparently ended up fighting with the local firm within minutes of getting there. His arse was saved by the police who locked him up for the night. The so-called holiday resort turned out to be deserted, one local remarking that the season was finished. This being the case we headed for Pisa the next day, but not before we'd had a couple of altercations amongst each other. Doddsy and Shell ended up rolling around on the floor and needing to be separated. Later the same morning it was Doddsy and Snapper who had a difference of opinion. With everyone becoming edgy and having a go at each other, I felt something heavy was going to go down as soon as we met up with the Eyeties.

We arrived in Pisa the next morning and sorted ourselves out with a hotel near the train station. Browny had been let off by the police and ended up in our hotel. This was the day of the match so we had a lot of drinking to do. First though I was hungry and sought out one of those famous Italian Pizzerias, after all we were in Pisa, the traditional home of the pizza. On asking a couple of locals, we found a restaurant which served up the worst pizza it has ever been my displeasure to try to consume. Oh how I longed for the delights of a Teesside 'Parmo'. The Parmo, or to give the dish its correct name 'Escalope Parmesan', is a traditional meal served only within the confines of the Teesside area (although word is spreading), consisting of a breaded pork or chicken fillet, covered in creamed parmesan cheese sauce and topped with melted cheddar cheese, baked under a grill served with chips and or salad. Fucking nectar. I tried a local hamburger that had some shite spicey bits ingrained into it. That got binned as well. For the rest of the trip I lived on crisps, chocolate and beer. No way was I going to waste any more money on the shite these bastards served up. Stevo was the complete opposite, the lad will eat anything, octopus, squid, horse, you name it he tried the lot. I wish I had a stomach like that.

As the day wore on our numbers grew as more Boro lads arrived. We had a tasty little crew of forty, all having a crack with the locals but no sign of Pisa's firm, in fact no sign of any Pisa fans full stop. As we slowly made our way towards the vicinity of the ground I noticed Lenny Lawrence and Steve Gibson having a drink outside a café. I must have a photo taken with these two, I thought, and they duly obliged as we all gathered around them for an impromptu photo shoot. The rest of the day is a bit of a blur as I consumed far too much alcohol. Then it was time to make our way to the ground. We expected some show from the Italians but nothing happened so we took up our seats and watched the game.

Pisa had a nice neat stadium that held 30,000, so it looked rather embarrassing, as the gate was only about 1,000 and a good proportion were of those from Boro. After the game we were all split up as we walked back to our hotels. I lost Bri somewhere en route and ended up with his brother-in-law and a couple of other lads. The streets were dark and forbidding and sure enough when you least want any chew it comes along by the bucketload. One particular stretch of road was flanked on both sides by narrow unlit alleyways and several unsavoury characters emerged from them, making our journey back more than interesting. One Italian was making the old throat-slitting gesture. Ted did not take kindly to this and walked over and offered him out one-to-one. The Eyetie did not seem to understand what he was saying, so Ted floored him on the spot.

I knew from my previous experience of Italy during the 1990 World Cup that they are the biggest shithouses walking if you stand up to them, and so it proved as we spent half the walk back chasing Eyeties back down the alleys from whence they came. The best thing about being English is that foreigners are very wary, even scared, of us and we used this reputation to our advantage by not showing any fear. I must admit that if they had not backed off I think it may well have been us doing the running. It's amazing how much bravado a few pints of beer can conjure up.

The rest of the trip saw us all on the piss and me getting so drunk I bought a can of red spray paint and took it upon myself to decorate half the city, with 'Boro' and 'Redcar' adorning the walls everywhere. I even intended to climb the Leaning Tower to spray Boro at the top but there was a high fence around it due to some restoration work being carried out. I'm glad I never got that far as I am a great admirer of ancient history and I don't think I could live with myself if I had ruined one of the world's greatest pieces of architecture. It just shows how stupid you can be when you have had too much drink.

On the last night we were all on the piss again when the local police decided to give us a painful reminder of our trip by ambushing us and weighing in with riot batons. We think it was because we were having a sing-song but they didn't explain. We'd been sat at this bar having a few beers when a police car pulled up with four officers, one of whom looked to be of a senior rank. He spoke a smattering of English and told us that the owner of the bar wanted to close up for the night. Why the owner didn't ask us himself is beyond me. Anyway we agreed to leave as long as the police officer had one last drink with us. He smiled then agreed to have a coffee as he was on duty. After the drink we started helping the barman collect his glasses and waved goodbye to the police. Everything was fine, we had all been good boys and were heading back to our hotel when one or two lads started a song going. Suddenly two vans full of riot police screeched to a halt and out piled twenty coppers dressed in all the riot togs, wading into us with those big long sticks. After thirty seconds of this they eased off and one (woman) riot cop ordered us to sit with our backs to the wall on the floor. One of my mates, Paul, was sat next to me taking the piss out of one cop who looked to be very young and had a baby face. 'You bambino,' he goaded him. Suddenly this little cop poked Paul straight in the eye with his stick, hilarious it was, what a good shot as well. Paul screeched in pain, clutching his eye. I couldn't help but laugh as the cop answered him, 'Me no bambino, you cry-baby.'

Eventually after we told the cops we were just on our way home they let us go – all except for Ted and Snapper. They were dragged to the local police station and beaten up with their hands securely cuffed behind their backs. The police did not explain to them what it was for either, they just let them go first thing in the morning with a friendly 'ciao' and that was the end of it. The trip finished as it started with two of the lads fighting among themselves at the airport. Snapper had fallen asleep and Snowy shaved his eyebrow off. As soon as he awoke that was the trigger for battle to commence. Then on the way home from Heathrow, Ted and Snapper started having a go with each other, so the trip started and finished with fights although most of them were between each other.

Back in the league our great start to the season was to be further underlined with a brilliant 4–1 demolition of Sunderland. The shine was taken off the victory by the disappointing gate of only 13,000. Live TV played a part but it was still a huge indication of how the fans felt towards the club for their failure to achieve anything. You could hear the Mackems laughing at the gate when it was announced (big crowds don't make a firm though). After that game we went on a downward spiral again, slumping to fourteenth by Christmas. Things were not going to get any better and the writing was on the wall for Lenny Lawrence. Some home gates had dropped to 7,000 and it was obvious that Mr Gibson needed to change things. Even the cups couldn't provide anything to smile about: we were dumped out of the League Cup by Sheffield Wednesday after a replay in round three and lowly Cardiff of the Second Division knocked us out of the FA Cup, though not without an interesting visit to the Valleys by Boro' s finest.

BEING DRAWN AT Cardiff on January 2 did not seem that appetising, but when you know of a firm's reputation and there's not much chance of meeting up with them again for a long time, then you just have to go. I had not heard of Cardiff's firm being called the Soul Crew before this game, however they were known as one of the top outfits on their day. After checking out the train times, we realised that there was no way we could get back to Boro, so we took a fleet of cars and minibuses as far as York and got the train from there. Our firm consisted of about forty lads with another 100 travelling down by various modes of transport. Our brief was to meet up at the nearest pub to the station.

Our crew were the first to arrive in Cardiff, so we made our way to a pub called the Albert not far from the station. This was to be our base. As more and more Boro arrived our numbers grew to over 150 and this, of course, had not gone unnoticed by the Taffies. One Cardiff lad was clocked making several visits to the pub to check out our numbers. Doddsy made conversation with him and let him know we were Boro's main firm. The Taffy agreed to leave things nice and quiet until after 2 p.m., when their firm would make a show.

Sure enough just after two a crowd of Taffies arrived outside, about 170 of them. The word went up and we all piled out and straight into them. Browny was first in closely followed by the rest of us. The pub was on a main road with another road adjoining it and as we emerged into the road we managed to drive a wedge through the Cardiff firm, splitting them in two. I don't think they were expecting such a positive response from us and after a short toe-to-toe battle they backed off. A few of them were caught in the doorway of the pub opposite and copped for a bit of a kicking. Half of the Taffies backed off down one road with the rest going up the main road. This worked in our favour as we were now in control of the junction and when either side came at us we could hold them off. The police arrived after about five minutes but by then the business had been done.

We were gathered together by the law and taken up to the ground. It seemed like every pub was full of their lads, all coming out to have a word. We just laughed at them and let them know they had been done. I personally could not believe we had just turned Cardiff over on their own patch and fully expected something more to happen. As we got close to the ground a few Taffs came out from a pub.

One shouted over, 'Where the fuck have you been all day?'

'Chasing your lot all over the fucking city you daft Welsh twat, you've been done,' replied one pisstaking Boro lad.

The same Taffy was told to go away by a copper, so he followed us up to the ground on the opposite side of the road, shaking his head and making threatening gestures. As we got to the away enclosure he shouted his final threat: 'See you after the game boys, we'll fucking have you then.' Everyone laughed at him as a copper started pushing him away.

The game ended up 2–2. When we left the ground the police collared us all and made sure nothing happened on the way to the station. Doddsy had swapped phone numbers with the Cardiff lad who had arranged the kick-off and later on he contacted him, only for the Taffy to claim that the mob we turned over was not their main lads, but that's easy to say after the event. Mind I must admit I did expect a bit more of a show from them. We had all our main players up for it in the replay but being a night match I suppose you couldn't blame them for not turning up. To make matters worse we lost the replay 2–1 and that was the end of our season, halfway through January.

Big developments were taking place off the pitch. One was the sacking of Lenny Lawrence but the surprise event of that summer was the appointment of Bryan Robson as player-manager. And so began the Riverside Revolution.

CHAPTER TEN

Walking In A Robson Wonderland

EVERYONE WAS FULL of expectation as the 1994/95 season got underway. Bryan Robson was in charge, we had made some new signings, breaking our record transfer fee, and the bookies had made us hot favourites for promotion. Our start was quite impressive as well, winning five and drawing two of the first seven games before losing a close encounter away to Port Vale. Apart from a 5–1 reverse at Luton we were flowing along quite nicely and by the time we played Sheffield United on Boxing Day we were top of the league. Off the field we were taking huge numbers away to every game although there wasn't any trouble, as a new breed of fan had emerged along with the new style of all-seater stadiums being erected throughout the country, ours being rapidly constructed on the blue banks of the River Tees.

On the surface hooliganism seemed to have gone away but it was still very much active, as I found to my cost away to Wolves on a night match. We travelled down in a minibus, leaving work at lunchtime. As we did not expect any trouble, Bri brought his fourteen-year-old son Robbie with us. We did not arrive in Wolverhampton until 6.30 p.m. so we parked up outside a pub about half a mile from the ground, had a few pints, then went to the match. Boro won 2–0, which upset the locals a wee bit, and as we were leaving the ground a few 'hard men' decided to have a go at young Robbie as it stood out that he was from Boro. We managed to sort it out at the time but knew that they would be having another go later, as we had to walk in the same direction. Bri and Robbie got out the way and headed away from the area back to a pub near our minibus. They were okay because the Wolves lads had their eyes on us. Once Bri had made good his escape we decided to split up and do the same. I was with a bloke called Arthur who was not what you'd call one of our firm, just a sound, honest Boro fan. As we neared a bridge I noticed some lads waiting on the far side. I warned Arthur to act normal as if we were locals, remarking that they looked like the same lads who were starting the trouble outside the ground.

Sure enough as we got to the point of no return we were sussed. Doozer, Shell and the rest were not too far behind us. They caught sight of what was happening and made off in the opposite direction. I waited until the Wolves lads were right on top of us, then told Arthur to get on his toes and did the same. I could have stood my ground and fought but there were too many, twenty too many, with a pub-full over the road to back them up. Being rather fleetfooted I left them trailing in my wake as I ran into a petrol station shop, thinking Arthur was behind me. I held the door open for him to get in only to find out that it was not him who was behind me but all the Wolves lads. I backed off as far as the counter, then about twenty of them came in, with this big, fat, yellow-haired, ugly cunt (one who was having a go at young Robbie outside the ground) at the front of them. I tried reasoning with them but to no avail as they weighed in with fists and boots, so I curled up in a ball and did my best to protect myself. None of the blows were really hurting as I howled my displeasure, apart from the last one that is; one of them shouted, 'Leave him, he's had enough,' and as I relaxed someone gave me a final hoof right in the ribs. That fucker did hurt.

Two Asians working behind the counter had called the police and when they arrived they asked if I wanted to press charges, as it would all be on video and they would be able to identify the lads responsible. I declined saying I was okay and that I just wanted to find my mates. The funny thing was, Arthur got clean away, making it to the pub where some of the lads off our minibus were sat having a pint only fifty or so yards from where I was taking a good kicking. I ribbed one of the lads all the way home, calling him a shitty-arse for not coming out to help me. I don't suppose I could blame him but he could have made a difference as he is a big enough lad.

Another trip where we had some chew was away to Swansea in the FA Cup. Well, we had done Cardiff the previous season so why not go for the Welsh double, especially as Doddsy had kept in touch with his Cardiff buddy, who promised us we would get a portion from their hated rivals. Now Swansea is a little further than Cardiff, so we arranged to travel to Leeds by minibus this time so we could pick up the train there. The minibus broke down between Wetherby and Leeds, leaving us to hitchhike in to Leeds. What a fuck about, just so we could get to a match without the Old Bill on our case.

The Taffy met up with us at Cardiff station and joined our firm for the day. When we got to Swansea it was the usual crack of nearest pub to the station, where we eventually numbered over 100 boys. Once in a town you do not have too much time before either the local law, or often your own spotter police, find you. The hard part is getting into a pub mobbed up in the first place. This much is up to the away firm; the home firm then need to come as soon as possible before the law clock you. The two spotters who were regularly following the Frontline lads around knew us all quite well, most lads were known by name and they had even pulled rank once or twice to get one or two of the lads off when they had been arrested, but at the end of the day they have a job to do and that job is to make sure no trouble occurs. The two Boro police spotters had sussed us out and had the local plod on our case straight away, so after a few pints had been downed we decided to move on towards the ground and, more importantly, where their lads would be drinking, directed by our accommodating Welsh host. We were immediately collared by the police. Bri and I decided nothing much was going to happen so we slipped away to get a drink in another pub. We met the rest of the lads in the ground and they told us they had managed to get a little bit with Swansea's mob, though it resulted in one or two lads getting arrested due to all the coppers in attendance.

The game finished 1–1 and we made our way towards the station, Doddsy and myself putting on a brisk walk to keep ahead of the police escort. As we turned a corner, the two of us were confronted by a dozen or so lads. Then we were at it with them. I smacked one and Doddsy was going at it with another lad. It only lasted a matter of seconds before the law split us up. One of the Swansea lads was quite brave, stood in the middle of the road wanting to go one-to-one with Doddsy, who in turn was only too willing to accommodate him if he would stand still for a moment.

Most of the Boro escort carried on up the same road, but about fifty of us went down the side road towards the town centre, where their lads were. The police did not stay with us, preferring to stick with the largest mob. This gave us and Swansea the opportunity to go for it, but where were they? Frustration led us to attack a pub to try to get them out for some action. This in turn attracted the police who caught up and got us together in an escort again. This time they made sure we did not get away and marched us all the way to the station, near which I made first sight of their full mob. It numbered something like 250. I cannot understand why they did not have a go at us earlier when we only had fifty with no law in attendance. As for the football, well we lost the replay (again) 2–1.

In the league things were going along nicely and Robbo was building up something of a cult status on Teesside as

Boro marched on towards the promised land of the Premiership. Yes we had been there before but not with this new-
found clout. Mind you we'd had a little bit of a slump in form
and had dropped to second in the league before we had to
make a visit to our most hated rivals Sunderland. These days
I had limited myself to going to the match just to watch
football and only get involved when it was needed against the
notorious firms that wanted it, such as your Swansea's,
Cardiff's and of course the Mackems. Theirs was one place
we had never had a lot of joy over the years. Myself and Bri
had been saying for years that we were going to knock it on
the head but there's just something there that brings it out in
you whenever these games come around.

So for the last time (I told myself) I was going up to
Sunderland with the mob to do the biz. Karen had reminded
me that I was thirty-six years old and that I should be standing
down to let the younger lads do all the business. Mind you,
when you go to Sunderland you need to go mob-handed or
you'll get turned over for sure, whether you want it or not.
Many a time I've seen old blokes of fifty and over getting a
smacking up there.

The game was a night match, so we arranged to meet in the
Boro before going up there. After much debate we agreed to
head for the Windmill pub near Seaburn station. 'You never
know, we might have it with the Seaburn Casuals,' one lad
remarked. The word went round and everyone set off, cars
and vans being the popular mode of transport. We got there
at about 6 p.m. and there were few Sunderland in the pub.
Within ten minutes we had a good firm of over 100, with
most of the top gadgies in attendance and more than a match
for anything that the Mackems could throw at us. These days
Sunderland's firm consisted of young lads who were poorly
organised, so it literally was men against boys.

Before the game Sunderland did not even show, leaving us
very disappointed. However Doddsy got talking to some of

their main boys before the game and we were promised a better showing afterwards. The game was good fare, with Jamie Pollock (ugly bastard) scoring the winner to put Boro back to the top of the league and fuelling the Mackems' anger to boot. The police did not hold us back at the end of the game, which meant that once outside we were able to mingle straight in with the Mackems, giving us those vital few moments you need to get away from the law's beady eye. About 100 yards up the road was a mob of Sunderland waiting, so we fired straight into them, sending them running through the terraced streets, save a few who stood their ground but got a pasting. In these situations you only have a matter of a couple of minutes before the police arrive on the scene, which turned out to be the case. They then escorted us up the road back towards the Windmill. There was this right arsehole on the other side of the road (apparently he was from Cardiff) trying to be the big 'I am'; he turned out to be the big 'used to be' after one of the lads crossed over and gave him a slap. So the business was done and we had the three points in the bag. Boro were to remain top of the league for the rest of the season.

Barnsley turned out to be a good trip when we took over their main pub (the Yorkshireman), but not so good for one of the lads who got his leg mutilated by a police dog during a kick-off with their boys outside the pub. We secured promotion after our home match with Luton, which also turned out to be the last match at Ayresome Park due to a new ground being built in the dockland area of Middlesbrough. It was quite an emotional day as we all turned up to say our farewell to Ayresome, the scene of many a happy occasion. I don't think I had ever seen so much colour at Boro, which made for quite a spectacle as the whole ground was bathed in a sea of red. The final match was away to Tranmere Rovers where we took over most of the ground, giving them their biggest crowd of the season. There was no trouble, just a good day out celebrating our return to the Premier League.

Big changes were happening throughout football, the crowds were coming back, everywhere all-seater stadiums were springing up. Families had started to go to matches and the boot boy era was coming to an end – or was it? I myself thought that the days of the hooligans were numbered, especially when I spoke to other fans I met while on holiday who remarked that their firm had more or less been disbanded or didn't 'do it' any more. Maybe it was time to knock it all on the head; I mean, you couldn't go to a game now without being singled out by the law and followed all over the place, while 'normal' shirt-clad fans were free to roam unheeded throughout towns and cities all over the country. The hooligan had gone from scarf-laden, easily identifiable gangs, to incognito, blending-into-the-crowd, organised soldiers, to planning 'kick-offs' with military precision, back to easily identifiable mobs due to the fact that they didn't wear colours. Everything appeared to have gone full circle. All that was needed now was for the mob to start wearing scarves and shirts again. The fashion had changed as well. Most game lads were identified by a new uniform consisting of expensive Stone Island and Burberry clothing. Not me mind, I have never paid more than £30 for a jacket in my life. It used to make me laugh when some of the younger members of Boro's firm would remark on how good or bad the opposition's mob were by their style of clothing, more like a fashion show than a battle half the time.

Anyway here we were back in the big time with Robbo leading the way and a ground called the Cellnet Riverside Stadium which had a capacity of 30,000 and record season ticket sales of 18,500. Surely we were going to do something special this time, especially with some of the signings we had made during the summer. Nick Barmby for £5 million set the tongues wagging.

The 1995/96 season started brightly enough with a live TV match away to Arsenal where we played quite well and came away with a creditable 1–1 draw. This was followed by a 2–0 victory in the historic first game at the new stadium, against Chelsea, one in which all the top gadgies turned out only to be let down by a disappointing turn-out of 500 by the Londoners and not a Headhunter in sight. The next match was away to Newcastle but fuck-all happened there as well, apart from my eyes taking half an hour to re-focus at the end of the game (I have never seen so many black and white stripes in my life). Oh and we lost. That was to be our only defeat during the first ten games, in which we reached the heady heights of fourth and also beat Arsenal to sign a player who was to become a legend in his time with Boro, the incomparable Juninho. Things were looking good. The signing of the 'Little Fella' had sold out the season tickets (Boro could have sold them twice over, such was demand) and the football being served up was a pleasure to watch. Ground attendance records were being set at almost every match, it just depended on whether the away club sold their allocation or not. As for the away supporters, well they had never had it so good at the Boro either. Gone were the daunting side streets and back alleys, to be replaced by a one-way-in, one-way-out bottleneck system, which was easy to police but shite for the lads. Most of the problems on match days at the Riverside were created by the lack of access. At Ayresome the ground was surrounded by tight terraced streets and back alleys on three sides, with a rabid dog on every corner. The fourth side held the hospital, where many an unlucky visitor ended up.

During this first Riverside season, quite a few away supporters would be stupid enough to enter the town centre for a pre-match drink, hence one or two slaps were dished out, but it was not long before the word went round that you just do not have a drink in the Boro if you want to stay safe. The exceptions during the season were Leeds, Everton, Forest and Manchester United from the Premier and Birmingham City in the League Cup. I paid out quite a lot of money for season tickets for myself and my two sons so I made sure I kept my nose clean, especially at home, as new laws meant that you could lose your ticket for the slightest misdemeanour. To be honest I didn't mind, as the football was so enjoyable along with the atmosphere being created. Away from home it was different; everyone still rated Boro's firm as the one to beat, resulting in one or two moments at Everton, Forest, Leeds, Man City and Birmingham. One noticeable aspect that was obvious to everyone was the fact that football had taken off in dramatic style all over the country, and though Boro were taking thousands everywhere, most of them were shirtheads. Our firm probably only numbered about 200 on a really good day.

On the football side Boro were quite content to settle for establishing ourselves in the Premier and having a go the following season, which we did in dramatic style. The rollercoaster ride started to gather full momentum to produce a season that I for one will never forget.

SEASON 1996/97 WAS to prove our most successful, yet also most disappointing in our history. I had always envied other fans when their team made it to the twin towers, and although we had been to Wembley once against Chelsea in the Mickey Mouse Cup, we had not graced the place in a major final. This season all our wishes came true two-fold in an amazing, thrill-a-minute ride that would capture the attention of the whole nation.

It started with the signing of two players, Fabrizio Ravanelli and Emerson, for a combined £12 million. Throw in the Little Fella and you have got one of the most exciting line-ups you are ever likely to see. Add more foreign quality in the shape of Festa, Kinder, Beck, Fjortoft and Schwarzer, along with Hignett, Barmby and several other half-decent homegrown players, and you have a squad capable of challenging for the highest honours. So where did it all go wrong? I would say with the men in grey suits down at FA headquarters, punishing us for not playing a game at Blackburn due to half the squad going down sick. This resulted in the loss of three precious points that could have kept the club in the Premiership and kept those superstars, but that's just my humble opinion. I mean what the fuck do I know, I've only been following Boro since 1966!

The season opened with a cracker against Liverpool, Ravanelli bagging a hat-trick in his debut to register a 3–3 draw and his actions leading to thousands of kids doing copycat shirt-over-the-head goal celebrations all over the country. In the league Boro were gung-ho, taking every game like a one-off cup match. Even if we went into the lead, we were so attack-minded we didn't know how to defend it, resulting in some bizarre matches that we lost when we should have won. But it was in the cup competitions where we came into our own, starting with the League Cup against Hereford. We won 7–0 in the first leg, Ravanelli bagging four, and 3–0 with a reserve team in the away leg. Next we dispatched Huddersfield Town 5–1 (credit must go to their fans, 5,000 of them sang their hearts out) with Ravanelli bagging another two. Newcastle came along for the fourth round and were destroyed 3–1 on an emotional night to set up a quarter final against Liverpool, where a tight game saw us come through 2–1 to put us in the semi-finals against Stockport and probably the best chance we were ever going to have of getting to a major cup final. During this time we had capitulated a bit in the league, nosediving to seventeenth. Our bad luck came to a head when we were disgracefully docked three points for not fulfilling that fixture at Blackburn Rovers. This would culminate in our relegation at the end of the season, something I attribute as much to Keith Lamb as the 'men in suits'. Mr Lamb must have known the rules before making the decision not to play the game. However we are all entitled to one mistake (what a costly one though).

One firm who did come to our place were Everton on Boxing Day, which was also significant to me as it was the last match I attended as an able-bodied person, due to my having a horrific accident the next day that resulted in nearly losing my leg and leaving me disabled for the rest of my life. I played football on the morning of the game in aid of a junior club that I was involved with. On arriving in the town centre with my two sons I noticed a couple of our firm who told me that Everton's mob were in town near the station. I told my lads to remain where they were while I went over to have a look. As I got to the bar opposite the station, fifty or more Everton lads came steaming round the corner. Fuck this, I thought. I joined a host of Boro lads coming out of the pub and got weighed in without even thinking. All credit to the Everton lads as they held firm under the bridge and stood toe-to-toe for a few minutes. Then as we were getting the better of it, one of them pulled a knife and managed to hold us off as they all ran towards police protection that had decided to make a show. The game was not too bad either as Boro won 4–2 in yet another thriller.

The next night I was at work and had a run-in with a six-tonne excavator shovel that took a dislike to my right leg, almost cutting it in half. I was in hospital for twenty-one days (I counted every one), underwent four operations and had steel clamps inserted in my leg for the next nine months. I missed the Liverpool game in the Coca Cola Cup, two away and one home league games and the third round FA Cup match against Chester which we won 6–0. I should have stayed in hospital longer but discharged myself in time for the next home game against Sheffield Wednesday. It was doing my head in just laid there doing fuck-all listening to the radio while Boro were involved in these titanic battles.

Boro were battling on three fronts now. We had all but secured our place in the Coca Cola Cup final by winning the first leg away to Stockport 2–0 and had been drawn away to Man City in the FA Cup fifth round. I could not go to this game as I was still under heavy medical treatment for my leg and it was deemed too dodgy to attend away games just yet, but the accounts I received from Bri and the rest of the lads almost made up for it. On the football front Boro beat City with a brilliant individual goal from Juninho to put us in the quarter final against Derby. As far as the lads were concerned, it went down as one of the best away trips for many a year, with Boro's firm battling from start to finish against a City mob who just love having it with us. Most of the lads I spoke to told me of backs-to-the-wall fighting all the way back to the station with not only City but also a firm of Hibernian lads who claimed to be there for a stag weekend. This mayhem left the police almost powerless to prevent the inevitable.

My mate Bri takes up the account:

> We arrived in Manchester Piccadilly early doors about 150-handed and were almost immediately picked up by the law and put into an escort. Some of us managed to slip the escort and found a pub near Oxford Road station. While in there a couple of Jocks came in to ask if anyone had any spare tickets, as they didn't know whether they wanted to join up with us or City. One Boro lad told them, 'Boro don't join with anyone.' They left to go back to their own pub. I went to the pub they were in and got quite a shock when I saw how many of them there were, something like fifty or so handed, all handy-looking fuckers.

> We got to the ground where we met up with the rest of the lads, all agreeing to meet out the back at full-time to get together. The game was class, with Juninho running the length of the pitch to celebrate his goal in

front of Boro's travelling army. As we left the ground
most of us, 100-plus, went to the left and down a main
road. Our Rob and about twenty others turned right.
We managed to give the law the slip and some lads had
a brief kick-off with some black lads outside a betting
shop, then we had City boys on the other side of the
road who were throwing fruit and vegetables at us from
a stall outside a grocer's shop. This attracted the law,
who moved in to break it up.

As all this was going on a mob of us broke away,
nipping through some side streets, across a kids'
playground and onto the main road leading back to
the city centre. Soon enough there was loads of City's
boys coming across the road at us from the right. To
our left was a fence surrounding a park, in front of us
were the fifty Jocks I had seen earlier. The police had
caught up with us a bit and were only just managing to
hold off the City boys, so we made a charge towards
the Jocks. A couple of flares were fired at us which
added to the commotion as we battled with the Scottish
mob. Now it was hand-to-hand stuff. One Boro lad
was caught on the wrong side of the road with City's
mob. When he came across to our side, Sparky laid
him out thinking he was City (he had a sky blue tracky
top on).

Things started to calm down as more police arrived,
ending with us all held in a tight escort. A bus pulled up
with some more of our lads on who had been fighting
elsewhere; apparently it had been happening all over the
shop. This was the end of it for us as we were taken to
the station under a heavy police escort.

Robbie takes up the story of the other mob who turned right
outside the ground:

As we came out we spotted some City getting into Boro ra-ras. Thinking everyone else was with us we piled into them, chasing them up a road. We walked down a few more streets in Moss Side before coming to a pub with scores of lads waiting for us. We only had about twenty lads but they were top quality: Doddsy, the Brick, Bowler, Spasky, to name but a few. We had our backs to a fence with the bigger lads doing most of the fighting, protecting us younger ones at the back who were chipping in with a few punches of our own. The Brick was knocking one lad after the other down, Doddsy was going at it hammer and tongs just throwing as many punches as he could at anyone who got anywhere near him. We were well outnumbered and things were looking grim as they continued coming at us, growing in numbers all the time.

A bit of respite came as two police vans crashed into each other. This distracted everyone for a short while. As more police arrived some joined in with us and actually fought side by side with us. Before long we were pinned into one small group and surrounded by police but what a battle we had. Our small but game firm held their own against all odds, one massive lesson for me that. We ended up getting taken to the train station where nothing more occurred.

Robbie was only seventeen years old at the time and still remembers this as one of the most frightening, as well as satisfying, moments of his time following the Boro.

Stockport gave us a fright in the second leg of the Coca Cola Cup by winning 1–0 at our patch but it was not enough to stop us recording our first visit to a major cup final. Add to this the fact that we had just dispatched Derby 2–0 the same week to go into the semi-final of the FA Cup against Chesterfield and you could see why we fancied our chances of winning something. Having to play three games a week wasn't helping Boro (or my pocket) so somewhere had to give and it was in the league that things started to go wrong. We were not losing too many games but we were drawing too many that should have been wins: Forest at home, West Ham away, Man Utd away (3–1 up only to draw 3–3), Blackburn away (0–0, referee refuses blatant penalty) and Leeds away, 1–1 in the final match which sends us down. If any of these games had been a win we would have stayed up, if we had not been deducted three points we'd have stayed up, and we would have probably won one of the cup finals as well.

The Coca Cola final was against Leicester City, and the whole country fancied us to win it. It was a nightmare for me travelling down to Wembley on crutches but I was not going to miss any of it and made the traditional trip to Trafalgar Square for the pre-match singing ritual as thousands of Boro took over the great landmark. On the day of the game I ra-ra'd it up to the stadium on my crutches with Bri, who stuck with me throughout when he could easily have fucked off with the rest of the lads. The game was not too exciting apart from two Boro streakers, the first of whom I knew from Redcar, a comedian called Chris who was wearing black suspenders and knickers and bouncing on a space hopper. Funny as fuck he is.

The second guy was bollock-naked apart from a smile, and he was the fastest thing seen on the pitch all day. I remember a streaker from Leicester coming on but he kept his underpants on and, after the Boro lads, came over as quite boring. Then with the game well into the extra-time period, Ravanelli struck to put Boro 1–0 up. What a sight it was to see him charging towards us with his shirt over his head as 35,000 fans sang his name. Then with the cup within touching distance, disaster struck as Leicester equalised with two minutes remaining. I felt like crying all the way home but it was not over yet. We could still win the replay – I thought.

The semi-final of the FA Cup followed straight after and what a game that turned out to be as 26,000 of us once again took to the road, this time to Old Trafford to play Chesterfield. Our tickets for this game took us to the very top tier of the new stand, a nightmare for me on crutches. Luckily the stewards allowed me in the service lift. What followed can only be described as one of the most remarkable matches it has ever been my pleasure to witness. The excitement started when Chesterfield stormed into a 2–0 lead. With Kinder getting sent off, Boro were down to ten men. Despair turned to hope as Ravanelli pulled a goal back, then Chesterfield had what looked a perfectly good goal turned down by the referee. That was the turning point, as Boro equalised through a Craig Hignett penalty to send the tie into extra-time. Boro scored again to go 3–2 ahead and just when we thought it was all over, Chesterfield scored with almost the last kick to earn a replay. What a match, it had everything and you couldn't help but feel sorry for them, although with this sort of luck we fully believed our name was on the cup.

Three days later we were off on our travels again, this time to Hillsborough for the Coca Cola replay with Leicester. Up to now I had not witnessed any trouble in any of the big cup games, mainly due to my physical condition I suppose. However at Hillsborough as I was stood with my twelve-year-old son waiting for my older son to go to the shop for me when some big brave heroes from Leicester tried to have a go at me because I was from Boro. Being on crutches made no difference to these hard men, and if it had not been for some police stood on the corner they would probably have given us a good hiding. I made a promise to them (and myself) that the next time I saw them I would not be on crutches but they might well be afterwards. Yet another spawny Leicester performance saw them walk away with the cup after extra time on another disappointing night for Boro, the only good part being the full-throttled rendition of 'We Shall Overcome', which almost brought tears to the eyes.

In the FA Cup replay against Chesterfield we comfortably tucked them away 3–0 on another great night to set up a final against Chelsea. Once again I travelled down to Wembley the night before, still on crutches – my arms were starting to get pretty strong with all this two hands, one foot effort! Once again we went to Trafalgar Square for the pre-match singing, even Steve Gibson turned up, absolutely rat-arsed drunk, proving that he is just one of the lads. Once again, however, we lost; when the opposition score after forty-five seconds the day does not bode well. Mind you I think we won the singing when I personally (I have witnesses) started a chant for three points that went round half the stadium and built up to a deafening crescendo, to let those wankers in the grey suits from the south know what we think of them. So we lost 2–0 and once again trekked home to God's little green acre with nothing to show for all our efforts. Was it all worth it? Too right it was and I would do it all over again, no hesitating.

AFTER THE DISAPPOINTMENT of those two Wembley defeats, coupled with relegation thanks to those tossers down at Lancaster Gate taking three points off us, we were back at square one. Juninho did a disappearing act straight after the cup final, not even having the grace to attend the open-top bus parade through the streets of Middlesbrough to say thanks to the thousands of fans who turned out to bid him farewell. Although I loved his performances and his attitude while he was with us, I still feel that once a player commits himself to a club he should stay through thick and thin. Maybe loyalty isn't something they teach you in Brazil.

So here we go again, another instalment of the great up and down life of Middlesbrough Football Club. We had made a few people sit up and take notice of us with some audacious signings and we were to continue in the same vein by capturing cokehead himself Paul Merson, and later in the season Paul 'Gazza' Gascoigne. After the early departure of Ravanelli, followed at Christmas by Emerson, our foreign contingent was down to a handful and were concentrating on promotion yet again, with solid British players digging out the results to get us back in the Premier. By the time we had played Stockport on Boxing Day we were sitting nicely at the top of the division, with Forest and Sunderland as our main rivals. Off the park it had been relatively quiet (no one came to Boro) apart from a dodgy trip to Sunderland at their new ground, the Stadium of Shite, where we won 2–1 thanks to a blockbuster from Emerson (thanks for the memories). I was still using a walking stick due to my dodgy leg but that didn't stop the Mackems as I was pushed, tripped and spat on all the way to the station. Later we found out that their 'hard men' had attacked a disabled supporters' coach after the match, leading to outcry back in the Boro (of course revenge was just around the corner, as they had to come to our patch).

Another eventful trip away was Man City, where we have had a lot of recent history. I can't really understand how or why this rivalry with City started. My own thoughts are that it began way back in 1976 when we played them in the semi-finals of the League Cup. We took a real pasting from them and gave them some of the same at our place, and maybe some people have never got over it. I know that City see their main rivals as Man Utd followed by the Scousers and probably Leeds, but I also know that their lads look for Boro's fixture with as much relish at the start of the season.

We travelled down by cars, minibuses and trains, all meeting up in a pub near the G-MEX Centre. I was on anti-depressants and couldn't drink, the side effects of the tablets making me very staid and sluggish. We thought we had managed to fool the law and we did do for a while, but eventually they sussed us out, so nothing went off before the match as about 150 of us were herded to the ground. The game was a bit of a let-down as we lost 2–0, and ten minutes from the end we all decided to leave en masse. The police didn't look twice as we left the ground. At the entrance to the back of one of City's ends, everyone just piled in – the temptation was too much for Boro's finest, I mean how often do you get the chance to do a top firm like City on their own patch? When we burst into the terracing the City fans shit themselves and ran away, jumping over the seats to escape. It was just like going back to the good old days. As we left the ground for the second time there was a welcoming committee from Mr Plod in large numbers. They were not best pleased. One copper on a horse seemed to revel in charging the animal into us, provoking a reaction from someone who sprayed the poor animal with CS gas, mind the same gadgie got arrested for it.

We had again been progressing quite nicely in the League Cup, dispatching Barnet, Sunderland, Bolton and Reading to set us up with a two-legged semi with Liverpool. The first game was at Anfield, where Merson put us 1–0 up only for Liverpool to come back to win 2–1, but we fancied our chances at home.

The home leg could not have started better with Merson banging in a penalty after two minutes, followed two minutes later by Marco Branca, who had signed for us that day. We hung on for dear life as Liverpool threw everything at us and survived the barrage to win 2–0, which meant we were off to Wembley yet again for the third time in less than a year. Who would we be playing? Chelsea, who else!

So once again the M1 and LNER throbbed to the sounds of Boro's travelling army as they made their way south for another Wembley showpiece. Surely we must win a pot this time? As in past visits, Boro fans adorned Trafalgar Square with red and white flags and scarves, singing themselves hoarse till the early hours of the morning in readiness for what we truly believed was to be our moment of glory. As we arrived at the Greyhound pub and prepared for the expected kick-off with Chelsea's firm, our numbers grew with a good covering mix of shirtheads and top gadgies. Where were the Headhunters? All we could amuse ourselves with were a few dickheads going past in open-topped buses, which were duly pelted with cans and bottles. We gave up on the notion of a big kick-off and went up to the ground, only to find out at half-time that some of our back markers got 'Japped' by Chelsea's finest just before the game. They're good at that sort of stuff those West London wideboys, maybe we were still learning, eh?

Boro showed a lot more commitment in this game than our previous Wembley embarrassment and we held the mighty Chelsea to 0–0 at full-time. The biggest cheer had been reserved for the debut of Gazza, who came on as a second-half substitute. Chelsea eventually ran out 2–0 winners, leaving us to head back up north with our tails between our legs yet again, but at least we weren't disgraced. The mob I was with did not see any trouble after the game but I did hear of Chelsea getting into some Boro fans in the car park of one of those hotels near Wembley Stadium, giving them a real good hiding by all accounts.

Now we could concentrate on the league as the old saying goes. We had slipped down to fourth place and desperately needed to string a run of results together in the last five matches if we were to have a hope of going up. This we did with sterling performances against Bury, Reading, Man City, Port Vale and Wolves, leaving us needing to win against Oxford in the last match to guarantee promotion. What a day that was. At half-time the score was 0–0 and Sunderland were winning away to Swindon; then in the second half Boro came out and totally demolished Oxford, winning 4–1, just as we had done thirty years ago at my first ever promotion season. The result was all the sweeter as it prevented the Mackems from going up and sent them into the play-offs, which they famously lost 4–3 to Charlton. The party went on into the night throughout Teesside as we celebrated our God-given right to the Premier League.

DURING THE SUMMER most fans take a holiday and recharge their batteries for the coming campaign. Being rather skint, I could not afford a holiday to Spain or even Scarborough, but I did manage to save enough for a tasty little pre-season trip to Holland. Word went round and a nice little firm of 30 or so went over to The Hague for a long weekend of drinking and football. We arrived on the Friday morning after flying out from Teesside, found some digs and set about getting well-oiled on the local ale. The first game was to be played that same night, so we set off for Den Haag's stadium on the tram; of course, nobody paid. At the ground we were disappointed to find a lack of drinking establishments and ended up in their social club right next to the ground, mind you it was really cheap and due to the state of my finances I found this most welcome.

We got talking to some of the Den Haag fans who seemed quite friendly, however I knew from my days following Feyenoord that they had a tasty firm and warned the lads not to become too complacent. We got a little bit of a warning as we walked round to our section of the ground, where we bumped into a handful of Den Haag boys. They let us know (in English) that today we were safe because we were playing Heerenveen but 'Sunday you fucking die'. As we entered our end I was pleasantly surprised to note that several hundred Boro fans had made the trip. We lost the match, although nobody seemed to be too bothered except when Merson was sent off for next to nothing.

After the game Bri, his son Robbie, my son Rob and myself made our way to the tram stop, where we were joined by a few other Boro lads from Stockton. Just then a car pulled up with some Dutch lads shouting out the windows and one of them waving what looked like a machete. One lad, known as TT, ran straight over to the car with his hands in the air shouting, 'Come on then you fucking cloggy wankers.' At that they shit themselves and sped off. I couldn't believe that was the end of it and felt sure they would return with a larger firm but the tram turned up and we managed to get away before they came back.

On the Saturday we met up with the lads in the Popeye the Sailor bar in Amsterdam, which is right in the heart of the red light area. I had been here before but the younger lads hadn't, so it was one hell of an eye-opener for them, and without mentioning names, one or two made use of the local delights on offer. One event that marred an otherwise perfect day was the arrival of the two spotter police from Middlesbrough, who pretended to be enjoying the scenery and claimed they had stumbled on us by accident. We were sat talking to some lads from Leeds who were on a stag weekend and most of whom were in Leeds's firm, the Service Crew. There was no trouble as far as we were concerned but when someone told them that the two guys outside were spotter police, they offered to give them a good hiding. We stopped them, as it would have made things worse for us in the long run. The Leeds lads were not best pleased, remarking how their spotter police were just the same. 'We'll just throw them in the canal then,' one burly lad joked. The two coppers could hear what was being said and worried looks descended onto their faces. The older of the two smiled nervously and, after supping his drink, made good his excuses and left, taking his younger colleague with him. I do believe they were shitting themselves. You could say they owed us one this time around, as these Leeds lads were genuinely going to do them over had it not been for us.

On the Sunday we arranged for everyone to meet up in the cheap social club bar so we could get together for the battle we had been promised by the local boys. We numbered about forty but the locals didn't materialise and the match passed off peacefully, with Boro winning 3–2. At night we bumped into the players as they were let out for a few beers, one or two taking the opportunity to try the local ale with more than a little relish. Paul Merson was true to his word and drank only soft drinks but Phil Stamp, Curtis Fleming and Andy Townsend were knocking them back big style, even bought me one. We stayed in The Hague, but the lads who had made their base in Amsterdam bumped into the some Boro players after I had told them how to get to the red light area, and one player who shall remain nameless sampled the delights of the windows. Monday morning and we flew back home to God's little green acre, looking forward to another season that was to promise so much yet fail to deliver.

Apart from travelling to Amsterdam for the weekend I couldn't afford much of a holiday and spent most of the summer saving up for the coming season. I enjoyed watching the World Cup on TV and with a bit of luck was hoping to be financially better off to be able to afford going to the European Championships in 2000. During the summer months we normally find a bit of an excuse to get together, usually as a result of someone's kid being christened or some poor soul tying the knot with his beloved (I know, I've done it myself, twice). Now and again we would all just arrange a night out, usually towards the start of the pre-season games.

CHAPTER ELEVEN

Back Where We Belong

THE YO-YO SPECIALISTS had done it again. This roller-coaster was one that no-one wanted to get off and such was the demand to see the Boro that they added another 5,000 seats to the ground capacity. Another thing we were becoming well known for was not being able to hang on to our top players for more than a season and so it proved again as Merson became yet another star to leave the club in acri-monious circumstances, his parting shot being that his teammates were a bunch of pissheads who drank and gambled too much (my kind of boys). He left us to go to a 'big' club. Aston Villa, big? They only fill their ground when they play Man Utd or Liverpool. I don't think Merson realised that most clubs have a group of players who enjoy going for a few drinks and socialising, but with Gazza in the camp maybe the temptation was too much. Merson comes across to me like an ex-smoker or Catholic convert, preaching to all and sundry.

During the past couple of years I had been living on bugger-all money since my accident and my finances were very short. This meant I had to stay in most weekends to save money for my 1998/99 season ticket. Although I had managed to attend about half the away games during the promotion year, I had to face up to the fact that while I was unemployed and living on benefits I would have to limit my away games even more during the next season. I would manage to get to only four away matches all season.

The season started fairly slowly but picked up when Boro went on a run that took us up to fourth in the league, culminating in a brilliant 3–2 victory away to Manchester United. This prompted Bernie Slaven to show his arse in a local high street shop window, much to the amusement of hundreds of Teessiders. Of course, it was then typical of Boro to go ten games before we were to win another. But we steadied the ship and ended the season in ninth position. Off the pitch, nothing untoward happened other than Man United's boys getting a good slapping on their own patch. We took a crew of seventy Frontline boys through to Manchester by train, managing to dodge the law. At Oxford Road we met some of their boys, with Doddsy and a few others leading the charge into them, right up into the station itself. Not being as nimble on my feet, I had to be content with walking up after them all and by the time I got where the action was it had ended. All I saw were their boys legging it across the railway lines. The fighting on the station had not lasted too long as Doddsy and co. did not hold back. One of Man U's boys phoned one of the lads later to claim that the firm on the station were only small fry, not their top boys. All the same, they were done.

Up at the Theatre of Dreams, Fazza, who'd had a few too many on the train down, got lifted when he punched a Man U fan who confronted him, right in front of a copper as well (perils of drink once more). Everyone else had ignored the clown except Fazza, who was oblivious to all around him. Oatsy and a few other lads got ejected from the ground early doors and ended up having their own little private battle near the bridge just up from the stadium. Oatsy told me there were only a handful of them up against superior odds, real 'backs to the wall stuff' with our lads coming off worse. One young lad from Redcar called Paul took a kicking and was on the floor getting a pasting when a copper came in and nicked him, the poor fucker; I mean, beat up then arrested for it, not a good day.

We drew them in the FA Cup as well but none of our firm went down as it was live on the box; anyway, why give them the opportunity to get one back on us? Of course the phone calls came in stating that we had bottled it, but what some other firms don't understand is that we can't afford to go everywhere. Unlike the big cities like Manchester where they can call on hundreds, we are fairly limited in numbers and have to pick and choose our games. Our last home match was also against Man Utd and for the first time in ages they brought a bit of a crew up, mind it was nigh on impossible to get anywhere near them as they were too well protected by what can only be likened to European-style riot cops, hundreds of them. Credit where it's due though, they came up for an off and it was not their fault that half of Cleveland police force turned out for them.

The Frontline all turned out for this game as word had gone around, along with a few phone calls from Manchester, that they were bringing, quote, 'Boys from all over the country, Scotland, London and Salford, the biggest firm you've ever seen.' The police had also got wind of what was going down and one of the biggest operations I had seen at Boro in a long time went into full swing. One lad likened them to Robocops. I saw one bobby with what looked like a scuba-style tank strapped to his back; apparently it was CS gas. There was not a chance in hell of anything going off before the game, as their mob were collared the minute they arrived. All tickets were checked before they were escorted up to the stadium, while those without tickets (they must have numbered fifty or more) returned to the station under escort and were sent back whence they came.

After the match, which United won yet again, Boro's firm tried all they could to get at them. Fair play once again to United's boys as they too looked to escape the police, but as anyone who was there will testify it was nigh-on impossible. The law won the day but not without some cost to the rate-payer (that's me and you); the whole operation must have cost thousands in police resources. A documentary shown a year or two later showed some of the technology that was used, pioneered by Cleveland Police. This included a video camera hidden in the helmet of a mounted police officer, catching clear pictures of any would-be perpetrators. I could pick out several Frontline lads clear as day.

The last game of the season was an away affair at West Ham, and also one of the lads' bachelor nights. Young 'Pikey' had not been running with the firm long but a good crew of lads turned out in Southend for his stag do, followed by West Ham on the Sunday. The theme of the party was Seventies-style skinheads, with about seventy lads – a good proportion of Boro's firm – heading to Southend dressed in Dr Marten boots, jeans, braces and shaved heads. Nothing happened on the night as we were all having a good time, and in the morning we set off for West Ham. We embarrassed them by taking over the Queens, one of their main pubs, at 11 a.m., making it ours for the day. Mind you, you couldn't blame them not having a go at us; with the rest of our firm coming down we had a 150-strong mob in and around that pub, all game as fuck and right up for it. I spoke with a big black lad who was ex-ICF. He told me that most of their lads he used to go with had knocked it on the head. One or two were now running the doors and drug scene over in Spain and Tenerife. He told me that West Ham were now much more of a family-orientated club, then reminisced about the old days when they ruled the roost. I didn't argue with him; they were awesome in their prime. Boro lost the match 4–0, most of us leaving after the third goal to partake of a few beers back in the Queens. Once the game was over we headed off back to Kings Cross where we had parked our minibus. Some of the lads went back to Southend to get their coach and by all accounts had a laugh stripping the groom naked at a service station on the way home. A happy end (apart from the result) to the season of reconciliation.

'1998/99 WAS A season of stability,' said Bryan Robson.

'Yeah, we'll take that,' said the fans.

'1999/2000 will be the season we chase for honours again,' said Robson.

'You better be fucking right,' said the fans, as we once again renewed our season tickets by the truckload (I could sense a little discontent amongst the troops, especially the Juninho bandwagoners).

As for our famous hooligan element, well they'd be happier in the lower reaches going up against the Millwalls, Cardiffs and Manchester Citys of this world. Life was becoming a little bit too predictable in the Premier League. The law had things well sussed, even to the point where they were talking to the main players on first name terms, in fact having the audacity to ask where and when they were having the next off. Do our job for us lads, eh!

It was also becoming obvious that someone deeply involved with Boro's firm had been tipping the wink to the law, as they always seemed to be in the right place at the right time when the lads had something planned; too uncanny to be true for me. I brought this to the attention of some of the top lads, who agreed that someone must be opening his mouth a bit too loosely to the local plod, possibly without realising it. These new days of internet technology were leaving things open for any Tom, Dick or Harry to broadcast where the big kick-offs were going to occur. All the police had to do was log on and they would have a pretty good idea where and when things were going to happen.

The main ideas to come out were that maybe the police had something hanging over one of the lads and were using the threat of arrest to extract information; another was that someone really didn't fancy getting 'done' and made sure that the law were there for protection. It was possible that someone was being paid for the inside nod. Everyone had seen the film *I.D.* where a couple of undercover cops were placed with a firm, but personally I didn't think things had gone to that extreme. The one thing that could not be proved was who the mole was. I knew most of the lads and they had all been going for a long time, all getting involved in some shape or form. The internet was also a chief suspect, and once I finally figured out how to log on to the hoolie sites I could see where a lot of their info was coming from. One new toy that did have its uses was the mobile phone. It could enable a firm to travel in to a town in small groups, where they could call each other and meet up out of sight of the law, then give their rivals a bell and arrange for a set-to. This was all a far cry from the old days but as Bob Dylan once said, 'The times they are a-changing.'

I had got to the stage now where I didn't even bother going down the town early when we played the top boys, because I knew only too well that nothing would occur. Now I went to the match with my youngest son and Karen's son for company, picking up Bri and his son en route. We'd have a couple of beers before the match with the lads, watch the game and go straight home. The only time we would have any sort of crack was at the odd away match and even then it would depend on who we were playing.

Take the 1999/2000 season. We started against newly promoted Bradford, who brought 3,000 shirtheads through with hardly any lads and nobody coming into the town for a drink. Chelsea at home, no fucker, they only bring about 700-800 up to Boro, all shirtheads. I mean no disrespect to them but even they don't do it any more. Sunderland at home, all on official coaches, straight in the ground and straight home after, all you got was a few slaps dished out during the 200-yard hike to the coaches. This after their lads had been in contact to say they were coming mobbed up and every man and his dog was out for this one (where have we heard this saying before?). Leeds, Newcastle, Man Utd, the list goes on, absolutely nothing at home. The big question on all our lads' lips was, has our reputation gone too far? Is every fucker scared to come here? Surely not, even Boro have a big following of shirtheads, I mean our firm only numbers fifty at some away games. Maybe it's all over, the hooligan has had his day – then Stoke, Cardiff, Millwall, and Leeds and Arsenal in Europe remind us that it will never go away.

Away matches: that's where a fan was rated in the old days and that's where we found our only bit of crack. Chesterfield in the second round of the League Cup does not sound too exciting and the game wasn't, ending 0–0, but myself, Bri and about a dozen or so young lads had a fair old bit of fun with a firm of their lads. In fact we thought we were gonna get done momentarily, as forty or so faced up to us in the street without a copper in sight, but because we stood our ground after knocking two or three of their leaders out, they were not confident enough to go at us. Then the law arrived and the moment was gone. Wrexham in the FA Cup looked to have all the hallmarks of a classic English–Welsh encounter and I felt sure we would get a portion there, especially as one of the lads was in constant contact with one of their main boys. But when we met up in one of their town centre pubs and they saw the size of our firm – over 100 – they phoned to say we were too strong so they weren't 'coming out to play'. We got beat 2–1 as well after leading comfortably at half-time.

The best away crack we had considering the situation was at Sunderland's Stadium of Shite. We travelled up on the early train, numbering about 150 and totally unheeded by the law, arriving in Sunderland at 11 a.m. We went straight in to one of their main pubs, the Aviary, and completely took it over. Doddsy was quite friendly with one of their boys, who rang him on his mobile to find out where we were. When he told him, he couldn't believe it and paid credit to our tactical nous. This would give the Mackems a good three hours to get a firm together to have a go at us, so from here on in we were expecting them to attack at any time.

By 2.45 p.m. nothing had been forthcoming, so we decided to head up towards the Wearmouth Bridge, as that was where we expected it all to go off. As we moved off we were immediately collared by the Old Bill, and as we got to the bridge a small band of Mackems tried to have a pop at us. A couple of lads burst away from the escort and sent them scurrying back where they came from. At the trading estate near the ground another firm started throwing bricks and bottles but that was about as good as it got before the game. After the match, which we drew 1–1, the police held us back as the Mackems did their usual 'We hate Borra' routine outside the ground. Eventually we were released and started to move towards the trading estate, suddenly turning towards the Wheatsheaf pub. At first the police didn't know what was going on and we nearly got through, but I think the overhead helicopter must have alerted them and they managed to cut the majority of us off before we got there. Twenty or thirty of our firm got away and apparently had a little set-to with some of their lads before they were rounded up by the law.

Another one I had better mention before they get upset was away to Man Utd. We could only manage to get about forty lads together for this one, as it was straight after New Year. We travelled by train and hit Manchester early doors. The law were waiting in large numbers, as they had heard something big was about to occur. They insisted on us going straight into a nearby pub called the Waldorf, which they duly surrounded. At about noon Bri's young 'un knocked on the window from outside the pub to announce that their mob were here. Fuck me, as I looked out of the window there they were, on both sides of the pub, at a guess I'd say over 100 armed with bricks and bottles, which they duly dispatched towards the doors and windows. We were powerless to leave the pub, as the police made a line in front of the doorway. After two or three minutes everyone managed to push through and out into the street, but by then the Mancs had decided we weren't coming out and had fucked off. When we had all got back in the pub one of their firm rang up to start calling us worse than shite for not coming out of the pub. I don't think he realised the situation we were in, bless him. Funnily enough, whenever any of us meets a Manc they always ask, 'Why didn't you come out of the pub?' Is that your only claim to fame? Put another record on for fuck's sake.

The police wouldn't let us walk to the ground (I was fucking glad as well, some hike that is, as I found out on later visits). They insisted that we got on the train straight to Old Trafford and went straight into the ground. We lost the match thanks to a missed penalty and used the train service to go back to the main station, all save five lads who missed it and ended up on a tram. These five consisted of some of our top lads, including Doddsy, Baba and Hindo, who kept pretty much to themselves. However Hindo, who never can keep shtum, got into an argument with a United lad and decided to spark him. This in turn led to attention the lads did not want, and when the tram stopped forty or more Man Utd got dug into our intrepid five, who commendably held them off in a toe-to-toe battle. Mind, poor old Baba got pulled from the tram and received a good kicking, although when they had finished he had the cheek to turn round and say, 'Is that the best you can do?'

The last match of the season was away to Everton and also doubled as Stevo's stag night, as another of our fine firm decided to tie the knot. This meant 100 lads descending on Blackpool on the Saturday night to give one of the old firm a good send-off. Everyone had a good time, Stevo didn't even get stripped or tortured in any way, sad really, then we headed for Everton and were ambushed by squads of police, who took us to a pub near Liverpool's ground. As we marched up to Goodison, we had a firm of about 130. An embarrassing mob of about thirty Everton lads tried to have a go at us. The way I saw it was that if that's all a once-respected firm like Everton can put out, I think it's time to pack it all in. So yet another season over, with Boro finishing in tenth position. Not only had the excitement gone off the pitch but even the football had stagnated as well, leading to some fans calling for Robson's head.

I had settled my compensation claim for my leg injury (nice little earner) and had started work as a civil servant, be fucked! So although I had already made my mind up to stop getting involved with the mob culture, my new job dictated that I had to. Sometimes, though, you just can't help yourself, I mean it's hard enough for a drug user to give up but when you have spent over thirty years with the same bunch of lads getting in and out of all sorts of situations, then the bond is nigh-on impossible to break. This new season was to prove the acid test as to whether or not I had managed to break the mould. To make the break in full would have meant severing all ties, but I was not prepared to do that; no, what I tried to do was keep in touch with the lads whilst avoiding any potential set-tos.

The Boro had signed a few players for season 2000/01, including Alen Boksic, Christian Karembeu, Joseph Desire-Job, Noel Whelan and Paul Okon, and this had me and most other fans feeling optimistic for the coming months. We started quite well, winning away to Coventry 3–1, but as usual the nosedive followed and by the time we had got to the end of November we had hit rock bottom, winning only two games (both away from home) out of fifteen. Something had to be done and although I had always been one of Bryan Robson's biggest fans, I thought it was time that we had to make a change. Some fans showed their dislike for Robson by chanting, 'You don't know what your doing,' and, 'Robson out.' I did not join in with this because I would not boo anyone publicly like that, although I knew where those fans were coming from. Bizarrely most of the firm were quite happy with the way things were going, especially as relegation would mean meeting up with the likes of Millwall, Pompey, *et al.* Personally I prefer the Premier League; maybe I was going soft in my old age.

Maybe it was something to do with the fact that I was about to tie the knot with Karen; yes, I had decided to get married when she proposed to me on Valentine's Day. The wedding was set for October on the same day that England played Germany in the World Cup qualifier. As I had come away with a healthy settlement from my accident, I splashed out and held the wedding at the only cathedral I have ever worshipped at: the Riverside Stadium. It turned out to be a brilliant day (and night). My best man was Bri, of course, and the show was timed to finish just before the England match started. Perfect, apart from the score (the bastard Krauts won 1–0). My stag night had been held in the Boro, although originally we were supposed to go to Blackpool followed by Man City away, but this was scuppered by the petrol strike. The Guvnors were not wearing that, and promptly accused us (via the web) of being scared to turn up. Come on City, get real.

Back to the footy and the next two results went in the same vein, with defeats at West Ham and Sunderland. Then the Messiah arrived in the shape of Terry 'El Tel' Venables, who immediately transformed the club by his very presence. His first match in charge was at home to Chelsea, which we won 1–0 (no they didn't bring a firm up yet again). This was to be the start of ten matches without defeat, a run that would hoist us out of the bottom three. It was a start, but that's all it was. The big work was still to come.

What was happening off the pitch? Nothing really, except for one away trip to Sunderland. The police had got the club

to put on a fleet of FREE coaches to transport our fans to
their ground in the hope of preventing any trouble. Did we
make use of them? Did we fuck like, we were going to use the
train like last time but rail track work stopped all that. So we
decided to make our way up in taxis. Yep, a fleet of taxis
transported sixty of us up to the Windmill pub. The plan was
so good I couldn't miss it, even though I was trying to keep
away from any trouble. Sometimes the urge is just too much
and you get carried along with all the euphoria. I mean, when
you're stood in a town centre pub in Middlesbrough at
10.30 a.m., frustrated because you can't get to a derby match
because the police say so or because the trains are fucked,
then someone comes up with, 'Why don't we just order a load
of taxis, it's only up the road,' you just cant help but get
caught up in it all.

When we had made base in the Windmill, I thought, if the
law don't suss this out there's gonna be one hell of a kick-off.
Unluckily (or luckily) for us, PC Plod walked in within fifteen
minutes of us arriving. They said they thought something was
afoot when they got a report of a convoy of fifteen yellow and
black taxis coming up the A19. After being searched and
questioned, we were told we could have a few pints until two
o'clock, then we would be taken up to the ground by a bus
they were laying on. This pissed everyone off, however at
least we had made a show against all the odds and we could
have a drink as well, which we wouldn't have got using the
free buses. Bang on two the bus arrived and we were
unceremoniously cleared from the pub, herded on board and
taken up to the ground. As I was walking up to the turnstile,
flanked on both sides by police, I could hear the Mackems
giving it the usual 'We hate Borra' chant. I responded with a
'So what, we hate Sunderland', to which a copper took
exception and promptly arrested me. I tried to argue that I
had done nothing wrong but he was not having any of it and
plonked me in a cell for the duration of the match, keeping me

there until 7.30 p.m. before letting me go without charge. Although I had missed the match and had the inconvenience of having to make my own way home from Sunderland, I was at least consoled by the fact that I did not have to go back for court and wouldn't lose my job.

CHAPTER TWELVE

There's Only One Ernie Ragbo

SO TEESSIDE TEL was here and had made his mark by taking us on a run of ten games without loss. I managed to get to two away games during this run, at Leeds, where nothing happened other than we were followed everywhere by police, and at Aston Villa, where all the old hands came out for the day to pay homage to one of the most respected Frontline gadgies who had passed away: big Ernie Ragbo. Ernie was the epitome of the northern, Seventies-style hooligan. He had been following Boro for as long as I could remember and had been leader of the B Farm Boys and one of the top gadgies in the Holgate stretching over twenty-five years or more. Famous for holding his own in the Roker End at Sunderland during the 1970s, standing alone when most of the lads he was with had long gone on their toes. Famous for going into the Gelderd End at Leeds in 1974, fighting his way through to the front then turning round to go back to help his mates out when lesser mortals would have played safe. He was a large, beer-gutted guy with his front teeth missing, loved his beer and must have clocked up over 1,000 games in his lifetime. He died of a heart attack while earning a crust working in the South (London I believe); maybe all that weight he carried and beer he drank caught up with him, but what a solid gadgie, respected all over Teesside.

This trip to Villa came about when we all heard of the death of Ernie, a well-respected Frontliner whose CV dated

back to the early days of the Ayresome Angels. He had not
been involved with the lads for a while but his past glories
had gone down in Boro folklore and even lads not been born
when he was in his heyday had heard of him. A few of his
best mates got their heads together and decided to have a
day out at an away match to remember him. When everyone
else heard about it, one thing led to another and one coach
turned into ten coachloads of Boro's finest, past and present,
wanting to pay their respects. A venue needed to be chosen
that could accommodate the ticket demand and Villa it was,
due to the large allocation we would receive. When I heard
how many boys were going I could not help thinking what
would have happened if we had gone to somewhere like
Sunderland with such a mob, although the police would
probably have stopped it somehow. As it was we actually
had the law's blessing on this. We kept them up to date with
what it was all about and they promised to keep a low
profile.

The day was organised with almost military precision. We
had a local working men's club booked, with a blue comedian
and strippers laid on, within walking distance of the ground.
After a few presentations to Ernie's sons, a raffle for various
donated Boro goodies and a good old-fashioned sing-song,
we made our way up to the ground, all walking behind a
huge banner which read, 'ERNIE RAGBO, HE WAS THE
HOLGATE'. I don't know what the locals must have thought
as about 600 boys paraded through the streets, but it must
have looked pretty impressive. Some lads didn't go to the
match and preferred to stay in the pubs drinking, and when
Villa went 1–0 up another 100 or so left the ground to join
them. I stayed until the end of the game, which was a draw by
the way, as I still had doubts about whether the police were
going to stay so lenient for the whole day and could envisage
an ugly scene developing once they tried to get everyone back
on the coaches, as proved the case.

We left the ground for the coach park and once aboard the coaches it was obvious that we were a couple of hundred bodies short. After waiting twenty minutes, I could see a large crowd of our lads having it with the local police up the road as they were making their way back to the coaches. It didn't take Einstein to work that one out. Once the majority were on board the police made all the coaches leave, resulting in about fifty being left behind. Apparently they all managed to get home by train. Once back in the Boro the organisers had a count of the day's proceeds and we had managed to raise around £3,000 for Ernie's widow. Not bad for a bunch of thugs, eh?

The next game was at home to Southampton, which brought to the end our unbeaten run with a 1–0 defeat. I was to attend two more away matches that season: Newcastle and the last match at Bradford. For Newcastle I was just going to go with Bri in his car but he had to work on the day, so I went with all the lads on the train. We had to go via Darlington due to work on the lines, which suited the lads down to the ground as it gave a good opportunity to get into the city centre pubs. When we arrived at the Central Station, the local law were waiting in full battle armour. We were given the ritual 'behave yourselves or else' warning and escorted to a 'chosen' pub. We had to stay there as the police threw a protective guard around the doorways, not letting anyone leave.

At about 1 p.m. I looked out of the window to see a hail of bottles coming over a fence and smashing on the road outside the pub, this being the Gremlins' way of trying to get us out to have a go. What they didn't realise was that we were powerless to leave even if we wanted to, thanks to the friendly advice offered by the Tyne and Wear police force. At around quarter past two, the police ordered everyone out of the pub and escorted us to the ground. A few Neanderthals tried to have a token go at us but we just laughed at them as we marched up to the ground observed by all and sundry, including scores of faces at pub windows, shedloads of police and a helicopter overhead.

Newcastle's ground had been changing constantly season after season and the addition of an enormous new stand made it more imposing than ever. The away end was accommodated in the highest vantage point available, making watching the match akin to a game of Subbuteo. 'No chance of us invading the pitch from here,' someone remarked, tongue in cheek. The game turned out to be rather good from a Boro fan's point of view, as we won 2–1 with ten men thanks to a brace from super Alen Boksic. We left the ground to find that we had a free passage into the street, unaccompanied by the police – at least, for long enough to send what few boys the Geordies had running like mice. Once the law realised we were loose, they collared us and held us in the middle of the road while the Geordies let fly with a volley of bricks. And that was it, another trip to Newcastle that promised so much yet failed to deliver.

We lost the next match at Chelsea (again) and drew at home to the Mackems (nothing occurred), then travelled down to Arsenal and stuffed them 3–0, yes Arsenal! This result handed the Premiership to Man Utd, who we were due to play shortly. Of course they didn't thank us by any means and promptly beat us 2–0. Although we had been getting some excellent results away from home we were still in deep trouble and went to the last away match at already-relegated Bradford still unsure of our fate. Christian Karembeu spared our blushes with a superb equaliser to send me and several others onto the pitch in celebration, ensuring yet another season in the elite. The last match saw us beat West Ham 2–1 and also saw the end of Bryan Robson as Boro manager, forced out by the boo-boys who roundly jeered him at the end of the game.

Venables was offered the manager's job but turned it down in favour of a lucrative TV deal, so Gibson appointed Man

Utd's first-team coach, Steve McClaren, as the new boss. This was to be the beginning of a new era in the story of Middlesbrough FC, one which was to bring a little history to our new home by the Riverside and the return of a famous adopted son of Middlesbrough.

WHEN STEVE GIBSON released Robson from the club, he also let his backroom staff go. As usually happens in these cases, McClaren brought in his own people, who all seemed to be called Steve: there was Steve Harrison, Steve Round, oh and another guy by the name of Bill Beswick. Now all the Steves had impressive coaching CVs and were experts in their own right, however no-one had really heard of this Bill Beswick fella except maybe a few basketball freaks. Sports psychology was his field; ah well, let's see. The 2001/02 season was to start with a home match against Arsenal. McClaren promised a more entertaining style of football and for the first forty-five minutes or so things didn't look too bad. Then class took over and we ended up getting stuffed 4–0. This was followed by defeats at Bolton and Everton. Next up was Newcastle. Good start, 1–0 up early doors, dodgy penalty, 1–1, keeper sent off, dodgy penalty to us, missed, open the flood gates, battered 4–1. Four straight defeats, great start, is this where this Beswick guy comes in or what? Off the field? Nothing for the umpteenth season running, a no-show from the Mags, where are they?

It was the worst start possible for a new manager cutting his teeth, but credit to the fella he never gave up and steadied the ship somewhat with the signing of Gareth Southgate. The next five games produced two wins, two draws and only one defeat. Another signing, Frank Quedrue, played his home debut against the Mackems (no they didn't bring a mob either) and scored the first in a 2–0 victory to become an instant terrace hero. Boro lost away to Spurs in the next game and then beat Derby 5–1. This sort of erratic form continuing for most of the season, however the ship had been steadied and Boro had got away from the relegation places, sitting nicely just below mid-table and giving Mr McClaren a little breathing space and time to start his re-building plan.

Off the pitch things had begun to stagnate. It was getting near to December and I don't think Boro's firm had seen a sniff of trouble all season. Following on from the previous season we had decided to pick a game to remember Ernie Ragbo, Freddy, Bunty and all the other lads who had died. This season it was to be Blackburn's turn to put up with Boro's finest, with a night out in Blackpool thrown in for good measure. Around 200 lads made the trip, all booked into a club in Blackpool not far from the big coach park. There were a couple of strippers on, I ran the karaoke and a comedian (from South Bank in Middlesbrough) was the main act. The karaoke went down okay, the strippers were a pleasure but the comedian never had an earthly chance as he was hammered from the moment he stepped on stage. His first joke, if you could call it that, was to insult Boro's finest. One lad took exception and threatened to throw him off the stage. The comedian, probably used to regular working men's club crowds, tried to call his bluff. Wrong move. Up stepped the same lad and literally threw the bloke off the stage. That was enough for the joker, who walked off, end of show.

Around half the lads stayed in Blackpool filling themselves with booze instead of going to the game. I went to the match, which we won 1–0, hurrah! Meanwhile back in Blackpool the rest of the lads were having a right old piss-up and one or two altercations, though nothing serious. When we arrived back from the match, half of them were scattered all over the town. I found my way to the Castle pub along with Doddsy, Spasky, Dooza, Robbie and a couple of other lads. The place was fairly quiet with just a few locals sat in a corner near the door. While we sat and chattered away about the match, Dooza, who had not been to the game and was a bit rubber-legged following an all-day drinking session, had ended up sat with the locals having a bit of crack. Suddenly there was a commotion over near the door and when we looked over there was Dooza on the floor with a few lads getting stuck into him. Well, red rag to a bull and all that, we were all straight in. These locals must have thought he was on his own and got the shock of their lives when half a dozen of us piled in to them. It was one of those good old Western bar-room brawl jobs. Doddsy put one lad into the middle of next week and the others took a couple of smacks from the rest of us. One lad stood taking on all-comers but eventually went down when Ecka, an old hand, walked in behind him and swung a bar stool across the side of his head, sending him crashing to the floor and his mates bolting for the door.

We couldn't stay so we headed for the Tower Ballroom, where we found most of the rest of the lads. The place was fairly quiet but livened up as the night wore on, with all the lads up dancing and having a bit of crack with the talent. As usually happens there were one or two scuffles, soon suppressed when any chancers saw the strength of our numbers. As I left with a couple of other lads, we walked into a fight involving some more of our lads. This was not so much a fight as an annihilation. I saw only the aftermath but you didn't need to be a genius to realise what had gone on. One lad was laid prone on the floor, blood leaking from his head, people were gathering round and you could hear the sound of police and ambulance sirens. Time to leave, this had nothing to do with me.

As I made my way to the coaches, I noticed one of our lads getting locked up, apparently for the earlier altercation in the Castle. The police presence was now growing quite significantly. I managed to grab a takeaway and boarded the coach for home, leaving this as one of those 'funny' days out, almost surreal you could say.

CHAPTER THIRTEEN

The Men In Black

BORO LOST THEIR next four matches: Liverpool, Man Utd, Newcastle and Arsenal. Should we hit the panic button again? Time for that Beswick guy? Nah, just a blip Everton were beaten next 1–0, courtesy of Uncle Festa.

Man Utd came up well mobbed with a good firm of lads. While I didn't expect anything to happen, mainly due to the fact that United are lucky to get 1,500 tickets from us, I still made this game one of the main attractions of the season. Around 11 a.m. I got a call from Bri saying that a mob of about fifty of their firm had been clocked by Doddsy near Redcar train station. One of them had told Doddsy, 'We're gonna take that pub of yours, Gilzeans.' By the time I had sorted myself and picked Bri up it was around 11.30 a.m. On arriving at Gilzeans it was obvious they had not managed to take the place. The funny thing is they probably could have, as there was only a handful of lads in attendance. The police had met them at the station and escorted them straight into the Bridge pub.

I noticed my daughter Emma with her boyfriend Darren and my granddaughter Miamh, who was only a few months old, coming out of the station. 'Dad, Dad,' our Emma gasped, 'we've just been on the train with all the Man U lads, all big gadgies, bloody Darren was sat staring at them all the time.' Darren was quite a handy young lad and I could imagine him eyeballing them, even hoping one of them would say something. Emma continued, 'They were all dressed in like black gear, y'know all that Stone Island stuff, they never said nowt though, no singing or owt.' I asked if she was all right and gave my granddaughter a kiss. 'Tell you what though Dad, there weren't any young kids amongst them, these were proper hard-looking gadgies, about thirty years or older.' I told her I'd watch myself and keep away from any bother and they went on their way into town.

I spoke to Doddsy in Gilzeans and he confirmed what Emma had said. He had met them in Redcar and said they were all main Salford firm, led by a fat Jock called James. As they had parked up in Redcar, most of Boro's mob agreed to make their way there straight after the match. The lads who were not going to the match went down to Redcar even earlier, along with lads carrying banning orders. I of course went to the match, where there was a predictably heavy police presence. Nothing happened and at full-time there were not even the usual lads hanging around outside. This must have spooked the police a wee bit. I drove back to Redcar and instead of going straight home headed to a pub near the station – like I wasn't going to miss this!

The place was packed with scores of lads from Boro, Stockton and Redcar, all waiting for the train to arrive. A couple of bobbies stuck their heads in to have a look and before long half the police from the match turned up. The lads who had come down earlier made sure the Manchester transport was fucked by slashing the tyres to prevent a swift getaway by these 'Men in Black'. For the next hour a new-style game of cat-and-mouse developed with Boro's finest doing all they could to get at their Manchester counterparts, nipping in and out of the back alleys and streets near the car park, while police on horseback and in vans chased and thwarted every move. Not a punch was thrown, in fact I don't think anyone got within fifty yards of them, mind they must have been counting their lucky stars all the same.

A lot of the Boro lads who had come down stayed in Redcar for a few beers and you could see the disappointment on every face. 'Looks like it will be up to us down their place again,' one lad complained. A few phone calls were made and the accusations thrown at each other, Man U's lads complaining that it was out of order slashing the tyres (something I agree with, wouldn't like it myself), Boro claiming that they shouldn't have come into town too early, both sides with their own reasons for this or that not happening. Personally I gave them credit for trying to do something different in the first place. At the end of the day the law won yet again. Oh yes and Man Utd won the match through a spawny Van Nistelrooy tap-in.

The FA Cup had thrown up Wimbledon away for the 3rd round, bit of a banana skin but we drew and then beat them in the replay. Next up was Man Utd in the fourth round at home. Now, would they get the full allocation? Would their mob come back? Would we beat them? No they didn't get the full allocation, only 2,000 (well out of order, that) and yes their mob did make another show. This time their firm did not show before the game even though Boro had a massive turnout for them. With the game being live on TV and MFC upping the prices, the crowd was way down on expectations, with only 17,000-odd turning up. I took my usual seat in the North Stand next to Bri for the first half. Noticing that the East Stand was half empty, we decided to move there for the second half to get a better view. On walking round, I noticed one or two Man U fans in the concourse. This got me thinking that there may be more keeping quiet; interesting if they score, I thought.

It was Boro who scored first, sending our small but vocal crowd into raptures. Just behind where I sat, some Frontline lads had clocked a handful of United fans sat lording it without a care in the world, either brave or just naïve. Anyway the goal was the perfect opportunity for the same lads to be subjected to the ritual kicking. With all the excitement in the crowd the police didn't notice these poor fuckers getting slapped and then legging it out of the stand. With only a couple of minutes remaining, Boro scored again. Heaven: Boro beating Man Utd 2–0, shove that in your pipe and smoke it. The final whistle brought the biggest roar of the afternoon.

Bri and I decided to celebrate with a pint at the Navigation pub just along from the ground. The place was packed so I stood outside the front entrance, smiling and slurping away salubriously. All the talk was of who we'd play in the next round. Suddenly I heard this shout – 'RED ARMY, RED ARMY' – and this big fat gadgie with a black hooded jacket came charging into us, followed by twenty others bouncing around in the middle of the street, arms out giving it the big come on. At the same time several Boro lads came flying through the doors into the street, forcing them to back off a little. Fuck me, it was their mob. For a couple of moments I was frozen with shock. I had thought at first the Red Army chant was from a happy Boro fan – it's something you can hear regularly at Boro matches.

The police were in very quickly to stop anything, although they didn't exactly escort the small but very game mob of Man U, allowing them to walk off away from the area. Several Boro lads made their way across the waste ground to try to head them off further up. I tentatively picked my way across the sodden ground trying to keep up. Ahead of me, the two mobs of fifteen Boro and twenty United met. A few punches and bricks were exchanged before the police once again intervened, although from what I saw Man U had the upper hand throughout. Late arrivals, who could have made the difference, turned up only to be chased off by the law. Fair play to these Men in Black, it was maybe not a victory but a lot of credit was earned in my eyes.

★ ★ ★

THROUGH TO THE fifth round and another home draw, this time against Blackburn, who brought a paltry 600 through, mind we dispatched them to progress through to the quarter-finals. In the league Boro had followed the cup win over Man U with a victory at the Stadium of Shite. A very heavy police operation and the fact it was a night match put paid to any chance of a dance with the Mackems. We continued this good form with a run of five games unbeaten in the league before capitulating away to the Hammers.

In the quarter-finals of the cup we had drawn Everton at home and things were looking good for a trip to the semis. The TV pundits were claiming the game would end up a goalless bore draw. How wrong they were as Boro stormed to a 3–0 victory to shut the gobs of Lineker, Hanson and Brooking. Surprising this one: with 5,000 Scousers on show you would have expected something to go off, but little action was to be seen all day.

Onto the semi-finals then and who do we get? Arsenal. Well, if we're to win the cup this year it's going to be the hard way. The game was to be played at Old Trafford, but first we had to visit there to play Man Utd in the league. Around 100 lads travelled down on the train, with a reception committee from Greater Manchester police waiting at Piccadilly. We stayed on until Oxford Road station to throw a spanner in the works. We alighted and quickly headed for a pub in the hope that we would get a peaceful drink for once. No such luck. PC Plod and his cronies had us all hemmed in within half an hour; 1–0 to the cat yet again.

Just after 2 p.m., a senior officer came in to order everyone out, as they are escorting us to the ground. 'No fucking chance,' came the reply, 'have you seen how far it is?' The police wouldn't listen and proceeded to force-march over 100 lads, including shirts who had travelled by train, up to Old Trafford. I tried to explain to one copper that I had a disability and needed to take a taxi as I couldn't walk such a distance.

'Tough shit,' he replied, 'you either walk or face arrest.' No wonder they're so hated. I tried explaining to him and showed him my leg in order to convince him I was genuine.

'What do you think I'm going to do in this condition, you fucking clown,' I snarled.

'Get locked up if you don't watch your lip, you northern wanker,' came the officer's sarcastic reply.

Our trek, which took well over an hour, resulted in us missing twenty minutes of the first half and Alen Boksic scoring the only goal of the game. A few 'Men in Black' tried to get at us on the trek up, fair play, but I don't think they got any nearer than 100 yards before the boys in blue had them on their toes. After the game the police made us march the same trek on the way back and this time there was no show from the Salford boys. I was fucked by the time I got back home and spent half the day on Sunday with my leg in a bowl of cool salty water taking the swelling down.

Next up it was the Arsenal for the semi-final on a memorable day where fortune did not favour the brave. Thirty thousand Boro fans had bought tickets for this one, with the same number coming up from London. Win this and it was looking like we would be facing our old adversaries Chelsea in Cardiff. A mob of Boro lads travelled down to Manchester on the Saturday, meeting up with Arsenal's firm, who knew Burner and some of the lads from England matches. Craggsy told me what occurred: 'We were sat in a pub in the city centre on Saturday night with most of Arsenal's top boys in attendance, everything was going swimmingly until Burner and a few others left to get something to eat. Two Gooners stood at the bar were overheard saying, "Let's get into these Boro wankers." That was all it took for Simmo and Totty to respond, starting a mass brawl with Boro taking it to the Gooners all the way. One or two Gooners were trying to calm things down, saying, "Leave it out," but it was too late. Boro had them all cowering and backing off. Yeah, we took them out quite easily.'

I travelled down on the morning of the game, arriving at 11 a.m. Once we had parked up and looked for a pub, it was plain to see that a lot of Boro had already arrived. The pubs near our end were chock-a-block with Boro fans. Myself, Bri and a couple of others made for the Arsenal end of the stadium, only to find the streets full of Arsenal fans unable to get into the pubs due to Boro having taken over most of them as well (even our shirts usually arrive early to get a drink). We hailed a taxi and went to the city centre to meet up with the rest of our firm, finding most of them in the Waldorf. No chew, just a good bunch of lads having a pre-match drink. The police were in close attendance but they needn't have bothered as no-one was going to have a go at this firm. We made our way up to the ground by tram and got in for about 2.50 p.m., just in time to take our seats for the kick-off.

Things went quite well for the first half as Boro took the game to the Gunners and my confidence grew as the game went on. Arsenal were struggling. Then disaster struck. From a Henry corner, Festa shinned the ball into his own net. Boro battled on but all was in vain, the minutes flew by like seconds and before you knew it the final whistle had gone. The Gooners were strangely quiet and subdued throughout the match and anyone watching would have thought it was us who had won. The TV and the next day's papers said we were unlucky but I didn't buy that anymore. I was sick of being unlucky. At the end of the day the history books will show 1–0 to the Arsenal, not how unlucky the losers were. Some people were saying how they enjoyed the occasion, what a great day out, etc. Not me. The great day out was in 1990 at the Zenith. Now we need to win something, I'm not satisfied with great days out any more, a great day out for me will be when we win a pot. After the final whistle I headed straight for our coach. I just wanted to get home. I was sick. A couple of lads came on to say they had seen a mob of Boro lads dragging some Arsenal out of their cars and giving them a slapping. I suppose some people just have their own way of dealing with a defeat.

The rest of the season held half a hope of qualifying for Europe through a high finish in the league. Sitting ninth, we had a chance if we could keep our form and remain unbeaten but we ended the season as we started it with four straight defeats. The final game was away to Leeds. Now Leeds have always bugged me personally. I have often read about and seen many times the efforts of the old Service Crew, but they have never really done anything other than rip up seats or attack young kids and shirts against Boro. For many years in the Seventies and Eighties Leeds travelled all over the country and Europe, taking impressive followings, kicking off here and there, but never at our place or even at theirs against us.

End of season games usually have that little bit of something, maybe the police switch off, maybe the nice weather goes to people's heads, but something always seems to occur, so Leeds by train was the order of the day. We arrived early at eleven bells, as usual, something like fifty-handed with more to come. Surprisingly no law were waiting at the station so we calmly marched unhindered to a pub nearby. Within an hour we had upwards of seventy lads in the boozer, then in walks Plod to scupper any chance of having any fun. I got out and into a boozer round the corner before the law collared everyone, met a handful of lads and decided the goose was cooked as far as the rest of them were concerned. The police commandeered a bus to transport the rest of the lads up to the ground, leaving just our small bunch in this huge pub alone. One of the lads I was with knew a Leeds lad who phoned him to warn us to get out of the pub, as a crew of their firm were coming in shortly. Seeing as there was only a dozen of us, we vacated the area moving to a quieter place where we had a few more beers before heading up to Elland Road by taxi (walk? Do you think I'm daft? It must be at least two miles).

We had been given only 1,700 tickets (by request of our football club, it has to be said), which limited the number of lads we had there. The game was a drab end of season affair which we lost 1–0. I then got split up from the rest of the lads as they went walkabout into the estate at the top of the road up from the ground; I don't know why because there's fuck-all up there, certainly no Leeds boys anyway. I walked off in the direction of the city centre, half hoping to flag a taxi down, as I didn't fancy the walk. I could tell where the Frontline lads were by the helicopter buzzing overhead, then I spotted the Shadow, who winked in acknowledgement. He was walking in the same direction keeping a thirty-yard distance between us.

I walked across a footbridge over the motorway, which led to a pub that had a fair-sized mob of Leeds lads sat outside. I kept my head down as I strolled past and no-one took any notice of me, as all eyes were attracted across to the mob of Boro on the other side of the motorway. I looked over myself to see what only amounted to half of what was in attendance earlier, something like forty lads with only a couple of horses and a few police on foot keeping tabs on them. As I moved further away from the pub and closer to the mob of Boro, I noticed a fat Leeds lad with his mate alongside me.

'Who's that lot there?' one asked.

'Follow me and you'll find out, daft cunt,' I said. I couldn't resist it.

The fat one started bouncing about behind me, saying, 'Come on then Boro, do ya want some.'

I laughed as he backed off without me doing a thing, then a couple of Boro lads ran past me to confront the main Leeds boys, who had come charging down from the pub. A couple of punches were thrown, then it was all over as more police arrived and started to crack skulls – Boro skulls, that is, as the

Leeds were long gone. One lad who is deaf and dumb took a real pasting from three coppers with their truncheons and another Boro lad who tried to help him got the same. As the police went in even more severely, a tall skinhead took a crack across the head that split his skull wide open. Then to cap it all several lads were arrested, all for nothing. The police held us for a short time while a bus was brought up to take us the rest of the way to the station. Thank fuck for that, I thought, I didn't fancy walking all that way with my leg and all. So that was it, end of another season, things were getting very tight as far as kick-offs were concerned. I had not seen anything to set the pulse racing; maybe this was the death knell of the football gang culture, maybe the police had won, only time would tell. Boro finished in twelfth position, McClaren had almost sorted the wheat from the chaff, next season should be one where we progress even further.

DURING THE SUMMER things didn't ease off with the World Cup in Japan, which seemed to confirm what I had been thinking about the end of hooliganism. McClaren had strengthened his squad with the addition of Massimo Maccarone (£8 million), George Boateng (£4 million), Geremi (loan) and, the icing on the cake, the return of the little fella Juninho (£3 million). Season ticket sales rose again, we had a good pre-season and the boys were also in action off the pitch at Hull. I couldn't get to Hull but asked one of the lads who went what had happened. Craggsy, one of our younger but fair-minded and knowledgeable lads, always spoke the truth and I knew that his version of events would be accurate. Craggsy takes up the story:

> We set off from a pub in Boro at lunch-time, four minibuses, around sixty lads all told, with a few more coming by cars. We got into Hull in the late afternoon, around 4.30ish, parking the buses in a side street 100

yards or so from the Silver Cod. As we walked towards the pub, we clocked half a dozen Hull lads sat outside who 'did one' on seeing our firm, obviously off to find their mates. We all piled into the pub expecting a kick-off straight away, only to find no more than a dozen locals, some of which were lads but not worth attracting the law's beady eye so early. So as not to spoil the crack we all left and moved off towards another boozer called the Tam Tam bar.

We had been there for a couple of beers and around 5.30 p.m. we noticed one or two Hull boys mooching about. On looking up the road towards the Cod we could see Hull's lads mobbing up. Too early yet for anything to go off, so we let their numbers grow. Shortly after this we get the shout that they're here, everyone piles out only to come face to face with a handful of lads. A false alarm, everyone goes back in the pub. A few minutes later I was stood outside with a few of our lads and clocked a mob coming down the road from the Cod. I told one lad to get the lads out, they were here. Looking up the road I would say they were about forty-handed at the front with another fifty or sixty lads straggled behind, all told maybe a 100 altogether.

We were straight into them with a few bottles being thrown by both sides. We had them on the back foot straight away and kept backing them all the way up the road right back to the Cod. As it was all going off one of our lads was run over by a BMW car. There weren't many punches exchanged by either side but quite a lot of dancing about, mainly by Hull who were backing off all the time. This all lasted only a matter of minutes before the Old Bill turned up to separate both factions, but all the same it was quite long by today's standards.

Once the law had it all under control we moved back to the Tam Tam pub and stayed there for a few beers.

After 7 p.m. the law came in to escort us all up towards the ground, or at least that's what we thought was going to happen. They held us in a park, gathering more Boro fans, putting them with us and eventually escorting us all out of town. We didn't even get to see the game. Apparently the police blamed Hull City Football Club, saying that they wouldn't foot the bill for the high expenses. Either way we were not allowed to even leave that park until they had got all the vehicles together and escorted us away.

By all accounts the Hull lads did try to get at Boro's mob but ended up attacking the police instead out of frustration. Once again though, as has been the case in the past, you can only beat what's put in front of you and Hull's young charges learned a hard lesson.

CHAPTER FOURTEEN

The Yids

OUR ONE AND only home friendly before the 2002/03 season started proper was against Oviedo (you know, that team who had the classic 5–4 UEFA Cup final against Liverpool). It was also the first showing of our new signings and the return of Juninho, drawing in a decent crowd of 20,000-plus. Some impressive attacking football had me and the rest of the crowd drooling as Boro went 3–0 up before McClaren put the 'stiffs' on to let the Spaniards back into the game. The final score was a respectable 3–2. What I saw convinced me and several thousand Boro fans that we could shake a few clubs up this season. Then disaster struck as Juninho tore his cruciate ligament in a nonsensical friendly game in Italy a week before the new campaign got underway. Some people remarked that one man does not make a team, however the next few months were to prove that Juninho is not just an ordinary man, he is something quite special.

The season began away to Southampton, which I travelled down to, a drab 0–0 draw which Southampton probably deserved to win. This was followed by a home match against Fulham resulting in another draw, though Boro showed a lot of promise in going two-up before letting Fulham back in the game with only a couple of minutes to go. One good thing was the form of Maccarone, who looked every inch the perfect striker. Things augured well. We won our next match against Blackburn followed by a night game at Man U, where we were robbed by a penalty decision which bordered on the ridiculous. Van Nistelrooy dispatched the spot kick to give the Mancs a fortuitous victory.

Next up was the Mackems from up the road, who tamely surrendered as we stuffed them 3–0 (no sign of their boys either, where have they disappeared to?). So, five games in and Boro were sitting pretty in sixth place with some entertaining football served up. The next big game to roll off the line was away to Spurs, who had been shaking up a few clubs on and off the pitch. They were undefeated in the league and ruling the roost in the capital by all accounts. Victory would have moved us up to third place, so the stage was set. Boro sold out all tickets for this one – at £30 as well, you greedy cockney twats – and word went around that the Yids would all be up for it. They had been ruffling feathers all over and wanted to take a big scalp by turning the Frontline over.

I travelled down on the early morning train with several other lads, arriving in Kings Cross at 9 a.m. We went for a breakfast in a café we had used several times in the past, near Euston. By 10.30 a.m. most, if not all, of our lads who were attending had arrived. Craggsy got a phone call to say that there was a pub nearby which had opened early and where we were going to meet up. On arrival at said pub, which was full of Boro lads, we had only one drink before leaving to head on up to Tottenham. I'm not a lover of the tube and persuaded Pinky and Robbie to share a cab. En route we received a call instructing us to head for a pub called the Ship, which was where the early arrivals had made base.

As soon as we pulled up and exited the taxi, I clocked the law making their presence known with a video camera filming all who entered the pub. 'Game's up already,' Robbie remarked grudgingly. True, I thought, here we go again, no peace for the wicked. By 12.30 p.m. most of what was coming had arrived in the pub, something like 100-plus. The Yids were fully aware and had kept their distance, parking themselves in a couple of nearby pubs, the Elbow Room and another just over the road. Our landlord had recruited some extra staff to cope with the demand. He needn't have bothered though, as one of the lads had already relieved the cellar of several crates of bottled lager, passing them out to all and sundry. There was a huge police presence outside the pub and it was plain that nothing was going to occur before the match, so everyone settled down to enjoy a few beers – everyone except Hobnail, who for some reason seemed to have something of a death wish, being prone to wander off alone to meet up with home fans, which he did yet again. He had apparently met a Yid on a previous visit and went off again for a drink with him. He didn't have a ticket for the game either so we resigned ourselves to the fact that we wouldn't see him for some time.

There were quite a few Boro lads without tickets. Some were subjects of banning orders and others just didn't manage to acquire one, so something like fifteen very handy lads would be left in the pub after we had made our way up to White Hart Lane. The police insisted on marching us up in an Eighties-style escort, with odd Yids walking alongside knowing they were safe, making the usual mimed threats and talking on their mobiles (probably to their missus telling her what they wanted for tea).

I took my seat and watched what can only be described as the best away performance I have seen from Boro for as long as I could remember (that includes the 5–0 mullering we gave Swansea back in 1981). The first half was one-way traffic, with Boro dominating proceedings. However we went in only one-up at the break courtesy of Maccarone. During the break I went out the back to find the lads, one of whom had received a phone call saying that the fifteen lads left in the Ship had been attacked by a mob of Yids after we had left. The windows had been smashed, CS gas used and there had been a good old battle in the doorway. We all agreed to meet just before the end of the game so we could march out mob-handed.

The second half was even better than the first, with Boro once again taking the game to Spurs. Soon enough they cracked and Geremi sent Boro 2–0 up. Shortly after, Joseph-Desire Job scored another. This was now fantasy football and Spurs didn't have an answer. Boro were rampant, hitting the bar and taking pot shots for fun. It shows how well you have played when the other team's keeper is their best player. The final score was 3–0 to the mighty Reds (it should have been six). I met up with the mob out the back and we left the ground along with the crowd.

Outside there was a heavy police presence, ensuring everyone went in the same direction, towards the road leading up to Seven Sisters tube station. As the crowd neared the corner where the two roads met, I noticed that the Yids were waiting on the opposite side being held back by a thin line of police. As we turned left onto Seven Sisters Road a shout went up, 'Here, here, on the left, it's their mob.' I looked to my left and coming through the alley at the side of a pub were several boys dancing about shouting, 'Come on Barra, let's have it then, come on.' Sure enough, Doddsy and a few others went charging into them, fists and boots were flying and after only a few seconds the Yids backed off down the alley.

A copper pushed me up against a wall with his truncheon across my chest, telling me, 'Stay where you are, don't move.'

At first I thought I was nicked and protested, 'Here I've done nowt.'

'Just making sure you don't, now stay there,' the lanky officer retorted.

Another shout went up, 'Here, they're coming on the right.' I was helpless to do anything with this copper pinning me against the wall and contented myself with watching a full-scale fight go off right in front of me. I noticed big Paddy and Craggsy going at it good style with a couple of Yids, then a police van screeched in to split the two warring factions apart. At this, the copper holding me released me and steamed into the mob, swinging his baton for all he was worth, in fact I would say he was enjoying himself. This to-ing and fro-ing went on for quite a while with the Yids on one side of the road and Boro doing all they could to get across to confront them. As always happens, the police eventually managed to calm things down and slowly escorted us up to the tube.

I later found out that Hobnail, who had been drinking with one of the Yids main lads throughout the day, had been subjected to a severe kicking as the Yids turned on him and took their frustration out on one lone soldier. Hobnail ended up in hospital with a broken ankle, two steel plates in his face and a couple of months off work. If it had not been for a couple of his mates, who actually managed to break away from the escort and steamed in to help him, he could have been in a worse condition.

The day was over and for once we could return home from London with a comprehensive victory, a nice kick-off with a respected firm, no casualties (Hobnail apart), no arrests (I don't think so anyway) and the opportunity to thank this wonderful team of ours for a great day out (McClaren and his heroes were on the same train home, fucking tortured they were). So Boro were riding high in the Premier League; I know it was only early days but it was much better than last season's start and once this team gels together, who knows where they could go, we thought.

Third place was consolidated with another convincing win over Bolton. Teesside was buzzing, as were Boro's firm. Some lads recounting the events at White Hart Lane said it reminded them of the old days. The Frontline website had Yids coming on trying to claim a draw, but no matter how you look at it, Boro took it to them all the way, we were the travelling firm, it was their territory and we entered almost unmolested. In this day and age that was a result. The way things are nowadays with the police having everything sewn up, it's classed as a result if you make it into the hometown pub!

ON THE PITCH Boro were going through some indifferent form, losing away to Charlton and the Mags (aagh, ripped off for two stonewall penalties) but drawing against Leeds (they attacked some shirts at the Navigation pub, my son and Darren copped for a slap, Leeds tried to claim a result, oh go on then) and beating a previously unbeaten Liverpool side (1–0, cheers Mr Southgate) who looked to have aspirations of the title. An excellent game at Chelsea followed where Signor Ranieri declared we were the best side he had seen this season, small comfort though as we lost. Newly promoted Man City, led by Kevin Keegan, were next. Now they have a bit of history, however a no-show from the Guvnors scotched any chance of something going off, mind a 3–1 result helped as far as the Boro were concerned.

Our next away game was at the Hawthorns against another promoted club, West Brom. Nothing was expected to go off as far as the Baggies were concerned, but a little matter of the Yids being in the 'second city' to play Birmingham enticed a large turnout from the Frontline, eager to continue this little mini war that had started. I was asked to drive a minibus down by the Redcar lads, and with it being Bri's birthday, I agreed. It was also Mossy and Jimmy Violence's birthdays, resulting in us taking two minibuses down. Billy had a coach organised, along with another coach from the Boro and a couple more minibuses, which made for an interesting turnout from the Frontline boys, all eager to find the Yids and to avenge Hobnail's hiding. We kept away from West Brom, heading into Solihull, south of Birmingham. There we parked the buses, met up with Paddy, who knew the area well, and proceeded to Brum by train. There had been no sign of the law.

One of the lads took a call from the Yids, who said they were drinking at a pub near Moor Street station. As the train reached Moor Street, everyone got off. A couple of police officers on the platform asked where we were from. 'Tottenham,' came the one-word answer from a couple of voices. Out of the station and into the street, 'Turn left and down the bank,' ordered the Brick. Over 100 lads poured down the hill towards where the Yids were supposedly drinking.

Bri had attended the call of nature so I waited for him; as we caught up with the mob I noticed a squad of riot police chasing after them. 'Better hold back Bri,' I advised, 'looks like they've been collared.' Sure enough, as we slowly caught up they were hemmed onto the corner of the street surrounded by police, helicopter hovering overhead. 'They're bang to rights now Bri, come on let's get away from here before we get roped in with them.' We both crossed the road and found refuge in a nearby bar, where we came across a few other lads who had managed to slip away, including Jimmy and Paddy. Paddy was with a Brummie lad who took us to a pub in the city centre, a right dodgy-looking place full of Brummie lads all talking about Boro's firm. We didn't feel too safe here so we just had the one pint and made tracks up to the ground.

The match turned out to be a poor game as far as Boro were concerned: we lost 1–0 to a bottom-of-the-table side who showed more fight than us. I got talking to Oatsy, who had come on a coach from Stockton. He asked if anything had occurred with the Yids. I told him what had happened and he laughed, telling me they had gone straight to West Brom and had a nice little set-to soon as they got off the coach. Sod's law, I suppose. West Brom apparently had a load of lads out for the Frontline and actually thought Boro had not even turned up, mind you Oatsy and his crew gave them something to think about.

After the game we headed back to Solihull without anything happening, save for a few pints in Yates's, then drove to Wetherby for a night out to celebrate the three birthdays. The Yids were fully aware what had happened and from what I gather were well impressed at the effort made by the Frontline to actually get something going with them.

The next big game was Boxing Day against our old foes Man Utd. No Men in Black this time but a very convincing 3-1 victory to the Boro; maybe we could get that elusive European qualification after all. Once again Boro let us down after showing so much promise by going on a five-game run without a win. We had not managed a goal away from home since we had stuffed the Yids, though nobody had beaten us by more than a goal, which made it all the harder to take. Boro were still unbeaten at home but that was to change as Villa, who had not won away all season, not only beat us but took the piss, shoving five away in a 5-2 defeat. With our next match away to Liverpool, following a controversial post-ponement of the Newcastle fixture, things did not augur well. Anyway, we only go and scrape a draw at Anfield with a superb free kick from Geremi, who was proving to be one of the signings of the season.

Next up was away to the Mackems, who were well-positioned to make it into the Nationwide League, rock fucking bottom, ha ha ha. Boro received only 1,700 tickets, leading to outcry on Teesside, and more importantly, Boro fans buying tickets for the home areas of the ground. Alarm bells now rang loudly. Sunderland AFC insisted the police had told them to send a reduced allocation of tickets in order to avoid potential trouble (it makes you wonder if the police force have one brain cell between them sometimes). I managed to secure my ticket, along with Bri, Robbie and Pinky, but most other lads were unsuccessful. Doddsy and Craggsy got theirs through a Seaburn Casual who invited them as his guest, Paddy managed to get some for him and a couple of mates, so all in all Boro's main lads would not be going mob-handed but would be in attendance at the ground, incognito if you like. At the eleventh hour, the police allowed Sunderland to send a couple of hundred extra tickets through to Boro, which enabled a few lads to get hold of the 'gold bars'. The police tactics had failed and now they were about to come under severe criticism for a monumental cock-up.

Four of us travelled to Sunderland in Robbie's car, following Mossy's car with another four lads in. Mossy got there ten minutes ahead of us and phoned to say they had parked in the city centre and were in Yates's bar, which had another thirty young Boro lads in one corner. When we arrived the bar had a lot of Mackem shirts in attendance but no lads. We sat in one corner with another thirty-odd Boro youngsters who, it has to be said, were a game little bunch, which they proved later on. I only recognised a dozen faces, including big Gillo, Ecka and Danny, the rest were all up-and-coming young lads. Gillo recognised one of Sunderland's main lads as he came through the door, a big ugly fucker with a scar running down one side of his face. Mossy immediately jumped to his feet, telling everyone to stand, and the Mackem proceeded to order the rest of the Sunderland in the pub to attack.

Next salute there were bottles and glasses flying at us from the other side of the room. We were pinned in one corner and it was all we could do to hold our ground. One or two of these young lads looked worried and cowered behind tables. I picked up a chair to hold up as a shield. One bottle bounced off the top of my chest and a glass smashed into the seat of the chair I was holding. I could hear Mossy, who was stood right in front of them shouting, 'Stop throwing bottles and use your fists, you wankers.' Pinky was stood near the bar and systematically relieved the bar top of its contents, pelting glass after glass with, it has to be said, a fair amount of venom. This heavy bombardment and a careful advance towards the Mackems soon had them on their toes out of the doors, though a couple of Boro lads caught on the wrong side of the skirmish were forced out of the doors with them. Two bouncers tried to come between both parties and took a lot of the flak resulting in them both nursing a few cuts to their hands. Fair play to them, when the law entered the pub they defended us, saying that the Mackems started it.

The two Boro lads who were forced outside came back in, telling us that a few of the Mackems had cuts to the head and arms. 'Fucking claret all over out there,' one lad remarked. I surveyed the scene inside and was happy to note not one of our lads had suffered any damage, even Mossy and Bram, who were right in the thick of it. The bar was duly closed and we were led out by the police, who insisted on putting us on a metro train for the short trip over the river, but not before taking everyone's personal details and photos (they must have a half-decent album of me by now). As we walked the short journey to the station the lad with the scar was hanging around being the big hard 'I am', shouting over and being a general pest. A copper warned him to move away but still he continued and eventually ended up arrested, the lunatic.

While we were in the pub Robbie had taken a call off Craggsy, who was with some of Sunderland's main boys, asking what was going on, as they had heard about a mob of Boro being in town. Robbie told him what had happened and that most of the lads we were with were not even recognised Frontline lads. Craggsy took great delight in telling his host that they had just been turned over by Boro's second string, reassuring him that we had not come up mob-handed (it's a good job we hadn't, if they couldn't handle this). Next up we were in the ground and the game was underway, Boro comfortably handling all that Sunderland could muster, which to be honest wasn't much. I almost felt sorry for the Mackem bastards having to watch that crap week in, week out. Boro cruised into the lead courtesy of new signing Chris Riggott. His goal sparked several fights around the ground as Boro fans sat in home areas of the ground jumped up in celebration. When another goal, again by Riggott, flew in there was more violence as more Boro stood up to applaud. These fans were not all boys, some were older blokes with their wives and people on hospitality packages or winners of radio phone-in competitions. The police and stewards were quite powerless to prevent what was happening. One particular ruck looked very heavy from where I was sat and went on for quite some time in the upper tier of the North Stand. All I could make out was this enormous gadgie taking on ten or more and holding his own.

When I went out the back for a leak, I bumped into big Paddy and two of his mates being led through to our end by two coppers. Paddy had a couple of bruises on his head and one of his mates had damaged his fist.

'What happened to you lot then?' I asked.

'Didn't you see us in the North Stand fighting like fuck?' said Paddy.

'Yeah, was that you lot, fucking went on for ages before the Old Bill came in.'

'I think he's broke his arm, have you seen the state of his fist?' Paddy showed me his mate's hand, which was up like a balloon.

'Hospital job that, mate,' I informed the lad.

He just laughed and said, 'If we beat these fuckers, it was worth it.'

More Boro supporters were led through following attacks by Mackems. The second half began the same as the first, with Boro just stroking the ball around as they pleased, then out of the blue Sunderland scored through their one and only decent player, Kevin Phillips (the first time he had ever scored against Boro, by the way). The revival was shortlived as Boro almost immediately went down the other end to restore our two-goal advantage through Malcolm Christie, another new signing. It stayed 3–1.

At the end of the game the police held us all back but after only a few minutes the crowd forced through the police lines. About forty of us got together and walked through the trading estate towards the city centre, safety in numbers and all that. We had big Paddy and one or two extra from what we had before the game and these lads were all up for anything the Mackems could throw at us. Just before we got to the Monkwearmouth Bridge there was a short but lively altercation with several Mackems. Paddy knocked one lad clean over a low fence, Mossy was going at it with another and Ecka bust his glasses and cut his eye nutting another. Pinky ended up with a bloody nose from one Mackem who punched him as he ran past. Only when the law rounded us all up did the fighting subside. We were put on the metro to the mainline station, where we split up to find our cars and left for home. No casualties, a good set-to and a 3–1 victory over Sunderland to savour on our short journey to God's country. Very satisfying.

THE NEXT FEW games ended with positive results for Boro, including a 3–2 cracker against Leeds which I couldn't get to as I failed to get a ticket (they only sent us 1,700 again). I had to satisfy myself with watching it on the foreign channel. Juninho had come back from his injury and our good form had coincided with his return. Against Leeds he scored a superb individual goal, bettered by Geremi who chipped in a sublime effort from outside the box. The Newcastle game, which had been postponed due to a heavy midweek snowfall – amazingly disappearing by the morning of the game, by the way – had been rearranged to take place on a Wednesday night. When the original game should have been played we had a bit of an injury crisis, leaving Bobby 'Zimmer Frame' Robson seething and accusing Boro of underhand tactics. I actually agree that the game should have been played on the day but it was great to hear all the Geordies moaning, claiming they had been done out of a surefire three points. Mr Robson must be suffering from senile dementia or some form of memory loss because I clearly remember him doing the same thing back in the early Eighties when he was manager of Ipswich, calling off a game against Boro because he didn't have a keeper and had a severe injury crisis; there was less dusting of snow that day than you'd see on a jam sponge. I was there and had travelled all the way down; we ended up going to watch Colchester just down the road where the conditions were perfect. Anyway, would you know it but we stuffed them 1–0 (more comfortable than the scoreline suggests). Any chew? Nah, they haven't brought a mob to Boro since the early Eighties. West Brom brought up the best away support seen at the Riverside all season, they never stopped singing even though we stuffed them 3–0, boing, boing, baggy, baggy. I'll miss the Baggies, they were a breath of fresh air those Black Country lads.

With Juninho pulling all the strings in midfield (running the whole game on his own, bless him) and our team back to full strength, anything could happen. Even Europe was being talked about, especially through the Fair Play League, which we were contesting with Man City. Guess who was up next, yep Man City, for the last ever game we would be playing at Maine Road. It was sad really because that ground reminds me of Ayresome with its tight little side streets and back alleys, dodgy as fuck.

Well I had to go even just to say my farewell to the old place, plus the fact that most of the lads would be making a show. I travelled by train with most of the lads, getting into Manchester for 11 a.m. As usual we were met by a heavy contingent of police, although myself and a dozen other lads slipped away out of a side exit unnoticed. The main mob were escorted to the Waldorf pub and placed under guard. We made our way to a pub nearby, where we enjoyed anonymity until the Boro spotter bobby popped his head in whilst doing his usual round of pubs. Collared. Not fancying the long walk

up to Maine Road, I slipped out of the pub with Pinky and
Robbie and took a taxi to the ground. The others all wished
they had done the same as they were searched and had their
photos and details taken under the section 60 ruling, making
them late for the game as well. The match it ended up a total
bore draw, 0–0. You would have thought both teams were
scared to commit themselves or pick up a booking; talk about
trying to get into Europe through the Fair Play League, you
couldn't get any nicer if you tried.

It was not so nice outside though. The waiting police lost
us for a few fleeting moments as we scurried through the
dodgy back streets of Moss Side. Eventually they found us
just as we found the Guvnors outside this pub, I think it was
called the Tavern. The numbers were pretty even, about
forty-a-side, with the City firm inside and Boro on the outside
trying to get them out for action. Kidda was first in, trying to
get at a lad through the beer garden. He was immediately
nicked. Then some City boys tried coming out of the doors
throwing a few glasses and bottles but the lads in the front line
had them well shackled. A police horse came bowling in but
one lad gave it one hell of a slap on its arse, sending the poor
animal onto its back legs and almost flattening the copper as it
reared up and toppled over. With the law well in control that
was the end of any fighting. We were all duly escorted to the
station where Hindo, who was the subject of a banning order,
got nicked at the entrance.

The next game of note was away to Birmingham, with the
Zulus promising a big turnout. Once again we made our way
to Solihull, only this time the law had read the move and by
noon the cat had caught its mouse. On arriving at a satellite
station near the ground we met only a token effort from a few
Brummie shirts, who did no more than throw a couple of
bottles over. After the match, which Boro disgracefully lost 3–
0, we were collared by the law and escorted to Moor Street
station. Four lads managed to slip the escort but only ended

up getting attacked by twenty Brummies as they got into a taxi. One nutter put a steel bin through the window in his eagerness to get at them, another lad threw a tomato sauce bottle all over Mossy, the loon.

Our last home game was against Tottenham, who had promised a big turnout to finish what was started at White Hart Lane. With it being the final home game, most of Boro's lads were out in force, including Hobnail, who had now recovered from his injuries and was looking to get some payback. As always with the last match, I went up the town nice and early, leaving the motor at home and arriving at about 11.30, only to see several Yids marching into the Bridge pub. Two Boro lads were stood on the corner counting their numbers. 'That makes about a hundred of the fuckers,' one of them remarked. Myself and Bri made our way to Gilzeans to meet the rest of the lads. All the usual faces were in attendance and were well informed of the Yids' presence. Mobile phone calls were being made between both parties with the Yids stating their intention to try to get out and into the town for some fun and dancing. Credit to them they tried but the police had them well shackled.

Next up we get a call at about 1.30 p.m. saying that the Bridge was on fire! The fuckers had only set light to the curtains in a side room; these boys were desperate to get it on. I'd heard that Stoke had tried the same thing before, however this blatant disregard for Teesside property only served to see the Yids escorted into the ground. Nothing was going to go off before the match but one or two phone calls later it was agreed that the Yids would stay until the final whistle, coming out with the rest of the crowd, as this would give the best opportunity for an off.

The game started with Spurs taking the game to Boro and they actually had the better of the early exchanges. Once Boro settled into their stride it was one-way traffic with Christie opening the scoring, quickly followed by a Juninho penalty and another one by my man of the match Nemeth. Spurs were shell-shocked and so were their firm, who could be seen streaming down the stands into the concourse, apparently kicking off with a couple of stewards and riot police. The second half continued in the same way, with Boro scoring another through Maccarone before Spurs grabbed a consolation. There was no sign of any comeback though as their goal only seemed to anger Boro, Maccarone grabbing his second to effectively end the contest at 5–1. Spurs fans were leaving in their droves and by the time the final whistle went most of them, including their boys, were halfway to Darlo on the train. We gave a lot of credit to these lads though; at least they came up, which is more than most firms do, and at least they tried to get something on. But as I have said time and again, in recent years the police have always been on top of the situation.

The season petered out away to Bolton with not much to say other than we lost 2–1, nothing occurred and the poor old Hammers, who played some decent football, were relegated. Well at least there was an England game to look forward to at the Riverside and a couple of interesting friendlies coming up before next season: Hull, Sheffield United and Rotherham (were the organisers of these games just looking for trouble or what?).

CHAPTER FIFTEEN

From One Lion To Three

AS I MENTIONED at the start of this book, my love affair with football started during the 1966 World Cup, when our famous eleven won that thirteen-inch-high block of gold known as the Jules Rimet Trophy. It was a day that will live long in the memory of those who were privileged to witness it. What are the credentials that make me an England fan? Well for starters I was born in England, of English parents, who themselves were born of English parents, in fact I have traced my family name right back to Anglo-Saxon times. I'm also Protestant and a staunch Royalist. I suppose you could say I'm what's known as a WASP (White Anglo-Saxon Protestant), and proud of it. No I'm not a racist bigot, although I am proud of my race and culture. Why shouldn't I be? There's no shame in what my country have given the world over the years. The whole world would be in a much worse state if it was not for our forefathers. True they made some mistakes along the way and the twentieth-century generations are paying for it, but that's history.

Back to the football. As a young kid I never got the chance to see an England game in the flesh for one reason or another, and when I was old enough and could afford it, I had already sworn never to enter Wembley until Boro played there. In light of this my first England game was at Hampden Park against the hairy-arsed haggis noshers, who think they have a divine right to be the ambassadors of football. The daft bastards want their own country; personally I'd build up the wall again and declare them official enemies. Anyway we lost and I spent the best part of the day keeping myself to myself, as I lost our lot the moment we entered the stadium. After the match everyone covertly made their way back to Glasgow Central Station, me included, mind we had a nice little set-to with Hibernian fans on the way to Edinburgh. A lot was made of the English fans' unruly behaviour on the day but we were up against it as soon as we got there – and what about the Jocks at Wembley and our goal posts, pitch, etc? Oh no, that was just them having fun!

The next England game I went to was in Scotland again. This turned out to be very emotional for a number of reasons. Firstly, Custer had been tragically killed in a works accident, so we used the game to remember him by. Secondly Hobnail was getting married so it became a bachelor night. And thirdly, we beat the bastards 2–0.

Custer (Fred) was another well-respected Frontliner. He was crushed under a steel girder. As I have said before, Fred was well known by all Boro's top lads and when he was buried (midweek before the Scotland game) the top boys from all over Teesside came to pay their respects. There must have been well over 500 lads at the funeral, it was like a who's who of boys down the years. The year was 1989 and Boro just happened to have one of the top firms in the country at the time, so off travelled some very tasty, emotionally charged boys to Scotland. Custer's seat (already paid for) was left vacant.

On the way to Glasgow we were stopped by police who searched the coach and made a good job of detaining us so that we couldn't get to the city centre, where it would undoubtedly have gone off. At Hampden the streets were full of tartan-bedecked, pissed-up Jocks singing their ginger heads off about how much they hate us, Flower of Scotland and so on. To make matters just that bit more interesting, Crow started singing, 'We're going to Germany, you're not,' a reference to the forthcoming European Championships, in a street where we were outnumbered something like ten to one. The Jocks just passed him off as a drunk and chose to ignore his remarks.

None of us had tickets so we went to the ground, where some were on sale to English fans only. As we were stood examining our tickets, Doddsy came over shouting, 'Away lads, Hibs are here and they want some with the Boro.' We all made our way towards this excuse for a mob, only for them to turn tail and get on their toes. This action immediately dispelled any myths that the Jocks were untouchable on their own turf, and instant respect was forthcoming from the cockneys, who made a point of acknowledging that when you're in Scotland it's the northern clubs who run the show, especially Boro.

Inside the ground it was obvious that the Geordies and the Mackems couldn't see eye to eye, as a little tête-à-tête took place after a Mackem was pulled off a barrier by a Mag for displaying a St George cross with SAFC emblazoned across it. Some firms just will not let the rivalry stop, even when they are supposed to be on the same side. There were a lot of Wolves fans at the match who were there to see their hero Steve Bull, who came on and scored, sending them into raptures. The game ended 2–0 to England and we were ushered straight onto our coaches and escorted out of the city to avoid trouble, although the fans who were on the train had a fair old bust-up by all accounts.

We managed to persuade the driver to take us to Dumfries for Hobnail's stag do. When we arrived, we made our way to the first bar and set about on a night of drinking and eventually mayhem. As it was only early doors we were quite well behaved and had a bit of crack with the locals. In one pub we even got them to observe a minute's silence for Custer, which they did impeccably. The peace did not last long as word went round the town that Boro's and England's finest were in attendance. Soon enough it all kicked off, starting with Spasky getting refused admission into one of the more popular establishments. He attempted to gain entry using the soles of his Dr Marten boots, the end product being the demolition of one plate glass door. This was the catalyst that had the whole town out in the streets battling with us for what seemed like hours, and due to everyone being split into groups of between five and ten it was hard going. I was in a group of six with Bri, Tommy, Hobnail, Pidgy and Windows. Windows was having an argument with a local and had agreed to fight him one-to-one. Well fuck me, Windows gave everything he had but the Jock just stood there and took it all, then Pidgy took a pool cue to the poor fucker and still he wouldn't give up. Eventually we moved away and left the nutter, who by now was covered in claret but incapable of fighting.

It was going off all over and the police were beginning to take an interest. First they arrested Spasky and another lad for criminal damage, then they advised us to return to our coach. On the way we walked straight into a fight involving some more of our lads; Browny and Macca were hard at it with some younger Jocks. We joined in to put them on their toes, then as the police had almost succeeded in getting us all towards the coach, a load more Jocks came across the car park to set the ball rolling again. There weren't enough cops to control the situation and as more and more locals joined what was now a war, the police called in reinforcements. I noticed that the cops knew half the lads we were fighting and threatened them with arrest later on (probably a few early morning knocks to look forward to). Calm was gradually restored and we were ushered onto our coach and then escorted to the border, where the English police were waiting to escort us in turn to each county border before being handed to the next force, and so on until we were back in good old Redcar. What a day out. Custer would have been proud; I know Hobnail was.

The next big England match was a qualifier in Sweden for the 1990 World Cup. This was to be my first England game abroad, and the General along with Degsy had organised a cheap ferry trip to Gothenburg for £99 each. A lot of our mob fancied it and we numbered something like forty bodies among 500 or so England fans aboard the ship. The bars were open well before the ship set sail and the majority of England fans did not need much encouragement to set about drinking that Elephant beer. By nine o'clock most of us were pissed as farts, with the majority of the other England fans singing 'God Save the Queen' and 'No Surrender'. Our firm were not joining in, which had the cockneys asking questions. One geezer who said he was Chelsea asked the General why Boro weren't singing. The General replied nonchalantly, 'We don't, we just do the business.'

Later reports came in that some of our younger lads had just dusted Bolton. Then this geezer from Plymouth, who apparently was a Leeds fan, decided Boro were shite and upset one of the lads by insulting his girlfriend. This ended with a glass in the face for said Leeds fan and twelve stitches by the ship's doctor. A Millwall fan decided to have a go at Verb in the nightclub; they were both as pissed as each other, which made for a comical fight that ended with Verb head-butting the Millwall fan, leaving him flat out on the dance floor. The rest of the night continued in the same vein with everyone at some stage having a run-in with one of our lot, though each time we came out on top. Someone even spiked the DJ's drink with an Ecstasy tab, which sent him into another world.

The night came to a riotous finish, with the majority of the 500 England fans on board smashing up the ship. One of our boys, who shall remain nameless, let off several fire extinguishers, covering everywhere in white powder. He even found his way onto the car decks and covered them as well. Unbeknown to us, the Leeds fan from Plymouth had been given an E and jumped overboard, resulting in the ship circling all night searching for him along with the Dutch coastguard, to no avail. On the orders of the British police the ship was turned back, so instead of waking up to the sights of Gothenburg we found ourselves back at Harwich with hundreds of police in full riot gear waiting for us.

Needless to say we were unceremoniously kicked off the ship, although we were promised a refund on the fare. Apparently we were the talk of the nation as all the TV and newspapers clambered around trying to get the story of what happened. None of our lads spoke to the law or the press, thus resulting in all stories pointing the blame at the Boro crew. Some even made it out to have been a north versus south thing. All I know is that we took no shit from anyone. Thirty of us went to Belgium for a few days, as we had already taken the time off from work, and ended up watching the match in a bar in Ostend. A few lads from Oldham and Manchester tagged along for the crack.

After 1990, when Boro had reached Wembley and laid the ghost to rest, I decided to become a more regular visitor to England matches; after all, I was living and working in London so it was easier to get tickets. Wembley was so well policed for visiting foreigners that the only chew you got was from opposing domestic firms having a dig at one another. I did have one weekend of crack when we played Scotland and for once the English had the upper hand inside the stadium as well as outside. All the in-house rivalry was put to one side as we ran the Jocks ragged. Most of the lads had managed to secure tickets and we put a good firm from Redcar up at our gaff in Wood Green, north London. We met the General and the rest of the Redcar firm at Paddington and spent the day boozing in the Pride of Paddington pub. We numbered somewhere around the thirty-plus mark. On the way to Wembley our tube train came to a stop in a tunnel and we were stuck for what seemed ages due to some over-zealous Jocks fucking about with the doors. The General lost his rag with some in our carriage who were opening the adjoining doors to have a piss. At first I thought it was going to go off but they apologised and behaved themselves.

Due to this delay we were late getting in the ground and missed England scoring, but we arrived just in time to walk in on a full-scale battle with the Jocks. There was a mix of both sets of fans at both ends of the ground so it was going off all over the place. For the first time I could remember, England fans had the upper hand, taking it to the Jocks at all times. The newspapers later vilified us for it but what about all those years when the Jocks used to come down and take over the place, wrecking the pitch, demolishing the goal posts and kicking fuck out of anything in an England scarf? That was apparently acceptable; what was not acceptable was England fans getting their own back for years of grief from these tartan-clad louts.

There were some more little kick-offs outside after the match (which we won 1–0) and throughout the city all night. We stayed in the Wood Green area and had a trouble-free night, even as far as having a drink with some Jocks who didn't want any bother. We ended up with bodies kipping all over our gaff and in the morning I woke to find a Scotland flag on the floor.

'Who brought this shite in here?' I croaked, still half asleep.

'Och that must be mine,' piped up a squeaky Glaswegian voice from one side of the room.

'Fucking hell, how did you end up here, you haggis-noshing little fart?' I exclaimed in shock.

Out of one corner of the room came this skinny, spotty little excuse of a man, stumbling over several prone bodies still snoring away to collect his prized flag of St Andrew.

'Who said you could sleep here?' I enquired angrily.

'You did, last night in the kebab shop,' one of the lads on the floor shouted.

'Aye, ye did,' the Jock confirmed.

'Well you can fuck off now ye cheeky git, don't think you're getting any breakfast as well,' I joked. I must have been well-oiled that night.

I WAS WORKING in Holland when the 1990 World Cup tournament kicked off in Italy and had to content myself with watching all the early rounds in bars surrounded by orange-clad cloggies. They don't half go over the top. Every bar was decked out in orange flags and lions. As England progressed through to the semi-finals, I felt they could go all the way and booked a train ticket to Rome for the final, as I was due some holidays. As you all know, the bastard Germans knocked us out on penalties and we had to settle for the third and fourth place play-offs. I couldn't get a refund so I took the trip all the same, ending up in a bar with a few Chelsea lads watching the 'B' final in Rome (I couldn't get to Bari). These Chelsea boys were a bit warm like, wanting to fight every Eyetie going. I kept myself out of their dealings and slept overnight in the station before heading back to Rotterdam the following morning.

During Euro 96 my best mate Bri managed to get tickets for the quarter-final against Spain, a boring game which the Spanish should have won, but the atmosphere was unbeliev-able with all the England fans getting on well with one another. It's coming home, it's coming home, no it's fucking not, but it should have. The euphoria was cut short when the Krauts beat us on penalties yet again.

Following my accident I had to content myself with watching England matches on TV again, but once I was financially sound, it was back to Europe for the Champion-ships in Belgium. I had always fancied going away on one of these tours but for one reason or another had never managed it. This time I could afford it, and the tournament was held within reach, so along with Bri and a tasty firm of Boro lads I arrived in Brussels. Billy, one of our regular England travellers, had booked several rooms at the Hospitality Inn and fifty boys piled in, four or more to a room. We arrived on the Friday, twenty-four hours before the match against the Germans, but as we made our way to the big square where the English fans were gathering, we were surrounded by scores of Belgian riot police. They held us for an hour, checking passports, names and addresses before letting us go with a warning. During our detainment we could hear sirens and chanting coming from the square and at one stage a large armoured truck with water cannon trundled past, accompanied by hundreds of riot cops.

We decided to stay put, as the police informed us that anyone who entered the square could be liable to arrest. Some of our lads did not heed the warning and curiosity got the better of them. They ended up at the square, which was teeming with police and Turks, who immediately made any English the target of their aggression. The lads who went there ended up being surrounded by Turks armed to the teeth. A kick-off ensued and when the police moved in to break it all up it was our lads who ended up getting arrested, five of them. We had a bit of chew outside the bar we were in, resulting in a kebab shop getting trashed. As several lads attacked the shop, a hand came from behind the door holding a pistol and firing away. One Leeds lad thought he had been shot but the gun was firing blanks; on closer inspection he had been hit by the cordite expelled by the gun. We decided to get away from the area before the police started rounding everyone up.

It was not until the next morning that we heard of the lads who had been arrested. Worse still, they were to be deported. With it being the day of the match, we set off to Charleroi bright and early on the train. We were greeted at Charleroi by hundreds of riot police, who insisted on checking every passport before allowing us to leave the station. Once through their lines we were at liberty to go where we liked; well the nearest bar seemed the best choice and the drinking started. The weather was absolutely scorching, and with all the beer flowing so freely this was a recipe for disaster, and so it proved. By about midday we had worked our way up to the main square, which was bedecked with all manner of England flags and of course a smattering of Germans. Out of about twenty bars surrounding the central fountains in the square, all but one or two were populated by England fans. Bri and I were interviewed by a local TV company who expressed a desire to know when the 'English hooligans' were going to start rioting. Bri had a go at the reporter, telling him that it was them who were stirring up trouble just to get the pictures they wanted. I pulled him away before he got into trouble and we walked over to some German fans, who stood and had a drink and a chat with us.

Suddenly it all went off. A handful of English fans set fire to a German flag, which brought in the police heavy-handedly. This sparked a reaction from their mates and the next thing you knew the shit had really hit the fan. The water cannon started blasting away, which in turn set the England fans into a rampage, throwing chairs and tables. The German fans started running down the side streets to get away, leaving just the English and police in a stand-off. I must give credit to the law for one thing: although they overreacted they made sure with their tactics that nobody could leave that square or enter it. The whole area was totally sealed off. It took all our powers of persuasion for me and Bri to talk our way through the police lines, even promising that we were going to get the next train out of Charleroi in order to get through. As we left the area we laughed as we saw hundreds of England fans doing their best to get *into* the square.

As evening drew in and kick-off approached, I resigned myself to watching the game in a bar, as there didn't seem any likelihood of us getting any tickets. Bri was mortal drunk and insisted on going back to Brussels to watch the game. I argued with him that he would not even see the second half, as the game was due to start in a matter of minutes, but he wouldn't listen and staggered off to the station. I said, 'Fuck you,' and left him to watch the game in a bar. Every bar in Charleroi was packed with England fans and this resulted in the inevitable kick-off between rival factions; Derby had a good-sized firm and went at it with Leeds during the half-time break. I half expected Bri to turn up any time, but he didn't so I stuck with twenty of our mob that had not returned to Brussels or gone to the match.

At the end of the game, which England won by the way, we set off back to Brussels. The train did not go where we wanted to be, so we ended up having to walk through a right dodgy area before finding sanctuary in the area where our hotel was situated. Nothing happened on the way but the atmosphere was reminiscent of that film *The Warriors*; I could have sworn you could hear that haunting music. I was totally knackered and returned to the hotel room, content to spend the night watching the day's events played out on the TV. Bri came in about an hour after me with what he thought was a German flag but turned out to be Belgian; well the colours are similar. To top it all he announced that he had bought a ticket from some late-arriving England fans and had been in the ground for the match! 'You bastard,' I exclaimed, 'you fucking lucky bastard.' He had been on his way home the last I saw of him.

So yet another false dawn for England as we lost against the Romanians, thanks to Neville the tosser, leaving both ourselves and the Krauts to get the early plane home. Almost 900 England fans were arrested and deported, although only a handful were actually taken to court and prosecuted. The most famous of these deportees was a huge-beer-gutted, heavily tattooed Boro lad whose picture adorned every national tabloid's front page.

Following the World Cup in Japan, which I had to content myself with watching on the box, there was a new belief that the English curse had finally left the game. No crowd trouble, no riots, not even any racist chanting. How wrong can you be? The qualifiers for the European Championships in Portugal 2004 had put us in a group with Turkey, Slovakia, Macedonia and Liechtenstein, a group that ten years earlier would have meant guaranteed qualification. These days, however, there were no easy games at international level and Turkey had emerged as a powerful force, even finishing as semi-finalists in the World Cup.

Our first game was against Slovakia away, an old Eastern Bloc country that had emerged from the break-up of Czechoslovakia. From what I knew of other ex-communist countries I expected the Slovaks to be still set in the old ways, trying to come to terms with the West and sporting loads of young Seventies-style boot boys. A couple of lads I know who regularly follow England abroad had arranged to go on the promise of tickets and I decided to go with them, as I love visiting new places and had also been promised a ticket. Our route to Slovakia took us from Leeds to Paris with a connecting flight to Vienna. From there we had to take a bus to Bratislava which was only thirty-odd miles away. At Vienna I was not surprised to see England fans (mostly boys) arriving in their droves and our one bus turned into a convoy of several.

At the border checkpoint we were met by Slovak police, who boarded the bus requesting passports. Pinky had left his in his bag, which was in the boot. 'You go fetch,' came the guard's stern response. Another lad asked if he could go to the toilet. 'You piss yourself,' the guard snarled at him. After all passports had been checked we were allowed to proceed to Bratislava, where we met up with Paddy and a few more Boro lads who had made the journey the night before. The hotel where we met the lads was a real smart gaff, one of the best in Bratislava we were informed by a taxi driver. The beer was fairly cheap, retailing at £1.50 a pint, however when we went walkabout the local boozers were even cheaper, some charging as little as 20p a pint. Obviously we got well stuck into it at that price. One pub we were in ran out of beer. As it was pissing down outside we didn't fancy going too far, so took the advice of a couple of locals and went to another bar close by. We got talking to some local lads all dressed in skinhead gear – black Harrington jackets, Fred Perry T-shirts, braces, Levi jeans and Dr Marten boots. They told us of their hatred of blacks, Turks and especially Czechs, then started chanting, 'Nigger, nigger, nigger, rous, rous, rous.' And they meant it.

One Slovak asked which club team I supported. 'Middlesbrough,' I proudly declared. This guy and all his mates started to hug me, shake hands and offer me drinks. 'Nemeth, Szilard Nemeth, he plays for you, he is a hero in Bratislava,' one Slovak screamed at me enthusiastically. Any wariness I had was slowly disappearing and once they found out a lot of the other lads were from Boro we hit it off great. One particular Slovak had consumed more than his fair share of beer and insisted on pulling out a knife, periodically flashing it around. Craggsy told me to keep an eye on him. An hour or so later I was deep in conversation with a lad from London when I heard a commotion outside the front door. I could see Robbie holding his arms out in front of him and the drunken Slovak waving his knife at him. The London lad I had been talking to was out the door before me and with one swift movement disarmed said Slovak, leaving him stood empty-handed (I still can't figure out how he did it). Then Pinky put the Slovak on the deck with one punch. He quickly jumped back to his feet and along with his mates backed off up the road and round a corner. A few minutes had passed, with myself and Robbie expressing our thanks to the Cockney, when back came the Slovaks, this time with a few more mates.

Everyone came out of the pub to make the numbers even, one or two punches were thrown and off they ran again. A few more minutes and they came again. Once more their numbers had grown but once more we sent them scurrying up the street.

'Soon enough they're gonna come back with an army,' one lad remarked.

I took his point. 'Let's fuck off back to the digs before they come back,' I said. 'Here, we'll grab a taxi.' This place was getting naughty. Our digs were in a hotel on the other side of the city, where Baz, a Boro lad, had booked in for £7 a night. As the hotel was full we all stayed in his room, eight of us, on the floor or three to a bed, anywhere as long as it was warm and dry. The next day we heard that a couple of England fans had been shot not far from where we'd had the chew. Hmm, could have easily been us, we concluded. It was still pissing down and word was going round that the match could be postponed. We made for the posh hotel we had met Paddy in the previous day to find out more, as the press were based there. I got talking to John Motson, the TV commentator.

'Now then John, got any tickets?' I asked cheekily.

'Ha, ha, no,' he replied. 'How many are there without tickets then?'

'Oh, quite a few thousand,' another lad chipped in.

'I shall mention that in my commentary,' Motson replied in that distinctive voice of his. I moved away from the poor man as by now he was being tortured off several more fans.

Apparently both the FA and the police had met up through the night to discuss the situation, the outcome being that this game was going ahead 'no matter what', mainly to avoid any potential riot situations and, of course, following the two shootings they did not want the English fans returning to incite any more mayhem. Our tickets had not been forthcoming, so it looked like we would have to rely on the black market or buy a Slovak one. Throughout the day the bars around the city centre filled up with hundreds and hundreds of England fans, in fact there appeared to be more English than Slovaks in most of them. Myself and Pinky decided to go walkabout to sample the atmosphere and seek out tickets, meeting all manner of fans from all quarters of the country: Barnsley, Doncaster, London, Portsmouth, Leeds, Manchester, Hull, you name it they were all there. One set of about fifteen lads from Burnley had me smiling as they marched into the bar all wearing Burberry caps, shirts and Stone Island jackets, identical they were, all aged in their twenties. One of the Burnley lads put up a St George cross with BURNLEY emblazoned across it. This prompted the unveiling of the Boro flag, an enormous royal ensign with MIDDLESBROUGH FC across the middle.

Pinky suggested we make our way to the stadium to find some tickets, as it was 6.30 p.m. and we needed to get sorted. A taxi took us to the home area of the stadium, which was a hive of activity, England and Slovak fans milling around together. Pinky managed to buy a ticket for the Slovak section of the ground for £20 from an England fan. I found Hagar, a Boro ticket tout, who got me one for £20, which was also in the Slovak end, sorted.

While we were hanging around outside the England end a couple of lads from Hull came up and asked, 'Where ya from lads?'

'Boro" I replied.

'Fuck me, we had it with your lot in pre-season, what a game fucking bunch yous are.' Then they proceeded to shake hands.

One of them told us that England fans trying to get in their end had been refused entry, losing their tickets to boot. Straight away Pinky and I offloaded ours to two unsuspecting cockneys for £40 apiece (£20 profit as well, eh). We noticed that the police were only searching for weapons but not checking tickets, so we joined Paddy (who had a ticket) and squeezed our way with the crowd through the police cordon. At the gate (which didn't have a turnstile) we just strolled straight in without being asked for anything, as did hundreds of other England fans. The rain had subsided a little and the end we had was packed, with everyone stood up instead of sitting. It was supposed to hold 4,500 but had more like double that. Craggsy managed to get in before the gates were closed and Robbie scaled the outside fence, ripping his jeans in the process. In the end everyone of our lads made it into the stadium.

Shortly after the game began, Pinky nudged me and pointed to the far side of our end. It was going off between England fans and the police. I don't know what sparked it but a few heads were being cracked open. The police withdrew but as the last cop was heading back down the exit, someone threw a seat at him, smacking him right on the top of his head. I counted to three and sure enough back they came, this time lashing into all and sundry with their batons. It was total indiscriminate violence: women, young kids, they didn't care, the blood was flying all over, people were climbing fences and scrambling over one another to get away. This went on for a good few minutes before it subsided, then you could see a procession of people moving away from the area covered in blood. I noticed that the riot cops had black ski masks on under their helmets and no identity markings on their uniforms. To me they might as well have been hired bouncers such was their disregard for who they beat up.

Back to the match and Slovakia score through guess who, yep, Szilard Nemeth. We had congregated behind our giant flag emblazoned with MIDDLESBROUGH FC and it felt as if the whole England end turned round and stared at us, like it was our fault that a Boro player had scored. I caught the eye of an England fan below me and just smiled and shrugged my shoulders. Into the second half and England find the equaliser followed by the winner, thank fuck for that, 2–1 and the

Burberry-clad hordes were in full voice, 'Eng-er-land, Eng-er-land, Eng-er-land.' The police held us back for about twenty minutes at the end though it was obvious nothing was going to occur.

For our second night we had arranged to stop in Paddy's room at the Holiday Inn, which fortunately was only just down the road from the stadium. The bar was out of beer so we made use of a local Esso garage where you could purchase beer for as little as 10p a can. I sat up most of the night in the hotel lounge talking to lads from Leeds, Tottenham and Millwall. The Millwall lad was nearer my age and had been a Bushwhacker in his early years. He introduced himself by saying, 'There's only three firms in this country, Millwall, Cardiff and Boro.' It was obvious he wasn't Cardiff, so I sat and reminisced about old days and meetings we'd had. The night passed by fairly quick and following no more than two hours shut-eye we were on our way back to Vienna and the trek back home. All in all everyone agreed it had been a great weekend away, with the right result into the bargain.

Next up was Macedonia and a 2–2 draw, followed by little Liechtenstein, who we struggled to beat in a ground smaller than a non-league effort (with a bit of chew in Zurich by all accounts). Next up was the big one, with more than the result riding on it: a political and racial time bomb just waiting to go off. England versus Turkey.

IT WAS PLAIN and obvious that this game was going to be a tinderbox, firstly because two Leeds fans had been killed in Istanbul, secondly because of a host of other match-related incidents concerning the Turks, and thirdly because the game was a must-win for England. As it was being played at the Stadium of Shite and on my doorstep, I made every effort to get a ticket. I cut it quite fine as well but persistence prevailed and I managed to score for a £45 main stand seat. Word went round that something like 200 Boro lads had managed to get

hold of tickets, making for an interesting day indeed, as
obviously the Mackems would be making a show, along with
the Geordies and of course Leeds, who had more reasons
than any to be there.

The lads made their way up by various means, some by
minibus, some on the train and some in their own cars. I
travelled with Robbie and Pinky, arriving at the Burton House,
a pub on Borough Road in Sunderland at the opposite end to
Yates's. The pub already had about thirty Boro lads in,
including Doddsy, the Brick, Oatsy, Billy and a few other
well-known faces. Within fifteen minutes the place had about
seventy lads in and guess who turned up, yes our spotter
friends. By 1 p.m. the place was pretty much filled, with well
over 150 lads, all Boro I might add. I noticed that the police
had encamped outside and it was obvious no-one was going
anywhere without the law in tow. Pinky said, 'I'm not staying
here all day, it's shite stuck in one pub with the Old Bill
outside.' So the two of us went walkabout to a couple of other
pubs. One place just up the road had a fair old mix of boys
from Yorkshire, London, Lancashire and a few young Boro
pups. Everyone we spoke to kept remarking on the fact that
the Burton House was a Boro-only pub, and from what I
could see in this area it was the only pub that seemed to be
exclusively for one set of fans. I don't know what the case was
over the river, where I had heard that most of the Mackems'
main firm were, but it was unique all the same.

A few other lads, including Billy and Hindo, came in
to announce that most were setting off towards the
Monkwearmouth Bridge at 6.45 p.m. Pinky rang Robbie,
who said that they were on the move as they had heard that
Hull's boys were teamed up with the Mackems. Sure enough,
as we supped our pints off there was this long procession of
lads coming up the road from the Burton House. There must
have been well over 170 bodies, which made for a most
impressive sight. I left the pub to track the mob from a

distance of about seventy yards. Glancing up I could see the police helicopter overhead also shadowing their every move.

As the mob snaked its way on to the main road through the city centre, I passed a couple of lads with southern accents, one excitedly exclaiming to the other, 'They're facking Barra, they are, facking Barra, I facking knew they'd be here.'

The same lad walked up to me and asked, 'Where ya from mate.'

'Boro,' came my one-word reply.

'Is that your mob over there?'

'Yeah, they're on their way to the Wheatsheaf.'

'See, I facking told ya, what did I say, what did I facking say? I facking told ya they'd be Barra.'

This guy was really excited. He turned back to me and offered his hand, congratulating us on having the best mob he had seen all day. Pinky was almost falling over himself laughing.

We moved on, as the mob had already started crossing the bridge. I turned to Pinky and said, 'Hey, let's not get too close, this looks like it could turn nasty. There's police all over them. Nowt's gonna happen here other than getting your collar felt, just keep a sensible distance, I wanna see the game.' Pinky concurred and we took a different route adjacent to the mob. The bridge appeared to be undergoing some repairs and most of it was masked off. This was where we lost sight of the mob. As we exited on the other side we were met by several lines of police; it was obvious that something had gone off and even more obvious it involved the Boro mob, as everyone had dissipated in different directions. Pinky and myself continued walking towards the Wheatsheaf, spotting Billy and a couple of others on the way. Billy asked where everyone had gone.

'Don't know mate, we lost everyone going over the bridge,' I replied.

'Didn't you see what happened?' he said. 'A mob of lads came from the side and it all went off, then the law moved in and everyone scattered. The Mackems thought we were Geordies, they were all shouting, "The Mags are here." Daft fuckers.'

Billy was really excited and suggested we make our way towards the Wheatsheaf. Just as we got outside there was a large crowd of lads, not Boro. I suggested keeping quiet until we sussed out the situation. Then a big squad of police in riot gear moved in, charging everyone down a side street. I tried to stand in one place with my hands up defensively only to be shoved from behind by a rather large cop insisting I move away from the area. As I strolled down the same street I came face to face with a large, angry mob, teasing and chanting at the police, who made a baton charge. Away I went. I ended up walking through a trading estate back to where I had started near the bridge. I checked out the time and with forty minutes to kick-off I decided to make my way to the stadium.

I clocked Oatsy on the way and stood with him having a smoke and chatting about what had been happening. Then just outside the ground I noticed some Turkish fans arriving on buses. They were escorted by police vans and motorcycle riders with a helicopter overhead. That did not stop several hundred lads trying to have a go, and as the coaches slowed down I noticed some were trying to pull the doors open while others were throwing anything they could get their hands on. I spoke to some lads nearby who told me they were from Leeds and most of the lads having a go at the coaches were from Leeds. Understandable I suppose, but pointless all the same as several arrests were made.

The police were now getting very heavy-handed so I left to go in the ground and, I must say, even though I'm not too fond of our Mackem cousins, they do have a fantastic stadium and I always like to give credit where it's due. I have only ever been in the away end but tonight I had a seat in the main stand and what a good view I had, just above and to the left of the players' tunnel. The atmosphere was very tense, especially when the players lined up for the national anthems. Ours was sung with passion and gusto, as always, but the Turks' was booed and catcalled throughout.

The game got underway and England took the initiative from the off, with young Rooney putting himself about like a veteran. Southgate (shame on you Sven) had been left out of the squad to be replaced by Sol Campbell, who I must admit had quite a good game. The atmosphere was building up all the time and I feared the worst every time the Turks got near our goal but the lads held firm. If they had scored there would have probably been a riot. As it was England scored first to settle the nerves and send several Burberry-clad youngsters onto the pitch in celebration, joined (it has to be said) by the players. By the time Beckham wrapped things up with a penalty (and another pitch invasion) England were coasting. This great victory had put us top of the qualifying group and in the driving seat. I left the ground happy and looking to find our lads, who had congregated near the Black Cats club. Not only did I find them but so did our intrepid spotter police – they're getting good these fellas. With there not being any trains to the Boro we had to go up to Newcastle in order to travel down to Darlo – this is the twenty-first century as well. At Newcastle we found out the train was delayed, so I jumped in a taxi with Paddy and a couple of other lads, which only cost us a tenner each all the way home.

The following day I checked out the Frontline website (you find out more about what goes on there than in the papers). It was most amusing to read about the Mackems and Geordies getting pulled, along with a large Leeds lock-up rate, all for next to nothing. It seems the law can now lock you up just because you look as if you're going to cause bother. There were also a lot of posts congratulating Boro on turning out a 'most impressive firm' that had not gone unnoticed. I for one could not believe how many fans had been arrested, over 100. Yes there were a few minor altercations and yes some lads did have a token go at the Turks and yes there was some racist chanting and yes a few young boys went on the pitch to celebrate the goals, but let's look at the real story. A riot? No. Organised gang warfare? All a load of exaggerated hype brewed up by the media. And why is it racist when England fans sing certain songs such as 'Rule Britannia' and 'God Save The Queen' or boo another country's national anthem. The Turks call us 'infidels'; is that racism? They threaten to kill our fans and players; is that inciting a riot? The Scots boo our anthem and sing 'Flower of Scotland', a rebel song if ever I heard one; is that racist? I believe everyone is just going over the top on all this and making mountains out of molehills. In my opinion there's nothing wrong with other countries being proud of their own heritage just as I'm proud of mine, so Rule Britannia, God save her Maj and thank your lucky stars if you're born in God's green acre, wherever it may be. End of rant.

The next and I must say biggest occasion to follow England as far as I am concerned was not too far away. The Slovakia game was to be played at my beloved Riverside Stadium, although following events at the Stadium of Shite it was touch and go whether the game would be played behind closed doors or not. Sanity prevailed and the FA got stuffed for £70,000 (chicken feed) and a warning for the fans to behave or else. The internet was alive with threats about what was going to happen, who was coming to Boro mob-handed, who was going to invade Gilzeans, even some little cyber warrior from Slovakia got in on the act saying they were going to have us over. The Mackems threatened to send us back into our little smoggy hidey holes, Leeds as usual threatened to throw everything including the kitchen sink at us, all shite of course, but the police were straight onto it, believing every word and arranging a massive presence to ensure a peaceful night would be had by all.

If they wanted to know the crack they just had to look at where the tickets had been sold: fifty-five per cent to TS post codes, another ten per cent to South Durham areas and another ten per cent to North Yorkshire; that's somewhere around seventy-five per cent of fans more than likely to be from within a fifty-mile radius of Teesside and also more than likely to be Boro supporters. What does that leave? No more of a full following of away fans than you would get for an FA cup tie. Mind, you can't rest easy, as it only takes a couple of hundred to cause a bit of chew. Szilard Nemeth, Boro's Slovak import, had also stoked up things by being 'misquoted' in the *Sun* newspaper as saying, 'Middlesbrough was a dump, the food was shite and the lasses were ugly fuckers,' or words to that effect. We had heard all this before from other imports, and by the way Szil I've seen some of the 'dogs' in Bratislava and they don't exactly set your pulse racing either.

Word had got out about my writing this book and I was contacted by the BBC for a documentary they were making concerning the match. I met with one of their researchers and agreed to an interview, this resulted in me spending ninety minutes getting quizzed in a local bar while the England vs Serbia Montenegro game was on (one or two of the locals weren't best pleased as the cameras rolled). I made my apologies and probably I'll regret doing the interview, as those ninety minutes were to be edited down to three, not reflecting a true account of what I said. All the BBC interviewer was interested in was getting me to say something sensational, how the Frontline was planning to attack any visiting firms, and so on. I wanted to talk about my book and, although they promised to include a mention, they didn't. I was stitched up – they only made a brief mention of the book on the six o'clock news. Ah well, I've done some silly things in my time and this will rank among the silliest but as Andy Warhol once said, 'Everyone will be famous for fifteen minutes,' so this was to be mine.

On the day of the match, I went into Redcar for a few drinks in the Hydro. The police called in five times before 3 p.m. Apparently there had been a rumour that Hull (again) were bringing a mob to Redcar. There were some strangers in attendance, a group of six lads all in England shirts up from Stevenage; no problem lads, have a drink and enjoy yourselves. I moved on up to Boro for 3.30 p.m. to drink in the pre-match atmosphere. Surprisingly (not) there wasn't the huge influx of visitors that everyone expected. Sure I saw some lads from Manchester (good friends of Boro lads), some from Barnsley (decked out in England flags), and heard the usual sprinkling of southern accents (ones and twos, no mobs, where have they been hiding since Wembley was razed?). Oh and there was a 40-strong mob of Stoke boys who didn't want trouble but wanted to know why they had not got much of a mention in this book. Well sorry lads but if it hasn't happened it doesn't go in. One big rumour going around was that Forest had a handy-looking firm and that a decent mob of Hartlepool were in town (Hartlepool? Yep, Pool had a firm out).

After doing the rounds of a few pubs, including Lloyds bar, the Central, Wetherspoons and Huxters, I made my way to 'home base', Gilzeans, which, no surprise, was heaving with Boro's finest. Bri had took his son round to the Bridge pub to avoid what he thought might happen and as I went round to join him I walked into a fair old kick-off between some Boro lads and the mob of Forest I had heard about. It did not last long as the police were in quick but all the same a few slaps were dished out. As I made my way up to the ground I noticed one or two more little altercations though nothing serious. At the ground I met the BBC1 camera crew who collared me for a quick word on the day's events, very quick in fact as bugger all had happened to tell. Into the ground and the national anthems, impeccably observed by all; what else do you expect, I wanted to go to Euro 2004 as well you know.

The first half was absolute crap, with England struggling against a very ordinary Slovakia, who took the lead from an innocuous free kick (David James where were you?). The second half was something different altogether. England came out with purpose and soon had the fans rocking to 'Pigbag' (Boro's signature tune) as Michael Owen thumped in the first from the penalty spot and followed up shortly after with a superb header which screeched into the roof of the net, phew! With the Turks also winning on the night (amid crowd trouble it has to be said; Uefa wont ban them though) this made the result even more important.

After the game I made my way back into town with Bri and a few of the lads, clocking one or two little slaps being dished out though once again nothing more than you would see at most games. I had a couple of beers in Gilzeans and took a cab home as nothing untoward looked to be occurring. It was not the sort of great ending you might expect from a book about football and the violence associated with it. When I heard Boro would be hosting this match I fully expected every firm in England to come through to show their strength and even delayed the completion in the expectation that this final chapter would be the icing on the cake. Well as with football's greatest games, these things never pan out as you would expect.

CHAPTER SIXTEEN

Interrogation

YOU MAY RECALL earlier I told of a serious incident involving an attack on Barnsley's firm in 1984. On the Middlesbrough Frontline website was posted this account of a police interrogation on a lad involved and charged with the incident. I personally think it is very poignant and, above all, true. I know well the two lads involved.

Middlesbrough is a cold, unwelcoming place. A mad February wind whips off the North East coast, driving rain into your face with the force of air rifle pellets. A youth of seventeen years sits smoking in the warmth of a police station interviewing room. Two fat detectives sit across the table. The year is 1984.

Interview commences at 10.15 a.m., 20th February

Q. *Do you understand exactly why you've been arrested?*
A. *You've told me, yeah.*
Q. *You've been arrested on suspicion of assault, that is to say, we are alleging that you have assaulted some Barnsley supporters?*
A. *Yeah, right.*
Q. *I'm going to ask you some questions about your whereabouts and movements on Saturday, 11th February 1984, which is the date that Middlesbrough played Barnsley at home. Did you go to the town centre on that date?*
A. *I went to that match, yes.*

Q. What time did you arrive at the town centre?

A. Let me think, I finished work half twelve, went home, got washed and changed, had some scran then got the bus into town. It would have been about twenty-five to two.

Q. Which bus did you catch?

A. It would have been the number 94 or the 98.

Q. Cleveland Transit bus?

A. Yeah.

Q. What happened when you arrived at the town centre?

A. I heard there'd been a ruck and there were boys all over, like. Everyone was stood around at the lights near the town hall and the bank, watching what was happening. Big gangs everywhere and coppers everywhere. That's where I was. I went to see.

Q. Is this when you got off the bus?

A. Yeah.

Q. So, what you are alleging is that you arrived in the town AFTER the fighting at the Wellington public house took place?

A. Yes. Not long after, though.

Q. Well, we have interviewed many people regarding this incident and I believe that you were in fact present when the fighting took place and that you are not telling the truth.

A. Well, I believe this interview is a big waste of time and effort. You're just wasting paper on me.
(pause)

Q. I have examined your hands and noticed a one-inch cut on your right thumb.

A. So?

Q. Where did you get this cut?

A. Throwing some glass into a skip.
(longer pause)

Q. Do you know a lad called —— ———?

A. Yes, I do. Why?

Q. If he says he saw you on Albert Road and spoke to you … is he lying?

A. *Yes.*

Q. *Why would he make such allegations?*

A. *I don't know. Honestly, I can't remember if I spoke to him. I don't know.*

Q. *Did you speak to him at the match?*

A. *Yes, I think I did.*

Q. *What conversation did you have?*

A. *On about London, 'cause he said he'd been to London, gone to find a job or summat.*

Q. *Who else was present during this conversation?*

A. *Just me.*

Q. *Did you show him your cut?*

A. *Why should I show him my cut?*

Q. *It seems very strange indeed that he would know that you had a cut on your thumb in the exact same place as he told the police unless you pointed it out to him.*

A. *What are you trying to say?*

Q. *I'm trying to say that the injury to your thumb was sustained in a fight outside the Wellington public house on Albert Road on Saturday, 11th February.*

A. *Wrong.*

Q. *Are you denying that the injury was caused on that date and are you also denying that you showed the injury to —— —— —?*

A. *I'm denying the lot.*

Q. *You maintain that you were on Albert Road by yourself and that you were on your own in the ground?*

A. *Yes.*

Q. *—— —— says that when he spoke to you at half-time, we'll discuss that conversation later, you were with a friend. He said that you were with this same friend on Albert Road too, and that this friend was sat next to you in the Clive Road End of the ground. So, the question is, who were you sitting with?*

A. *I was sat with loads of people in the East End. A big gang of lads sit right behind that goal every game.*

Q. Who was the lad with his front teeth missing?

A. I haven't a clue.

Q. Well, it's strange that —— —— has made a statement saying he saw you in Albert Road with this character, he saw you at half-time at the hotdog stand with him and he sat with the pair of you for the whole of the second half.

A. I dunno, he may have done. I know loads of people. I'm well known. *(1)*

Q. So, we've established that what —— —— has said in his statement to the police is true in many respects. It's only the parts which implicate you in the fighting outside the Wellington pub which you are denying. And he must be psychic to know that you had an injury to your thumb.

A. I told you how I did the thumb.

Q. And you refuse to tell us who you went to the match with?

A. I told you I went by myself and that's true.

Q. I'll ask you again. Why would he implicate you in the fighting outside the Wellington public house?

A. Does he say he seen me fighting?

Q. Yes. He also implicates many others, some of whom have already been charged. Have you got an answer to that?

A. I don't believe he said it. I don't think I'll answer it 'cause it's pathetic.

Q. Why don't you believe that —— —— has made a full statement implicating you?

A. It sounds daft. It sounds as if you are making it up.

Q. I can assure you that everything I have said about —— —— — is true, because he was there and I wasn't. Do you understand?

A. Yes.

   (pause)

Q. Let us talk now about what was said during your conversation with —— —— at half-time, near the hotdog stand. What were you talking about?

A. He said that he'd been to London looking for work.

Q. Did you discuss the fighting outside the Wellington?

A. We were on about how there had been some fighting there, yes.

Q. What did you say?

A. That we heard that someone had been carved up. We were on about somebody being slashed.

Q. How did you know this?

A. Oh, you hear everything, don't you. There's that many mouths going, you don't know what's true and what isn't.

Q. He says that you understood there to have been six people slashed outside the Wellington, that the police would now be looking for you and that you and your mate would now have to sneak out of the ground at the end of the game.

A. He's talking rubbish! I've never heard such dribble.

Q. At this point I will ask you again, who is the other lad who was present?

A. Honestly, I don't know who it was. (long pause) All right, I'll tell you about it. I had just met two lads who came from the railway station. I knew they were from Redcar. As we were walking past the 'Welly' the doors opened and the Barnsley fans steamed into us. As we were fighting, a gang of Boro boys ran toward us and there was a battle. I never had a clue some of them had knives. Then the Old Bill turned up and I legged it.

Q. So, how did you get the cut on your thumb?

A. Dunno, it looked like a slash to me.

Q. Okay, so tell us from the beginning, after you left work that day, how did you get to Middlesbrough and what you were doing down there at the railway station?

A. I got off the bus next to the Cleveland Centre and walked up to the Zetland pub. That's where everyone hangs out before the match, like.

Q. Did you go in the Zetland?

A. No, I looked in the window but nobody was there.

Q. When you reached Albert Road, in company with these two lads from Redcar, who you say you met at the railway station, did you see anybody else stood about near the Wellington?

A. No.

Q. Well, the fighting you have described to us is an incident we believe happened some minutes after an earlier incident in which the police moved on numerous Boro supporters from the Wellington pub (2). I can't accept that when you came round the corner there weren't numerous supporters congregated on just about every junction, waiting for the Barnsley supporters to come out.

A. None that I saw. We were scrapping then they all came running toward us. There was about twenty Boro came running, against about sixty Barnsley.

Q. What you're saying is, basically, that you and your two friends were the first people to be involved in the fighting?

A. We had no other option. They came at us.

Q. What exactly were you doing when the Barnsley supporters came out of the pub doorway?

A. I remember getting punched on the back of my head and I turned around and there was these Barnsley lads swinging at me. There was no way I could get away, so the best thing I could do was defend myself.
   11.15 a.m. Break – Refreshments given – Meal refused.
   11.56 a.m. Resume.

Q. I'm going to ask you some questions now about your clothing that day. Can you remember what you were wearing?

A. Yes. Samba training shoes, faded jeans, T-shirt, I'm not sure what colour, and a pretty dark blue v-necked Fred Perry jumper. I might have been wearing my ski jacket, I'm not sure.

* * *

At this point, one of the interviewing officers waddled out of the room. A squad car was dispatched to an address in Grangetown, one of the most notoriously unruly council estates in Middlesbrough at the time. The authorities, ever keen to point out the positive aspects of this area would say, for example, that it was once the *home of popular comedian, Roy 'Chubby' Brown, who made himself a millionaire by swearing and telling blue jokes. Everyone in Grangetown swore and told blue jokes but 'Chubby' had the good sense to call it an act and the courage to get up on the stage. A very clever bloke. Personally, I think he's shite.*

One day, I was in Massey's newsagents on the corner of Bolckow Road buying some tobacco. The front page of the newspaper on the counter drew my attention. It was a picture of my next-door neighbours holding up a big rat by the tail. They said they had found it in their oven. The thing that puzzled me was why they were smiling in the picture, as if they had won the Lottery or something. Some months later, the whole street was knocked down. Everyone was 'relocated' and the council gave us all a cheque for a thousand pounds, moving allowance, so in a way that dead rat really was a winning Lottery ticket.

Anyway, to get back to the story, I had spent all that morning fitting some lino in the bathroom when there was a knock at the door. With Stanley knife still in hand, I absent-mindedly answered the door without first sneaking a look out of an upstairs window. I was met with the sight of two uniformed constables who explained that our kid had been arrested and that they had come to collect some items of his clothing. When I asked to see a search warrant they noticed and seemed very interested in the gap in my front teeth.

Q. On match, days you said that you meet your friends at the Zetland pub?

A. Usually, it depends who is playing.

Q. Why do you all meet there and not, say, at a pub nearer towards Ayresome Park?

A. Because, you might meet them off the train.

Q. Are you talking about away supporters?

A. Yes.

Q. Are you a supporter who could be described as one of the 'boys'?

A. Yes.

Q. What exactly are the 'boys'? What purpose, in football terms, does the 'boys' mean?

A. It's just a fashion, like punks or skins. The boys are the Service Crew, like the Chelsea Headhunters or the ICF from West Ham or the Intercity Crew from Leeds. They are runners. (3)

Q. So, when you are talking about Service Crews are we talking about football supporters who travel on the normal service trains and who look for fights with opposing supporters?

A. Yes, they are after a reputation.

Q. Are the Middlesbrough boys trying to get a reputation?

A. Yes, well, they've got one now.

Q. So, the purpose of you going on Saturday, to the Zetland, was to meet your friends and to see if any Barnsley supporters turned up on the service trains to have a fight?

A. Yes.

Q. Is it common knowledge amongst Boro supporters that the boys meet near the Zetland to meet opposing fans travelling on the trains?

A. If it's Chelsea or Newcastle there would be a big turnout but if it was Shrewsbury or Watford there'd be nobody.

Q. So, on that Saturday you went to meet your friends but there was nobody there. Where did you think they were?

A. I don't know. I don't think the Barnsley fans were expected because if they had been there would have been a big mob there and they wouldn't have got to the Welly.

Q. What would have happened?

A. They'll have been fighting as soon as they stepped out of the station.

Q. When the fighting took place, how many were from Middlesbrough?

A. About twenty.

Q. Would you say they were all boys?

A. You can't tell now, there's that many now who dress like the boys.

Q. Do you think it's a fair assumption to say that the word had spread amongst the Middlesbrough boys in the town centre that day and within a short period of time they had assembled near or in close vicinity of the Wellington?

A. They must have done.

Q. Well, how do you know that?

A. Because as soon as the Barnsley fans came out of the pub door and fighting started they turned up, so they must have been close by.

Q. So, do you think that the boys were waiting for the fans to leave the pub and start fighting then?

A. They must have known where they were to have come so quick. Soon as they came out.

Q. So, it's just unlucky, in your version of events, that you just happened to be walking past.

A. Yes.

Q. Who are these two lads from Redcar that you met off the station?

A. I don't know their names, and that's true.

Q. Were any of them carrying weapons? Were you?

A. No, I never get tooled up, no, it sickens me when people get tooled up, especially blacks. (4)

Q. Did you see anybody else with weapons of any description?

A. No, I was just trying to defend myself. You don't look what others are doing, do you?

Q. How long exactly would you say that you were fighting?

A. I don't know how long it lasted, about thirty seconds at most.

Q. Were you present all of the time between the Barnsley fans leaving the pub and the police arriving on the scene?

A. Yes.

Q. You have said there was about twenty Middlesbrough supporters and about sixty Barnsley supporters fighting, surely you could see if any of the Middlesbrough supporters had knives?

A. You don't watch other people fighting when you're trying to save your own skin.

Q. You have admitted kicking and punching Barnsley supporters and you have admitted being punched yourself. Is that right?

A. Yes.

Q. Were you shouting?

A. Why would I shout?

Q. Was there any shouting?

A. I didn't take any notice, there may have been some noise, yeah.

Q. You have said that Middlesbrough's boys have a reputation for not being runners, do you think this is an example of them standing their ground when they could easily have prevented the trouble had they left the scene?

A. It wouldn't surprise me.

Q. How many Barnsley fans did you hit?

A. Dunno.

Q. How did you get the injury to your hand?

A. Dunno.

Q. Who else did you see fighting?

A. I told you. I don't notice anyone when I'm trying to look after my own hide.

Q. You didn't see anyone you recognised at all?

A. No.

Q. Have you seen the newspapers? The names of the people who have been charged already?

A. Yes.

Q. Do you know any of them?

A. I've heard of —————— 'cause I used to live near him.

Q. Did you see him fighting?

A. I didn't even see him.

Q. Do you think it was a Middlesbrough supporter or a Barnsley supporter who slashed you?

A. I don't know.

Q. You have seen the amount of people who have been injured. Did you see the pictures on television of all the blood outside the pub? Did you see any blood on the floor at all?

A. No.

Q. *Did you see any Barnsley supporter go down?*

A. No.

Q. *Did you get your injury as a result of a direct slash to your hand or was it caused in the thick of the fighting?*

A. *I haven't a clue, it could have been some lunatic running through and swiping everybody for all I know.*
(pause)

Q. *Are you trying to tell me that you were totally unaware that any Barnsley supporters were in the Wellington before you got outside the public house?*

A. *Yes, the only time I knew who they were was when I was punched in the head and I turned round and saw that they weren't from Boro.*

Q. *Have you got any blood stains on your clothing that you wore that day?*

A. *I think I had a bit on me jumper, on the cuff.*

Q. *Has it been washed?*

A. Yes.

Q. *Did you have a handkerchief with you that day?*

A. No.

Q. —— —— *has said that during the match you produced a blood-stained handkerchief from your pocket and threw it to the ground.*

A. *I had a tissue. It was stained from my hand. I got it from the Central.*

Q. *He says further that when he stopped to talk to you, on Albert Road, you were with a lad who was about six foot tall with his front teeth missing, and he saw you with him in the ground. Who was this person?*

A. *I don't know who it was, there was no-one like that.*

Q. *Did you see a lad wearing a Burberry jacket outside the Wellington?*

A. No.

Q. *Did you see anyone with a hairstyle like* —— ——?

A. Can't say I noticed.

Q. How well do you know ———?

*A. I know him from the matches. I used to talk to him last season.
I seen him once at the British Steel Gala. I know him quite
well.*

Q. Is he a troublemaker?

A. I think so, yes.

Q. Did you see him fighting?

A. I didn't see anyone fighting.

*Q. I believe you were aware of the trouble that was about to take
place outside the Wellington prior to you getting there and
your explanations to date are not the truth. I believe that the
Boro boys were waiting on Albert Road. I believe that you
knew this and could have avoided the Wellington had you so
desired, and that when the Barnsley fans came out of the pub
you were one of the first group of Boro supporters to attack
them.*

*A. You're wrong. There was three of us. Do you expect three of us
to attack sixty? You would have to be a right birdbrain. As we
were walking past the doors opened, the Barnsley fans came
out.*

*Q. You say they outnumbered the Middlesbrough supporters, by
about three to one. Why do you think that the Barnsley
supporters suddenly came out of the pub and started fighting?*

A. Obviously, that is what they were after – trouble.

*Q. Judging by the injuries they sustained and the lack of injuries
sustained by the Middlesbrough supporters, they obviously got
the trouble?*

A. I should think so.

*Q. Is it usual for Middlesbrough supporters to drink in public
houses on away visits and then suddenly come out and attack
the first people they come across?*

*A. Well, if the Barnsley lads were getting taunted, they must have
come outside looking for trouble.*

Q. And then just happened to meet three Middlesbrough supporters who by your own admission look for trouble with away supporters anyway?

A. *Doesn't it happen? Obviously it happens 'cause it did happen.*

Q. *Do you think that any persons working on Albert Road, or walking along Albert Road, not connected with the fighting at all would have been frightened?*

A. *I should think they would be, yeah, they would be. (5)*

Q. *Do you still maintain that you were in no position, even amongst eighty people, to leave the scene of the fighting?*

A. *I didn't have time to think about getting away.*

Q. *Even if you had an opportunity to get away, do you think you would have gone away and left your mates?*

A. *No, I don't think I would have done.*

Interview concluded at 4.40 p.m.

To be in a police station holding cell, especially sober, is one of life's most depressing experiences. The buzzing noise drives you up the wall, the smell of well-used Dunlopillo mattress, but mostly the company one is forced to endure. I had the pleasure of meeting a facially tattooed paraffin lamp whose forte was hitting selected Asda customers over the head with an empty bottle then running away with the carrier bags. When my turn for interview arrived, I had to stop myself from hugging and thanking the policeman who came to fetch me.

In the interview room the policeman did the talking and a hard-faced blonde policewoman was taking his dictation. He began this long spiel, something along the lines of, 'I put it to you that on the 11th of February blah blah blah . . .' I said nothing for a good few seconds and he looked at me expectantly. 'Well?' he said. I retorted that he hadn't indeed asked me a question to which I could answer. The blonde one screamed loudly at me.

'Don't be so fucking pedantic!'

I didn't reply as she looked like she could handle herself. I stonewalled them for ten minutes or so until the policeman *sighed and handed me a ream of A4, helpfully pointing a fat finger at the paragraph that implicated me in the whole affair. My spirit was broken. It was a fair cop. They let me out on bail shortly after being interviewed and if Middlesbrough can be said to have any fresh air, I was breathing it in deeply at that moment.*

★ ★ ★

Time interview commenced – 6.35 p.m. – Prisoner cautioned.

Q. *Since we last spoke we have been making enquiries into the person whom we believe was with you outside the Wellington and who later accompanied you to the match that afternoon. Who do you say it is?*

A. *Dunno, is it one of —— ——'s mates?*

Q. *The description of the person we have been trying to trace is six foot tall, slim build, short brown straight hair and with teeth missing at the front. Do you know who this is?*

A. *It's the wrong description. There's nobody of that description with me or near me, I don't think.*

Q. *Do you go to many matches?*

A. *Not now.*

Q. *Who did you go to the match with on Saturday gone?*

A. *A bunch of lads from Eston. (6)*

Q. *Do you ever go with your brother?*

A. *No, he hardly goes, apart from cup matches and that.*

Q. *Did your brother go on Saturday, to the cup match against Notts County?*

A. *Yes.*

Q. *Can you describe your brother to me?*

A. *He's about six foot, slim build, skinny anyway, twenty-four, dark short brown hair.*

Q. *What about his teeth?*

A. *What's wrong with his teeth? You don't think it's him do you?*

Q. I'll ask you again, what about his teeth. Are there any missing?

A. I'm sure there isn't.

Q. I've just seen your brother and he has two teeth missing at least on the top palate at the front.

A. He hasn't.

Q. Look I'm not prepared to argue with you over this issue as I have just spoken to your brother. Furthermore, he says that on the day of the Barnsley match he met you near the Zetland and accompanied you to the match, which he regularly does.

A. He doesn't. Have you got him in, like?

Q. Yes, he has been arrested. Do you now wish to change your story concerning the events of this Saturday?

A. Yes, I do. Look, I'm sick of messing you about over this. I want to tell the truth.

Q. So you want to tell us all about it?

A. Well, I met me brother down the town. We saw a gang of lads walking over towards the Welly and we went over to them to find out what was going on. They said there was Barnsley fans in there. The doors were locked so we just began walking about in circles, just waiting.

Q. So, you met these lads who told you about the Barnsley fans and then you walked over to the Wellington pub with them. Did they have any intentions of causing any trouble?

A. That's what they were going round for.

Q. How did you know that?

A. It's obvious, innit? They were walking towards the Welly and there's Barnsley fans in there.

Q. Did you think that they were looking for a fight?

A. Yeah.

Q. After receiving this information about the Barnsley fans did you then join this gang and intend to look for a fight yourself?

A. Yes.

Q. Did you stay with this gang?

A. No. Me and our kid and this other lad began walking off.

Q. Who was this other lad?

A. Haven't a clue. He was quite small, short dark hair, burgundy leather jacket and a grandad shirt. He looked about sixteen or seventeen. Average build.

Q. Outside the Wellington, did your gang start shouting and taunting the Barnsley fans inside?

A. No. They weren't shouting. One lad, like, he was jumping on the windowsill and looking in.

Q. Who was he?

A. Dunno.

Q. What was he doing on the windowsill?

A. He was just looking in, shaking his head at them.

Q. Do you mean he was taunting them?

A. Yes.

Q. Were any supporters shouting words like 'Come on'?

A. There was no shouting.

Q. Do you think the Barnsley fans knew there was Middlesbrough fans outside?

A. Oh, yes.

Q. If the Barnsley fans had come out in an orderly fashion and began to walk up Albert Road towards the town centre, do you think it would have made any difference or do you think the Middlesbrough fans were intent on trouble anyway?

A. Trouble.

(pause)

Q. So, after you left the main gang outside the Welly where did they go and where did the three of you go?

A. Just walked round the corner, just walking in circles, I think.

Q. Were you waiting for the Barnsley fans to come out?

A. Yes, we were.

Q. So, you were walking past the Wellington entrance doors one time and then what happened?

A. We heard banging noises from inside and the sound of locks being undone then the doors flew open. Barnsley came out and ran at us. I was punched on the back of the head then I retaliated and ended up fighting about three lads until the others arrived.

Q. When you say fighting, what were you doing?

A. Punching and kicking.

Q. I appreciate that the Barnsley fans may have come out at first but in all honesty, do you think they had any other option open to them, after all, all of the Boro boys were going to start fighting anyway?

A. I agree.

Q. Did you see any others fighting?

A. No, I was too busy fending for myself.

Q. Did you enjoy it?

A. I enjoy a ruck but when I found out about the blades it made me sick.

Q. Finally, is there anything else that you would now like to tell the police about the incident, which you haven't told us already?

A. No, that's it.

   (pause)

Q. Your brother was fighting as well, is that correct?

A. Yes.

Interview and my liberty concluded at 8 p.m.

After a day-long interview my kid brother had bravely withstood every attempt to make him admit to seeing anyone but himself fighting. A devious copper, trained in the black arts of interviewing technique, caught him with a sucker punch right on the final bell. By relaxing his guard, by inwardly sighing to himself that it was all over, he wasn't mentally prepared for that final question, just like that fictional character in the film 'The Great Escape'.

   The case subsequently went to trial. The jury found us all guilty and the judge meted out thirty-nine years between the thirteen defendants. The harshest sentences ever awarded for football hooligan related crimes. The largest individual sentence was six years. In a cell below the courts, one of the defendants had burned in match smoke the words:

BORO 6 BARNSLEY 0

We had gotten for ourselves the reputation as the best hooligan outfit in the country. Some say that we were lucky to get thrown in jail as a lot of local noses were put out of joint by our actions, not least of which being the landlord of the Wellington public house. The football club we followed didn't appreciate our reputation as much as we ourselves did, as it kept away the frightened moneyed middle classes, who at that time preferred sports such as tennis and golf over football. Nor were potential commercial sponsors too keen on investing their name and money in a club whose public image had been so badly tarnished. In 1986, Middlesbrough Football Club couldn't afford to pay their players' wages and the gates to Ayresome Park were padlocked shut by the receivers.

They have since risen phoenix-like from the ashes, recently hosting the first full England International match in Middlesbrough since 1937 at their new multi-million-pound stadium by the riverside. This was voted the friendliest and safest stadium to visit in 2003 and boasts the highest percentage of female supporters in the country. Yes it's a whole new ball game these days.

* * *

Appendix

(1) *The youth appears full of pride in his notoriety. The boast of being 'well known' is more than mere bravado, though. In provincial towns like Middlesbrough the main hooligan faces really were as famous as most of the football club's players.*

(2) *The interviewing officer seems to be saying that the Wellington pub was cleared of Middlesbrough supporters in order to facilitate a large group of Barnsley fans known to be arriving*

shortly by train. This would explain not only the close attention they received by Middlesbrough supporters but also explains how the police arrived on the scene so soon after only thirty seconds of fighting.

(3) Notice here how happily this easily led teenager is singing like a bird about the 'new' fashion he has adopted, and his concern for reputation.

(4) This use of this word 'blacks' doesn't sit right. The interviewing officer may have misheard the word 'blades' as 'blacks'. This would make more contextual sense. A more cynical commentator could say it was an example of how the police used words in statements in ways that blacken the character of the accused (before taped interviews), such as leaving in local dialects verbatim (went round me dad's house, rather than **my** dad's house). Even though the police officer himself has the same dialect usage his questioning will use the Queen's English.

(5) By agreeing to this seemingly harmless question the accused has given up his relatively light common assault charge and has left himself open to the more serious charge of affray, and with it a likely jail sentence.

(6) Microsoft Word's spell checker amusingly offered 'Eton' as an alternative spelling.

CHAPTER SEVENTEEN

Songs For The Boys

I WAS ONCE asked the question, 'Why don't Boro's firm ever do much singing?' by a Chelsea fan at an England match. Well we usually leave that sort of stuff for your shirt-clad regular choirboys, who at times have been as impressive as the famous Kop at Liverpool ever was. I myself enjoy a good sing-song, as do most of our intrepid Frontline lads, however we usually have our own songs that are never heard at matches, songs that have stood the test of time but, because they contain several verses of more than twenty words, the choirboys are usually too thick or impatient to learn. The following are a few examples of our ditties.

> I love to go a-wandering, along the cliffs of Dover
> And if I see a Mackem scum, I'll kick the bastard over
> Tra-la-la, Tra-la-la, Tra-la-la, Tra-la-la-la-la-la-la-la-la-la.

> I found an old stocking and filled it with lead
> I hit a sad Geordie right over the head
> A copper came to me to ask me my name
> So I gave him the answer with a bicycle chain
> (this goes on for several verses)

> I was walking through the park one day
> In the very merry month of May
> To a Sun'lan' skin's surprise

T'was a bottle 'tween the eyes
And this is what the Holgate sang
Oh what a lovely bunch of dozy cunts
La la la la la la la la la la

With Ayresome Park in my heart, keep me Boro
With Ayresome Park in my heart, I pray
With Ayresome Park in my heart, keep me Boro
Keep me Boro to my dying day
No surrender, no surrender, no surrender
To the Sun-der-land SCUM!
(We also do the England version)

Beer, beer, we want more beer
All the lads are cheering
Get the fucking beer in
Beer, beer, we want more beer
All the lads are cheering NOW

From the blue banks of the River Tees to the shores of
     Babylon
We will fight, fight, fight for Middlesbro' till we're in
     Division One
To hell with Man United, Sunderland and West Brom
We will fight, fight, fight for Middlesbro' till we're in
     Division One.

Some of Boro's divisions had their own 'signature tunes', for
example, long before Man Utd ever started singing it the
townies had:

Country road take me home
To the place I belong
Middlesboro, south of Sunlan
Take me home, country road

The Redcar lads had:

> The old Starlight is big and bright
> Deep in the heart of Redcar
> You can get a fight if you play your cards right
> Deep in the heart of Redcar

The Dormo boys had:

> Rockin' rollin' ridin'
> All along the way
> All bound for Dormanstown
> And the ol' Fairway
> Somewhere there is sunshine
> Somewhere there is rain
> Somewhere there is Dormanstown
> And the 'ol Fairway

The Eston boys had:

> I was walking through Eston 'bout a quarter to two
> Saw my favourite honey an' she gave me a chew
> Nothin' could be finer, being a mad miler
> Chew, chew, chew, we are the Eston few

One that I and a couple of mates wrote, that everyone likes to join in with, goes:

> Sunrise, that was a bender the lads took me on
> I've never bin that drunk since I was twenty-one
> I'll do it again, have no fear
> 'Cos I did what I did for the beer.

> Last night went to a nightclub, stayed there till three
> Spent thirty quid not a penny on me

I know it's a lot and it's dear
But I did what I did for the beer

Midnight tapped up this girlie, she'd been looking at me
A real sausage queen, yes a one from Page Three
Grabbed me arm, I said, 'Ow listen here
Steady on luv yer spilling me beer'

Sunrise after the bender the lads took me on
The wife's packed her bags, to her mother's she's gone
She said, 'Mam it's quite crystal clear
It's not me the bastard loves, it's his beer'

Well, she's right in a way
For at eleven each day
At the bar I will stand
With a pint in my hand
I'll just down it in one
In ten seconds it's gone
A decision was made with no tears
I think I made the right choice, I chose BEER!

We've also done all the 'Delilah' stuff and enjoy impromptu sing-a-longs on coaches or trains returning from matches. Some of these nights have given me the best times of my life. Even nowadays we have little get-togethers after home matches and allow our wives and girlfriends to join in with the after-match crack. So yes, we do enjoy a sing-song but at the right time in the right place; other than that, as the General once put it, Boro's firm don't sing, they just do the business.

For those who are interested the following is my list of top firms based on their achievements against the Boro over the past thirty-seven years:

 1 Man Utd. Salford firm hot and cold but still very active, with 60,000-plus fans who wouldn't be?
 2 Sunderland. Hate to admit it, not so hot nowadays, firm consists of too many youngsters but so did ours once, these fuckers will grow up.
 3 Newcastle. The Mags are and always will be a threat, though the Gremlins aren't as active these days.
 4 Chelsea. Too corporate these days, although they're always in the back ground.
 5 West Ham. Very quiet in recent years but ruled the roost for donkey's years.
 6 Portsmouth. Not met them often but impressive just the same, still doing it by all accounts.
 7 Nottingham Forest. Still very much active, always up for some action.
 8 Man City. Always had fun and dancing with these since the early Seventies.
 9 Cardiff. Had to include the Soul Crew, although we have only really met the once, and what a meet, but they're still one of the most active firms in the country.
10 Millwall. Would appear top of anyone's list but until you've done it up here lads, you're staying lower than you should be.

Well that's it, the highlights of my life as a Boro fan from the Holgate to the North Stand at the Riverside. I still keep tabs with the lads and spend many an hour before matches reminiscing about the good times and telling the junior ranks stories of how it used to be but I tend to avoid the naughtier side of things now, preferring instead to take a back seat and let the younger mobile phone and internet types do the business.

When I was a fully active Frontliner, someone once asked me, 'Why do you do it?' At the time I didn't really have an answer. I don't suppose anyone can really explain something that another person can't comprehend. One explanation that one of the lads used has stuck in my memory and is about the nearest I can come to answering that age-old question. I quote him thus: 'I have had sex with many different women and I've tried most drugs, but the biggest buzz I've ever had is when I am stood with twenty mates having it with a hundred lads toe-to-toe, even if we end up with a good hiding.' It's a funny old game and so is the game played out between opposing fans. Thank you for taking the time to read my story and if I've offended anyone, then as Chubby Brown would say, tough shit.